GUNS OF
THE THIRD REICH

GUNS OF THE THIRD REICH

BY
JOHN WALTER

GREENHILL BOOKS, LONDON
STACKPOLE BOOKS, PENNSYLVANIA

for Alison and Adam, with love

Guns of the Third Reich
first published 2004
by Greenhill Books, Lionel Leventhal Limited,
Park House, 1 Russell Gardens, London NW11 9NN
www.greenhillbooks.com
and Stackpole Books, 5067 Ritter Road, Mechanicsburg
PA 17055, USA

British Library Cataloguing in Publication Data
Walter, John, 1951
The guns of the Third Reich
1.Germany. Wehrmacht – Firearms 2. Firearms – Germany – History – 20th century
I. Title
623.4'4'094309044

ISBN 1-85367-598-9

Library of Congress Cataloging-in-Publication Data available

Edited by Hugh Schoenemann
Typeset by Servis Filmsetting Ltd, Manchester
Printed and bound in the UK by CPD (Wales), Ebbw Vale.

Contents

List of illustrations

Line drawings

Foreword

My interest in German military firearms goes back many years to my childhood, a cap-firing 'Luger', and an early encounter with a Boer War Mauser rifle on display in Brighton Museum & Art Gallery.

Eventually – after a somewhat chequered career – I was asked to write a general introduction to the subject for Arms & Armour Press, which was then a division of Cassells. The result was *Guns of the Reich. Firearms of the German Forces, 1939–1945*, written under the pseudonym of George Markham and published in 1989. Part of a series of four, this was not only extremely successful but also generated some lively correspondence.

Since then, however, there have been very real advances. This is largely due to a change of attitude in Germany, which undoubtedly has its origins in the contacts made between British and American collectors and German enthusiasts. I can pinpoint one such year: 1979, when Joachim Görtz was employed by Motor-Buch Verlag to assist with the translation of *Luger* into German.

Joachim was convinced that information still existed in Germany to disprove many of the spurious claims being made in collecting circles; moreover, he embarked on a quest that led first to *Die Pistole 08*, published in 1985, and then to an obsession with details that he cheerfully shared throughout the 1990s with the gun-collecting fraternity.

The discovery of archival material is undoubtedly encouraging some researchers to delve ever deeper into the minutiae of Third Reich small-arms history, and collectors are persuaded to pursue 'variations' that can often be ascribed to nothing other than manufacturing tolerances. And while this is not to be taken as criticism, such specialisation handicaps the creation of any overview seeking to present information consistently.

Another problem concerns supporting evidence, as the most detailed studies are customarily peppered with notes that hinder the flow of narrative text. There was a time when narrative histories were concise and eloquent, but the trend now is often towards size, jargon and complexity. Fortunately, during preparatory work for this edition, I read and re-read Captain Sir Basil Liddell-Hart's classic *History of the Second World War*, which reminded me that even the most complicated historical study can be easy to read. If *Guns of the Third Reich* manages to tread the same path, I will have done my job well.

Yet I must now confess to a double standard of my own: I still believe that most footnotes are a repository for irrelevant information, to be discarded or integrated with text, but I also have to deal with information supplied by Joachim Görtz in the form of extracts from German military-technical periodicals such as *Allgemeine Heeresmitteilungen* and *Heeres-Verordnungsblatt*. These provide documentary evidence that my claims are not simply guesswork, but including them in the text risked too many abbreviations and too many German words – each obstructing the flow of narrative – and I reluctantly decided to use a few chapter notes myself! I hope that these notes do not intrude, and that they provide sufficient detail to allow readers to pursue their own interests.

2002 was a sad year, bringing the deaths of both Joachim Görtz and Anthony Carter, two of the leading researchers of German weaponry; and also of Ian Hogg, the best-known populariser of this particular subject. Herbert Woodend MBE, Custodian of the Pattern Room Collection – kept first in the Royal Small Arms Factory, Enfield, then in the grounds of the Nottingham factory of Royal Ordnance – died after a long illness in the summer of 2003. I counted all four men as friends, and miss the help that was always so generously given.

I must also thank Don Bryans of Salem, Oregon, for the support that I have never properly acknowledged; Warren H. Buxton, author of

The P. 38 Pistol; Brian L. Davis of Sanderstead, Surrey, for his unrivalled knowledge of uniforms and accoutrements; Claus Espeholt of Grenaa, Denmark, for sharing his knowledge of the Gew. 41 and Gew. 43; Dr Rolf Gminder of Heilbronn, for photographs of the Parabellum pistols in his collection; Tom Knox of St Louis, Missouri, long-time editor of *Auto-Mag*, the NAPCA journal; David Penn, Keeper of the Department of Exhibits, Imperial War Museum; Karl Schäfer of Pirmasens, for supplying details of the signal pistols; Joseph J. Schroeder of Glenview, Illinois, for sharing his knowledge of handguns generally and Mauser pistols in particular; Jan Still of Douglas, Alaska, for collecting so much data from German-marked handguns; Jim Stonley of Startforth, County Durham, for information drawn from his fascinating articles in *Guns Review*; and Henk Visser of Wassenaar, the Netherlands, for supplying information about the pistols in his splendid collection.

Lastly, I must once again thank Lionel Leventhal of Greenhill Books, for allowing me to continue the work begun with *Guns of the Reich* . . . and Alison and Adam, for letting me finish it more-or-less on time.

John Walter, Hove, 2004.

1

Prologue

The comparative single-mindedness of Anglo-American and particularly Russian arms-production contrasted greatly with the fragmentation of German efforts during the Second World War. In Germany, the armed services, the Waffen-SS and other paramilitary organizations each clamoured separately for attention. The situation was summarised by the late Ian Hogg in the original version of *German Secret Weapons of World War 2*, published by Arms & Armour Press in 1970:

'. . . It was not until the war ended and Allied investigation teams began to examine . . . the arms manufacturers and the files of the military departments, that the details of these developments (and of many more still in their infancy) came to light; the number of developments staggers the imagination.

'Indeed, it is this number which gives a clue to the mystery of why German technology failed to produce the superiority in armaments envisaged by Hitler. In Germany, however, no . . . central clearing house existed. Each service had its own research establishments, laboratories, proving grounds and ranges; each kept its researches secret from the other, and each scrambled against the others for factory facilities. If it were possible to get the ear of a high-ranking party official or, best of all, Hitler himself, then the most outlandish scheme had every chance to prosper . . .'

Millions of Reichsmarks were wasted in the development of legions of differing guided missiles – an area in which the Germans could have excelled had efforts been properly co-ordinated – and in the production of rocket-powered aircraft, resources for which would have been better diverted to the two outstanding jets, the Messerschmitt Me. 262 and Arado Ar. 234. Ponderous super-tanks were designed at a time when the Soviet Army was showing the merits of mobility; and huge railway guns were prepared when funds should have been allotted to anti-tank gun production.

Spreading resources across such a broad range of projects does not necessarily suggest that the German arms industry was always unable to achieve its targets. Indeed, paradoxically, so much was achieved that the results were impossible to prioritise. A fatal lack of unified control, particularly prior to 1942, ensured that projects competed against each other and designers were allowed too much independence. Even after being ordered to concentrate on bomber design in the immediate pre-war period, for example, Heinkel had obstinately continued to work on a fighter to compete first with the Messerschmitt Me. 109 and then with the Focke-Wulf Fw. 190.

Few other major participants in the war, excepting possibly the Japanese, proved less able to co-ordinate weapons development programmes than the Germans. The result was perpetual duplication and a tendency to encourage the unencourageable. Most ordnance departments contained visionaries who were customarily at odds with more analytical colleagues, but it was rare that the former were allowed to dominate the latter.

Britain had had experience with eccentric weapons designs, particularly when the threat of German invasion in the summer of 1940 seemed so real. Yet the Smith Gun and the Bates Six-Barrel Bottle Thrower made sense in the context of the Home Guard; and even the Giant Panjandrum, abandoned when it ran amok on trials, promised a simple solution to a perceived need. In contrast, the Germans seemed incapable of producing simple solutions. In the desperate days of 1944–5, when the *Gerät Neumünster* or MP. 3008 was being rushed into production, the designers could not resist adding a selective-fire capability to what was supposed to be a copy of the ultra-simple British Sten Gun.

The hypnotic effect of lunatic-fringe ideas such as the Zippermeyer *Wirbelgeschütz* ('vortex gun'), the sound cannon, the Hänsler Electric Gun and the *Tausendfussler* permeated downward even to the Heereswaffenamt. Though the curved-barrel project (*Krummlauf*) had a realistic goal, it was undoubtedly a waste of resources; the HF15 or *höherer Feuerfolge*, conceived by Hungarian Bela Zettl to achieve exceptionally high rates of fire, promised much but ultimately delivered nothing; Tromsdorff ramjet shells never achieved the requisite accuracy; rocket cartridges for small arms predictably proved to be useless; and even the *Fallschirmjägergewehr 42* and the first assault rifle, the MP. 43, conflicted with each other. The inability of the army and Luftwaffe authorities to co-operate resulted in two radically differing designs reaching production status when one would have been preferable.

Though these rifles have now achieved near-mythical importance in small-arms history, neither was an outstanding success prior to 1945. Production of the FG. 42 was interrupted initially by the withdrawal of vital manganese steel, causing a wholesale remodelling of the gun, and production totalling only a few thousand was scarcely significant when 200,000-plus MG. 42 machine-guns had been made in 1944 alone.

Far greater quantities of the MP. 43/StG. 44 series were made (about 285,000 in 1944), but the ambitious production programme was impossible to implement in the face of ever-increasing demands without encountering difficulties with sub-contractors who had no experience of gunmaking. Some parts were out of gauge, or simply would not fit; some broke, while others were made of the wrong material. So many minor changes were made to the master drawings that guns made in March were not necessarily the same as those made in February, or those that would be made in April.

Lack of co-ordination between the armed forces and the paramilitary was bad enough, but the German production effort was also hamstrung by high-ranking political interference; in 1941, acting on Hitler's instructions, the O.K.W. had cancelled defensive projects that could not be completed within a year – and Hitler had himself ordered the suppression of the Maschinenkarabiner project in 1943. He had also insisted that the Messerschmitt Me. 262 be used as a bomber, when its speed as a fighter would have presented a real threat to Allied air-raids; and the facilities at the Peenemünde research station were frittered away on the A-4 (alias *Vergeltungswaffe Zwei,* or 'V2'), simply to deliver small amounts of high-explosive to London, instead of perfecting the C-2 Wasserfall anti-aircraft missile.

Even without conflicting priorities, Germany would always have struggled to obtain the raw materials that were necessary to sustain pro-tracted campaigns. The perceptive Basil Liddell-Hart (*History of the Second World War,* Cassell, 1970) identified twenty raw materials essen-tial to war. He then continued:

> '. . . Germany had no home production of cotton, rubber, tin, platinum, bauxite, mercury, and mica, while her supplies of iron-ore, copper, antimony, manganese, nickel, sulphur, wool and petroleum were quite inadequate. By the seizure of Czecho-Slovakia, she had gone some way to reduce her deficiency of iron-ore, while by her intervention in Spain she had been able to secure a further supply of it on favourable terms, and also of mercury . . . Again, she had succeeded in meeting part of her need for wool by a new wood substitute. Likewise, though at much greater cost than the natural product, she had provided about a fifth of her rubber requirement from 'buna', and a third of her petrol needs from home produced fuel . . .'

The advent of war and the loss of the sea-lanes to the Western Allies hit German imports strongly. Industry coped as long as the Wehrmacht was ascendant, but the situation changed dramatically as the Red Army drove the Germans out of the principal coal-, ore- and petrol-producing areas they had seized in eastern Europe. As this all but coincided with demands to accelerate weapons production, the results were predictable: declining quality, a higher percentage of failures at inspection, and a general loss of confidence in the products.

A reduction in the quality of explosives and propellant had been forced by shortages of nitrogen. Before any hydrogenation plants were bombed, Greater Germany had produced almost 100,000 tonnes of nitrogen compounds monthly; by December 1944, the total had dropped to virtually a fifth of the original level, and substantial amounts of rock-salt additives were appearing in explosives. Not surprisingly, performance deteriorated.

The apogee of German small-arms production – judged quantitatively – occurred in 1944. According to Albert Speer's memoirs, *Inside the Third Reich*, the average monthly production of rifles (mainly Kar. 98k and Gew. 43, but excluding MP. 43) rose from 133,000 in 1942 to 307,000 in 1944; the figures for machine-guns were 7,100 and 28,700 respectively, the former being largely MG. 34 and the latter MG. 42; output of rifle ammunition, 76 million rounds in 1942, reached a staggering 486 million in 1944. However, increasing difficulty was being encountered in distributing the weapons to the soldiers in the field. The disruptive effects of Allied bombing had a gradual cumulative effect, particularly on the railway network, and the index of industrial production – 223 at the end of 1943 – declined from 277 in December 1944 to 227 in January 1945, 175 in February and 145 in March.

Had bombing offensives been directed specifically at the Achilles heel of the German war effort – the petro-chemical industry – rather than towns of cultural but no particular industrial significance, the arms industry would have been reduced to impotence more efficiently.

The inability of the German arms industry to supply sufficient small arms was initially camouflaged by reissuing obsolete German weapons, impressing huge numbers of guns that had been captured, and taking surprising quantities of firearms from civilian populations – especially in occupied territory, where the possession of a gun would inevitably bring a death sentence. However, unless they were despatched to unimportant defensive formations (the Channel Islands, for example) or fortifications such as coastal artillery emplacements or the Atlantic Wall, where they were seen only as a 'last-ditch' defence, non-standard weapons contributed little else than to release regulation weapons for front-line service. In this respect, and in many others, the Germans repeated mistakes that had been made in the First World War.

Impressed small arms did not compromise fighting efficiency as long as the Germans were in the ascendant, and as long as the ascendancy was great enough to keep unrest in occupied territories to a minimum. However, when the Germans were ultimately forced back, the balance of power shifted and the lack of large-scale reserves of ammunition for the impressments compromised the effectiveness of many German second-line units. The effects grew in proportion to the losses of arms and equipment, which were stupendous.

Though it is difficult to provide overall estimates for these losses, just as it is difficult to document the precise distribution of non-standard guns[1], surviving Wehrmacht records reveal that about 58,000 submachine-guns were lost in 1943 compared with deliveries of about 220,000, representing about a quarter of the potential increase in the inventory. In 1944, however, with the Germans in retreat across Europe, deliveries of much the same magnitude were counterbalanced by losses that amounted to 135,000 . . . more than *sixty per cent* of the new deliveries.

One of the biggest problems created by diversity was the supply of ammunition. By 1945, there were, for example, eight different semi-official handgun chamberings to add to the 9mm Pist. Patr. 08: 6.35mm and 7.65mm Browning; 7.65mm Longue (French); 9mm Browning Short (9mm Kurz, .38 ACP); 9mm Browning Long; 9mm Mauser 'Export'; 9mm Steyr; and .45 ACP. By the last desperate weeks of the Second World War, many non-standard small arms had ceased to be useful either because no ammunition was left or because supplies could no longer be delivered.

Postscript

Though the war ended for most of the arms makers in the spring of 1945, the best of their ideas soon reappeared elsewhere. The Allies spent several years sifting through millions of documents, confiscated valuable experimental data, and took away countless prototypes to test. However, interest was initially centred on the advanced forms of conventional weapon (notably the FG. 42, but later the MG. 42) at the expense of the intermediate-cartridge assault rifles, as most Western armies still believed that only powerful rifle- and machine-gun cartridges allowed long-range accuracy to be retained.

The Russians, who had no such preconceptions, were so impressed with the MP. 43 that comparable designs were being developed even before the end of hostilities. The S.K.S. semi-automatic carbine was

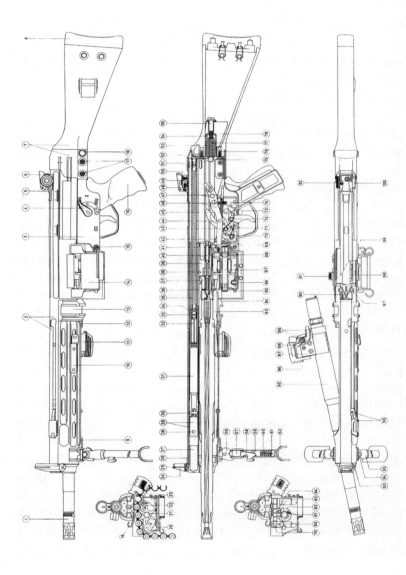

1. The modern Heckler & Koch machine-guns embody a roller-lock breech system adapted from the MG. 42. These drawings show a belt-fed HK11A1. The method of removing the barrel also has some similarities to the wartime design.

introduced in 1945 as an expedient, but the perfected A.K. (Kalashnikov) soon replaced it. Most other armies remained unconvinced of the value of intermediate cartridges until comparatively recent years, even though the U.S. Army grudgingly accepted the 5.56mm round in the 1960s.

The greatest achievement of the German small-arms industry was the iconoclastic application of simplified metalworking techniques to conventional service weapons, persuading other major industrialised nations that stamping, pressing and welding should not be destined simply for 'emergency' weapons such as the Sten Gun. The collapse of the Third Reich, accompanied by a dramatic extinction of the German arms industry, was not the end of the story.

Many of the best ideas simply migrated to neutral countries – as they had done twenty years earlier – and re-emerged under different names. The roller-locked breech, copied from the MG. 42, reappeared on the Swiss StGw. 57, and also in the SIG MG-710 series. It was embodied in the unsuccessful British Thorpe or EM-1 rifle, but the most important application was in Spain. There, the Mauser roller-delayed blowback system, developed by Stähle, Altenburger and Vorgrimmler and tested in the MG. 45V, Gew. 45 (M) and Gerät 06 (H), became the CETME of the early 1950s. Ironically, once the Bundeswehr had been allowed to re-equip to face the German Democratic Republic and the Soviet Bloc, the CETME rifle was adopted as the G3.

Originally made by Rheinmetall and Heckler & Koch (H&K), the G3 rifle provided the basis for the many H&K adaptations that helped to rebuild German arms-making capacity for the third time in seventy years.

In addition to the G3, design of which may be attributed to Mauser prior to 1945, the Bundeswehr of 1995 was still equipped with the MG3 (a slightly modified MG. 42 made by Rheinmetall) and the P1, a version of the Pistole 38 still made by Walther. But for the costly reunification of Germany, the Bundeswehr would have adopted the revolutionary caseless-cartridge Gewehr 11 . . . another idea that was developed, if not entirely successfully, during the Second World War.

Guns of the Third Reich attempts to tell the fascinating story that lies behind the development and use of small arms in the German armed forces, from the first days of the Weimar Republic – when controls imposed by the Allies were still in place – to the impressive large-scale rearmament endorsed by Adolf Hitler and, finally, the last desperate days of the Second World War.

2

The First Steps, 1919–33

Links between the history of the small arms of the Third Reich – the rearmament programmes of the 1930s and the campaigns of the Second World War – and the restrictions placed on Germany by the Allies at the end of the First World War, are undeniable. However, the story is now also shrouded in myth: the political 'stab-in-the-back' that cost the German army dearly in 1918, the Blitzkrieg ('lightning war') that was said to be invincible by those it crushed, and the progress of technology in Germany that was so superior that her enemies had no option but to capitulate. One consequence of elevating German military supremacy to mythic proportions has been that over-exaggerated attention has been paid to 'advances' that were either illusory or, in some cases, abject failures.

An unwanted, if immediate effect of the restrictions enforced by the Treaty of Versailles was to canonise many people undeservedly, and force underground the militarism that had previously been overt. The victorious Allies tried to smash German military traditions by destroying war matériel, and by redrawing the map of Europe in an attempt to control political development.

Article 180 of the Treaty of Versailles severely restricted the size and strength of the German armed forces (*Reichswehr*). At the time the treaty was signed, Germany had about 400,000 men still under arms. Though this was a fraction of the peak wartime strength, achieved by wholesale desertions and overnight demobilisation, the Allies imposed a reduction to 200,000 'within three months' and to the ultimate 100,000-man establishment not later than 3 March 1920. The issue of weapons was also to be strictly controlled, allowing the issue of merely 84,000 Gew. 98, 18,000 Kar. 98 AZ., 1,926 MG. 08 (Maxim machine-guns), 252 trench mortars (*Minenwerfer*) and 288 large-calibre guns. Armoured vehicles and aircraft were banned, the manufacture of small arms was restricted to replacements for weapons that had worn out, and the navy was reduced to a handful of obsolescent pre-dreadnought battleships and elderly torpedo boats.

Desperate to keep industry from participating in wholesale rearmament, the Allies restricted participation to only a handful of 'trusted' companies. Those such as Mauser and Deutsche Waffen- & Munitions-fabriken, which had supplied most of the pre-1918 small arms (especially the machine-guns) were prevented from making weapons. Consequently, the supply, repair and replacement of rifles, pistols and machine-guns was entrusted to Simson & Co. of Suhl, a Jewish-owned company that could be expected to resist pressure from German militarists; ammunition was made the exclusive purview of Polte-Werke of Magdeburg, with comparatively little blemish on its pre-1918 history; and the supply of propellants and explosive was given to Westfälisch-Anhaltische Sprengstoff AG ('WASAG') and Köln-Rottweiler Pulverfabriken AG. Primers for small-arms ammunition were to be made by Dreyse & Collenbusch in Sömmerda.

The manufacture of artillery, which had always been restricted to a mere handful of large industrial conglomerates, presented more of a problem. Eventually, the Allies were forced to accept that Krupp and Rheinische Metallwaaren- & Maschinenfabrik ('Rheinmetall') could not be excluded, contenting themselves with restricting the former to guns with calibres greater than 17cm and the latter to the smaller patterns.

It is easy to argue, particularly with hindsight, that the effects of the Treaty of Versailles smacked more of revenge than a long-term solution to European problems. The redistribution of territory from Germany and Austria-Hungary allowed the creation of new sovereign states, but these were often imposed more for geopolitical reasons – and a desire for punishment – than to address the needs of ethnic groups that had been freed from tyranny. Thus the return of Alsace and Lorraine to France, the integration of large parts of Schlesien (Silesia) in Poland, the detachment of the largely German-speaking Sudetenland to become part of Czechoslovakia, and the cobbling-together of a kingdom of Serbs, Croats and Slovenes (a mutually antipathetic mixture) all ultimately proved to be grievous errors of judgement. It is an interesting, if idle pursuit to debate what could have happened had the creation of new states been more logical, or if the punitive measures applied to Germany (in particular) had been less draconian.

The destruction of weapons, at least superficially, seems straightforward, but the reality was quite different. However diligent the Allied supervisors may have been, the official inventory was a sham. No-one knew for sure how much equipment actually survived the end of the First World War, how much had been left in places such as Turkey, or how much had been spirited away by disaffected groups on both wings of German politics. Much of the German battlefleet had been scuttled in Scapa Flow in 1919, huge numbers of small arms were consigned to the furnaces, and it was comparatively easy to destroy aircraft or tanks. But it was much less simple to account for the handguns and the rifles. The impressment of so many non-standard designs during the First World War – the *Beutegewehre* and *Behelfspistolen* – ensured that huge numbers of serviceable weapons simply disappeared into the hands of individuals who feared that revolution would fill the vacuum in German politics just as it had done in Russia.

Photographs taken during the early 1920s, when the Weimar Republic struggled to gain acceptance and a left-wing coup in Bavaria was brutally suppressed by the right-wing Freikorps, show no evidence of a scarcity of weapons. Though the rifles may occasionally have been obsolete, single-shot 11mm Mausers, Gew. 98, Kar. 98 AZ. and Maxim machine-guns clearly survived in quantity.

Despite the release of millions of men from military service, many angered and disenchanted by their experiences, it was soon clear that the left-wingers in Germany would never defeat the might of the church and the right-wing aristocracy that had traditionally provided much of the officer class that controlled the army. The activities of the armed forces may well have been radically curtailed, but the Allies tacitly accepted that the creation of well equipped police forces was essential to maintain civil order. Complaints about the niggardly scales of issue allowed the Reichswehr machine-gun quota to rise to 2,336 in 1921, and weapons were also retained for police 'internal security' purposes. There were also large clandestine stockpiles of what were called 'Black Weapons' (*Schwarzwaffen*, 'hidden weapons') kept well away from Allied view.

By the 1930s, the Prussian police had a strength of 85,000 men and an inventory that included large numbers of submachine-guns, machine-guns and even armoured vehicles. Britain and France were just as fearful as the German right-wingers of Bolshevism, and were anxious to ensure that Germany did not descend into anarchy.

The deep-seated resentment that had arisen in Germany was due to the loss of territory to its old enemy France and emergent Poland and Czechoslovakia, creating an ever-increasing desire to regain what had been lost. Power had been centralised in a constituent assembly after the dissolution of the state monarchies (the Kaiser had fled to the Netherlands), meeting for the first time on 6 February 1919 in the small provincial town of Weimar.

However, the near-anarchy of the early 1920s caused desperate hardship, and there seemed scarcely a chance that industry generally – much less the specialised arms industry – would ever recover its former glory. The Allies had presented a colossal bill for reparations in May 1921 after protracted discussions, but the French re-occupied the Ruhr early in 1923 in reprisal for non-payment, and the German currency collapsed.

As Germany could clearly not continue to meet her debts, important decisions had to be taken; gradually, with the assistance of American capital, the German economy was rebuilt. Yet this enforced rebuilding could not approach pre-1914 levels, and a combination of deprivation and weak leadership fostered the development of extreme opinions, just as it had done (and would still do) in many other countries. The politics that would triumph in Germany would be of the far right instead of the Bolshevik left.

The 'Weimar Republic' is generally reckoned to have lasted until the advent of the Third Reich in 1933, though the appointment of Brüning to the chancellory in March 1930 effectively ended the period of democracy; instead came what A.J.P. Taylor, in *The Course of German History*

(Hamish Hamilton, London, 1945), called 'demagogic dictatorship'. A primary cause of the change was agitation by the Reichswehr, which sensed that the rearmament programmes were not proceeding fast enough and which provoked a crisis that economic collapse subsequently sealed.

The phoenix rises

The restriction of the Reichswehr to a mere 100,000 men was one of the major catalysts of rearmament. There was still much sympathy among the old officer corps for the pre-1918 values, and the sudden reduction of the armed forces from the millions serving the colours in 1918 caused not only extensive hardship but also encouraged the formation of old comrades associations. In these lay the genesis of the paramilitary formations of the Third Reich.

Clandestine operations soon began in sympathetic countries such as the Netherlands, Denmark and Switzerland, where many 'import/export' companies were formed by arms makers who had seen their markets wrecked by Allied interference. Rheinmetall, Krupp and Mauser, among others, continued development work covertly – machine-guns were built in Switzerland; submarines, under Krupp supervision, in Finland. However, governmental support in 1924 could not be what it had been a decade earlier. This was partly due to the influence of the Allied Control Commissions, and to unannounced inspections of industrial sites to prevent large-scale rearmament.

However, Allied enthusiasm soon waned, and a conference convened in October 1925 in the Swiss town of Locarno had important repercussions. There the Weimar government officially (but unpopularly) recognised not only its borders with France and Belgium, but also the permanent demilitarisation of the Rheinland. Signed on 1 December 1925 by the three principals, and guaranteed by Britain and Italy, the treaty survived only until the Wehrmacht marched into the Rheinland in the spring of 1936. It is an open question, therefore, if the Weimar government ever considered the terms of Locarno binding; the German military most certainly did not.

At much the same time, the Germans embarked on the first of their rearmament programmes, carefully camouflaged by the introduction of manufacturing codes. As Johannes Preuss' fascinating book *Zahlencode Systeme des Heeres von 1925 bis 1940* shows, the idea was to hide the recruitment of new contractors by giving them codes that made each consignment appear to be just another 'lot number' delivery from the prime contractor. Consequently, all the ammunition-making businesses used a 'P' prefix designed to suggest that everything had been made by Polte-Werke. The coincidental withdrawal of the Allied inspectorate made this subterfuge easy to conceal, as the *volume* of new stores (which could have shown a dramatic increase) was no longer being subjected to such minute scrutiny.

French ties with Czechoslovakia and Poland were also ratified in Locarno, as were German arbitration agreements with the same two countries over its unsettled eastern borders. To a casual onlooker, the chances of lasting European peace had never seemed as promising, but there were important drawbacks: interest in the Great War had waned so greatly that the Allied controllers withdrew from Germany immediately after the Treaty of Locarno had been signed; the scale of reparations was greatly reduced in 1929; and, in 1930, Allied troops withdrew from the Rheinland five years ahead of schedule. These gestures were offered as conciliation (the British and the French feared the U.S.S.R. and wanted a sturdy buffer between them and eastern Europe), but were a godsend to German militarists and it is no coincidence that the *Inspektion für Waffen & Geräte* (I.W.G.) was formed in 1926.

Secret mutual co-operation agreements with the Russians, signed in Rapallo in 1922 and in Berlin in 1926, showed that the Germans were paying little but lip-service to the restrictions applied in Versailles. By treating with the Russians, whose politics were diametrically opposed to its own, the German government had shown its true colours. However, no sooner had clandestine rearmament begun than the stock market collapsed in the U.S.A., causing the immediate suspension of the second US-backed recovery plan. This plunged the German economy, recovering from the dark days of the early 1920s but still fragile, into a severe decline.

The Reichswehr-backed appointment of Chancellor Brüning in 1930 led to a suspension of parliamentary democracy, and when the German banks closed temporarily in July 1931, six million people were already unemployed. The route to salvation was once again seen to be in militarism; and there was a sudden surge of enthusiasm for men such as Hitler who, with an untainted record in governance, could promise to repair national fortunes without the necessity of delivering it immediately.

The peace of Europe was being chipped away; in the Reichstag elections of 1930, the *Nationalsozialistische Deutsche-Arbeiterspartei* (N.S.D.A.P., 'Nazi Party') had been the second largest. Elections held in July 1932 returned more N.S.D.A.P. candidates than any other, though the party had failed to secure half the votes cast and had no overall majority. Reichpräzident Hindenburg, a field marshal in 1918, initially snubbed ex-corporal Hitler, but a campaign of political trickery – supported by the thuggery of the rapidly-growing *Sturm Abteilung* (S.A.) – forced a change of heart. Hitler became Reichskanzler ('State Chancellor') of a coalition government on the last day of January 1933; the march to war had become a trot.

Restricted leadership was not what Hitler sought. The burning of the Reichstag (parliament building) so soon after the election, in highly suspicious circumstances, provided an ideal way of denouncing the Bolsheviks and all other left-wing groups. By the spring of 1933, Hitler had become the virtual dictator of Germany, and the death of the geriatric Hindenburg in 1934 removed the last barrier to his ambitions.

To revitalise the flagging German economy, however, only massive investment in re-armament could substitute for an inability to recreate the lucrative export markets that had once made imperial Germany Europe's leading industrial power. In the autumn of 1933, therefore, Hitler withdrew from the League of Nations conference with the comment that Germany could not be expected to remain helpless while the Allies would not themselves disarm.

It was an astute move; excepting France, which vehemently opposed any conciliatory gesture, the remaining Allies – suspicious of French expansionism – agreed to permit the Germans to re-equip. The signatories realised neither the extent of clandestine development nor that Germany could re-equip fast enough to threaten the Allied power-base. They were soon to be proved wrong.

Hitler had formed a council for national defence immediately after withdrawing from the League of Nations conference, and such great progress had been made in the development of aircraft, submarines, vehicles and small arms that re-equipment began almost immediately he had left the conference table.

The guns of 1918

Machine-guns.   The machine-gun, exemplified by the ponderous but exceptionally reliable Maxim, had been one of the revelations of the First World War. Derided at the outset by most military hierarchies, almost always dominated by opinionated cavalrymen who scarcely saw beyond the nose of a horse, the machine-gun had brought a new tactical dimension to warfare. Head-on attack was no longer merely a matter of sufficiently superior numbers. A few well-sited machine-guns, as long as ammunition supplies could be maintained, had beaten off even the most determined assault, even though the advent of man-portable 'light' guns such as the Lewis had swung the balance back towards offence.

When the First World War ended in November 1918, the principal German service weapons were the water-cooled MG. 08 and MG. 08/15 Maxims, though many air-cooled Maxims and Parabellums (the latter with an inverted toggle-lock) had been pressed into service alongside the Bergmann MG. 15 and a tiny number of water-cooled Dreyse ground guns.

The Maxim, originating in the 1880s, had excited the interest of many armies. Germany had purchased a few in 1896, mainly for naval use, and then issued small numbers of MG. 99 and MG. 01 for field-service trials before adopting the *Maschinengewehr Modell 1908* ('MG. 08'). Vickers, Sons & Maxim had already granted a production licence to Deutsche Waffen- & Munitionsfabriken ('D.W.M.') of Berlin, and the rifle factory at Spandau delivered the first government-made guns in 1910. The links between D.W.M. and Vickers, Sons & Maxim were due to the German Loewe family – majority shareholder in D.W.M., Mauser and Fabrique Nationale d'Armes de Guerre. Loewe had also acquired substantial shareholdings in Vickers in the 1890s, and Sigmund Loewe had served as a Director of the British company until his death in 1903.

D.W.M. also offered an M1909 'export' version of the Maxim on a lightweight tripod, and then the 'S. M. Gew. M. 1913'. Better known as the 'Parabellum', the latter was basically a lightened Maxim with an inverted toggle-lock.

The MG. 08 was quintessentially Maxim; the barrel and breechblock retreated through about 17mm, securely locked together, until the barrel stopped and a locking toggle broke upward to allow the breechblock to run back alone. After withdrawing a new round from the fabric feed belt on the rearward stroke, the mechanism returned to re-load. The toggle then snapped back into place and the main spring pushed the barrel/breech assembly back to its initial position.

The gun operated reliably, but the cyclic rate of the earliest guns was only about 300 rds/min. Experience of trench warfare suggested that this was too slow to halt large-scale attacks, and a recoil booster ('*Rückstossverstärker S.*') was developed to increase the fire-rate to about 450 rds/min simply by deflecting propellant gas to increase the rearward thrust on the barrel.

The MG. 08 was heavy and cumbersome, weighing about 26.5kg, and the perfected sledge mount (*Schlitten 08*) contributed an additional 32kg. When the first Lewis light machine-guns were captured on the Western Front, the Gewehrprüfungskommission ('G.P.K.') immediately refined the basic Maxim into a more mobile weapon. Credited to Oberst von Merkatz of the G.P.K., the MG. 08/15 had a small-diameter barrel jacket, thinner receiver walls than the MG.08, a new pistol grip and butt, a bipod and a simpler back sight.

Weighing nearly 18kg, the MG. 08/15 was much more cumbersome than the Lewis or the Madsen. However, being water-cooled and based on well-tried components, it was more reliable and could sustain fire much more effectively than air-cooled rivals that tended to overheat if used too enthusiastically.

Production of German Maxims was entrusted during the First World War principally to Deutsche Waffen- & Munitionsfabriken (marked with a D.W.M. monogram) in Berlin; to the government rifle factories in Erfurt and Spandau; to Rheinische Metallwaaren- & Maschinenfabrik ('Rh.M.& M.F.') in Sömmerda; to Siemens & Halske ('S. & H.') in Berlin; and to Maschinenfabrik Augsburg-Nürnberg ('M.A.N.').

Only about two thousand Maxims were available in August 1914, but wartime production was spectacular; the Inter-Allied Military Control Commission ordered the destruction of all but four of 87,950 machine-guns collected together in 1919!

A belated attempt had been made during the First World War to develop a simplified machine-gun for universal ground use (the so-called *Einheitsmaschinengewehr 16*), but development of this water-cooled adaptation of the MG. 08/15 was abandoned in 1917 to prevent interfering with production of the regulation patterns. The only tangible result of the Einheitsmaschinengewehr programme was the adoption of the tripod, or *Dreifuss 16*, as a substitute for the *Schlitten 08*.

The German armies had impressed large numbers of ex-Russian Maxims, in addition to some of the guns that had been used in the navy. The few surviving pre-1908 ground guns were issued for training purposes, freeing the MG. 08 for front-line service; captured Vickers and Lewis Guns were turned against their former owners; and ex-Austrian Schwarzlose machine-guns were also used in small numbers. Small batches of 8mm-calibre Madsen 'machine rifles' (which were really light machine-guns) had been purchased in Denmark, mainly for the Gebirgsjäger, and similar guns chambering the rimmed 7.62×54mm round had been taken from the Russians on the Eastern Front.

Automatic rifles.   Very little progress had been made with automatic rifles, even though the desirability of increasing infantry firepower was universally accepted. The Germans had tested many guns prior to 1914. Mauser's vaunted reputation had often persuaded the G.P.K. to issue his complicated, cumbersome and expensive recoil-operated rifles for trial – including the so-called C/98, C/98-02, C/06 and C/06-08 – but none had been successful. A clutch of Mannlichers had been submitted by Österreichische Waffenfabriks-Gesellschaft, together with toggle-action D.W.M. guns designed by Luger and Borchardt, the Danish-designed Bang rifle and, presumably, others as yet unknown.

The only semi-automatic rifle to be officially approved during the First World War, however, was the Mexican-designed Swiss-made *Flieger-Selbstladekarabiner 1915* ('F.S.K.' or Mondragon). Adopted on 2 December 1915, the gas-operated Mondragon fired Belgian-made 7×57mm cartridges rather than the standard 8mm S.-Patrone. About three thousand guns were purchased from Schweizerische Industrie Gesellschaft, where they had been stored since the Mexican revolution of 1911. As the G.P.K. considered the original small-capacity box magazine inappropriate for aerial combat, about 20,000 *Trommelmagazine* (drum- or 'snail' magazines) were made by Hamburg-Amerikanischen Uhrenfabrik of Schramberg. The guns were subsequently issued to the Fliegerkorps and the Kaiserliche Marine, but were withdrawn once efficient aircraft machine-guns became available. The F.S.K. subsequently appeared in the trenches, but disappeared again when their susceptibility to jamming became obvious.

Tiny quantities of the stupefyingly-expensive 8mm-calibre Mausers were procured in half- and full-stocked variants (designated *Selbstlade-karabiner* and *Selbstladegewehr* respectively), each costing six times as much as a Mondragon. The fully stocked Mausers had standard Gew. 98 nose-caps, accepted the standard bayonets, and were intended for the army. However, experience in the air, at sea and in the field convinced the G.P.K. that the simpler gas-operated Mondragon – though far from perfect – was preferable to the clumsy recoil-operated Mauser.

Rifles.   When the First World War ended the principal German service rifle was the *Gewehr 98*, adopted on 5 April 1898. Its action was a standard Mauser turning bolt, with a third (or 'safety') lug and an internal five-round box magazine loaded either from a charger or with loose rounds. In an attempt to isolate the effects of the bayonet from the rifle barrel, the Gew. 98 had a sturdy twin-band nosecap supporting an unusually long attachment bar. The bayonet, therefore, had an elongated attachment slot to impart sufficient rigidity to the mount without requiring a muzzle ring. The original 8mm Patrone 88 was replaced by the 8mm S.-Patrone, adopted on 3 March 1903.

Gewehre 98 were made by the four state-owned arsenals – Amberg, Danzig, Erfurt and Spandau – as well as by Waffenfabrik Mauser AG of Oberndorf; Deutsche Waffen- & Munitionsfabriken in Berlin; and Simson & Co., C.G. Haenel Waffen- & Fahrradfabrik and V.C. Schilling & Co. in Suhl. Small quantities were also made by Waffenwerk Oberspree, Kornbusch & Co. in Niederschönweide, near Berlin, until the company was acquired by D.W.M. in 1916.

Several unsuccessful carbines had been produced early in the twentieth century, but the excessive flash and muzzle-blast of the Patrone 88 or S.-Patrone caused the original short-barrelled Kar. 98a to be abandoned. The replacement was a much longer 'carbine' – a short rifle comparable with the British S.M.L.E. – called the *Karabiner 98 mit Aufplanz- und Zusammensetzvorrichtung* ('Kar. 98 AZ.'). Adopted on 16 January 1908, this had a full-length handguard above the barrel, a simple tangent-leaf back sight, a unique hinged nose-cap and an ultra-short muzzle. The front sight had prominent protectors; a piling rod protruded beneath the nosecap; and a hemispherical bolt handle turned down into the stock, its back face being chequered to improve grip. The Kar. 98 AZ. served throughout the First World War with only the minor modifications necessary to facilitate mass production.

Anti-tank rifles.   The Germans had also made substantial quantities of the first effective man-portable riposte to the tank. The appearance of the first British tanks in combat on the Western Front (15 September 1916), and the subsequent massed use of them, caused great panic among inexperienced German defenders. Though the land-ships were impossibly clumsy and unreliable, they had considerable offensive capability; initially, they seemed invulnerable to anything less than an artillery shell. However, the Germans had an effectual 7.9mm armour-piercing bullet, which, developed for aerial use, had proved itself against metal vision-slit protectors and was widely issued for land service. These projectiles could pierce the 10mm armour of the earliest tanks, but only if they struck perpendicularly ('normal') to the plate surfaces; an angular strike usually caused a ricochet, though it sometimes detached fragments of the inner surface of the armour plate to the discomfort of the tank crew.

The G.P.K. soon realised that greater penetrative power was needed, but also that no existing gun could be adapted to the task. Consequently, the authorities set about developing two projects concurrently: a large-calibre rifle, for immediate issue to the infantry, and a machine-gun for land and aerial use. Towards the end of November 1917, the G.P.K. had instructed Waffenfabrik Mauser to develop a manually operated anti-tank rifle even though the cartridge had not been agreed. Owing to the urgency of the situation (the priority was identical with the submarine-building programme) the cartridge had been tested and the prototype gun delivered to the G.P.K. by mid-January 1918. By the end of the war, about 15,800 *Elefantenbüchsen* ('Elephant Guns') had been made. They were known as 'T-Gewehre' or, later, 'T.u.F.-Gewehre'.

Measuring about 1.7m overall, with an 87cm four-groove barrel rifled with a clockwise twist, the T-Gewehr weighed about 17.8kg with its MG. 08/15-type bipod. Though it had a modified Mauser bolt action similar to that of the Gew. 98, the standard gun was a single-loader. Mauser did make a handful of improved rifles, with a five-round box magazine beneath the stock ahead of the trigger and a sprung butt-plate, but none had been issued by November 1918.

The 13mm cartridge measured about 133mm overall and weighed about 116gm laden; its 63mm steel-cored bullet contributed 51.5gm, while the charge of flake nitrocellulose provided 13gm. Muzzle velocity was about 780 m/sec, resulting in an impressive penetrative capability for its day. Allied representatives were mortified to discover at a test-firing that the T-Gewehr bullet went straight through a 28mm-thick 'bullet proof' plate placed at a distance of fifty metres.

Shortly before the war ended, the Germans had introduced a heavier bullet in which the entire core surface had been hardened; the core tips of the earlier lightweight bullets had shown a tendency to snap off when striking obliquely, considerably reducing the T-Gewehr's effectiveness.

Submachine-guns.   Though many light machine-guns had been issued for general service, and the twin-barrelled Italian Villar-Perosa had been chambered for 9mm pistol cartridges, it is generally agreed that the Germans developed the world's first true submachine-gun. The Bergmann *Muskete* or MP. 18,I., developed by Hugo Schmeisser a year previously, was introduced in 1918 to arm raiding parties and 'Stormtroops' (*Sturmtruppen*). Standard infantry rifles were too clumsy in this role, even the lightest of the standard light machine-guns being too heavy, and the long-barrelled Parabellum pistol – the LP. 08 – was semi-automatic only.

The MP. 18,I., however, presents something of a puzzle, not only owing to odd nomenclature but also to its questionable official status. The first patent protecting its action (DRP 319,035) was granted to

Theodor Bergmann of Gaggenau, Baden, on 30 December 1917; an additional patent to allow the mainspring to double as the action-locking catch spring (DRP 334,450) followed on 26 April 1918. In April 1918, too, the first manual was published. However, *Leitfaden für die Maschinenpistole 18,I. (M.P. 18,I.)* holds no clues to the odd suffix; additionally, the omission of a Druck-Vorschrift identifier may indicate that the gun was never adopted officially. It was plausibly suggested by the late Joachim Görtz, in "Wieso Maschinenpistole '18,I'?" (*Deutsches Waffen-Journal*, December 1983) that the '18,I.' suffix referred to the relevant portion of the military budget – Chapter 37, Title 18 of Artillerie-und Waffenwesen – and, consequently, was linked to the year of its first military trials by nothing other than coincidence.

Claims that more than fifty thousand guns were 'in service' by the end of the First World War are probably inflated. However, as gun 17677 bears pre-1918 army inspectors' marks, production was undoubtedly substantial.

The MP.18,I. – whatever its genesis – was a simple but sturdy blow-back firing 9mm pistol cartridges automatically at about 450 rounds per minute. Measuring 815mm overall, with a 200mm barrel and an empty weight of 4.18kg, it had a distinctive ventilated barrel jacket and a wood half-stock with a grasping groove in the fore-end. The most obvious feature, however, was the diagonally projecting feedway for the standard Trommelmagazin 08. This was presumably an expedient: the TM. 08 had a comparatively large magazine capacity (thirty-two rounds when fully loaded) but was heavy, clumsy, and less reliable than a simple box pattern. The MP.18,I./TM. 08 combination, therefore, was far from ideal.

Handguns. The principal regulation handguns in 1918 were the 9mm Parabellums ('Lugers'). The first substantial purchases of these guns were made by the imperial navy or Kaiserliche Marine in 1904, and eight thousand had been ordered from Deutsche Waffen- und Munitionsfabriken.

The *Selbstladepistole 1904* was officially renamed 'Pistole 1904' in 1907, and the operation of the safety lever was reversed in 1912 to prevent the safety system unlocking itself as the gun was thrust into the holster. The mechanism was altered so that the lever worked in reverse, but remedial work proceeded so slowly that in 1914, when it was decided to eliminate the grip safety entirely, the imperial dockyards were ordered to stop work until alternatives were considered.

Shortages of handguns had become so acute by the autumn of 1914 – Kiel dockyard had only six navy-type Parabellums in store by October – that a supplementary order was immediately given to D.W.M. Another followed in August 1916, though these were essentially long-barrelled Pistolen 1908 with short frames and army-style manual safeties.

Navy guns had distinctive proof marks in the form of an imperial (squared) crown, 'crown/M' inspectors' marks, and markings on the front grip strap that were usually applied by the Kiel or Wilhelmshaven dockyards.

The German army provisionally adopted the 9mm Parabellum in March 1907 for the four experimental infantry machine-gun detachments, and, in August 1908, the '9mm self-loading pistol Luger with flat-nose steel-jacketed bullet' was adopted to replace the ageing Reichsrevolvers.

An order for 50,000 pistols had been given to Deutsche Waffen- & Munitionsfabriken in 1911, and a duplicate production line was created in the Erfurt rifle factory. The Pistole 1908 was similar to the perfected navy Parabellum, with a coil-type main spring in the back of the grip and an extractor/loaded-chamber indicator set in the breechblock. However, the separate mechanical hold-open had been omitted and the grip safety had been replaced with a simple radial lever that raised a vertical plate to act directly on the laterally moving sear bar.

Experience soon showed that the lack of a hold-open was a backward step, and the omission had been rectified in 1913. A stock lug had been added in August 1913, and the design of the sear had been altered in 1916 to allow the mechanism to be cocked even if the safety catch were applied. The Parabellum performed well enough if kept reasonably clean, though the exposed sear bar could bind unless lightly coated with oil, and key components (particularly triggers, sears and trigger-plates) were often hand-fitted to ensure satisfactory performance.

A decision had been taken as early as 1907 to equip field artillerymen with long-barrelled pistols, and the *Lange Pistole 1908* (LP. 1908) was adopted in 1913. It was little more than a standard army-type Parabellum with a 20cm barrel and a tangent-leaf back sight on the barrel ahead of the receiver. Some guns used after 1917 were issued with the Trommelmagazin 1908 ('TM. 1908'), which contained thirty-two rounds instead of the eight in the standard box magazine. The TM. 1908 relied on a spring-driven follower to push cartridges around the helix in the drum and up through the pistol butt.

Wartime manuals optimistically suggest that the LP. 1908 was effective against head-size targets at 600m, and that 'accuracy to 800 metres' was possible if the back sight had been adjusted appropriately. However, many long-barrel guns were withdrawn from the army in 1918 to be issued to the crews of gunboats and inshore minesweepers.

The Parabellum had a characteristically slender barrel, tapering to end at the muzzle in a band for the front-sight base. The barrel screwed into the receiver, which in turn slid within a frame that was open at the top and the rear. A multi-link locking system, attached to the breechblock, could slide within the receiver, and an adjustable two-position 100m/200m back sight (navy guns) or a fixed open 'V'-notch sight (army guns) lay on the back toggle link. The sharply raked extension of the frame contained the detachable box magazine.

When the Parabellum fired, the barrel/receiver and breechblock groups moved back until sturdy grips on the toggle struck the ramps formed in the back of the frame, lifting the transverse joint between the toggle links above the axis of the bore. This broke the lock; barrel and receiver were brought to a stop by an abutment on the frame and the toggle links continued to fold upward around a fixed pivot in the rear of the receiver until the breechblock could be drawn back behind the magazine well. The spent case was ejected upward during the opening motion.

Once the breech had opened to its limit, a spring in the back of the grip (attached to the back toggle-link by a bell-crank lever and a stirrup) returned the breechblock. This stripped a new round into the chamber, closed and then re-locked the action as the toggle links rotated over-centre. When the last spent case had been ejected, a hold-open ensured that the breech remained open and the toggle broke the line of sight to show that the magazine was empty.

Pressing the magazine-release catch, on the left side of the frame behind the trigger, released the magazine. The toggles were pulled slightly upward to disengage the hold-open once a replacement magazine had been inserted, the action closed and the gun could be fired. On army-type guns, a safety lever set into the rear left side of the frame could be rotated to block the laterally moving sear.

Most pre-1918 Pistolen 1908 were marked with either the 'DWM' monogram or 'crown/ERFURT' on the toggle link, though a few were assembled by the Revisions-Commission at the end of the war and are marked 'crown/SPANDAU'. Guns made for the army after 1910 had been dated above the chamber, and, at least until the programme was suspended in 1916, could have unit markings on the grip straps.

Shortages of serviceable handguns during the First World War forced the German authorities to accept a variety of substitutes for the Parabellums. These included all the ancient Reichsrevolvers that could be pressed into service with munitions columns and similar formations, and a huge variety of simple 6.35mm and 7.65mm pistols that could be issued to officers, NCOs and military officials away from the front line.

These guns have been the subjects of several highly detailed studies, but were discarded – or 'retired' by individuals – after 1918. The only other pistol to see combat in large numbers was the 1896-pattern Mauser, designed in the early 1890s by the Feederle brothers, which had competed unsuccessfully against the Parabellum in the German military trials but had had a far greater impact commercially prior to 1914. When the war began, many guns of this type were already in the hands of individual officers (who were expected to purchase their own personal-defence weapons), and a contract for guns chambering the standard 9mm service-pistol cartridge was passed to Mauser in 1915. These had 500-metre back sights and a large '9' pressed into the grip to remind the firers of the chambering.

When the Mauser fired, the barrel and the receiver was run back until the locking piece in the receiver was cammed down into the frame-floor to disengage its lugs from the bolt. The barrel and receiver stopped against an abutment in the frame, allowing the bolt to run back alone to eject the spent case and cock the hammer. When the opening stroke was completed, the main spring within the bolt, which was compressed against a bar running transversely through the receiver, returned the parts. This movement stripped a new round into the chamber, cammed the locking piece back into engagement, and propelled the barrel/receiver unit back into battery.

The action was held open mechanically after the last spent case had been ejected, allowing the magazine to be refilled with loose rounds or from a charger. The bolt was then pulled back to disengage the hold-open, and then was run forward to strip a new round into the chamber. This also left the hammer at full cock.

The basic design had been finalised by the spring of 1897, once a ring-head hammer had replaced the original spur and a second lug had been added to the locking piece, but the design did not stabilise until the adoption in 1912 of the *neue Sicherung* ('New Safety', 'N.S.') that moved upward to lock only when the hammer was cocked.

The C/96 had a distinctive deep slab-sided frame containing a magazine ahead of the trigger aperture. The grips were customarily finely ribbed walnut, held in the frame by the only screw in the action, and a lanyard ring lay on the base of the butt. Magazines usually held ten rounds, and the back sight was either a fixed open notch or an adjustable tangent-leaf graduated as far as 1,000 metres.

The Mauser was a clever design with parts that interlocked without screws, bolts or springs, but it was also unnecessarily complicated and costly to make. Yet the introduction of copies in Spain in the 1920s eventually persuaded Mauser-Werke (as the company had become) to improve the basic design. This led to the detachable-magazine and 'Schnellfeuer' or fully automatic guns described below.

The guns of 1933

The pre-1918 small arms that survived to serve the Reichswehr gained a '1920' date in addition to their original marking, but the so-called 'Double Date' has a simple explanation. The extensive looting of military stores by Freikorps and revolutionaries hindered the control of the military inventory that was demanded by the restrictions of the Treaty of Versailles. Consequently, on 1 August 1920, the Reichswehrministerium directed that all small arms and accessories should be marked '1920', in

3.1mm-high numerals, so that the source of stolen weapons (otherwise indistinguishable among the flotsam of the First World War) could be readily identified.

Work began in September 1920 and was stopped on 8 April 1921 by the introduction of new unit markings, but it is possible to find guns, ranging from Parabellum pistols to Gew. 98, dated '1920' *and* '1921'; the former is the property mark, the latter is the date of manufacture.

Machine-guns.   Few changes were made to the Maxims during the Reichswehrzeit, apart from the addition of anti-aircraft sights, adapting the back sights for s.S. ball ammunition, modifying the feed for canvas or metal-link belts, and adding limit-stops and trajectory tables on the Schlitten 08.

Though the Allies were keen to prevent replacement of the ageing Maxims, it soon became obvious that they would not be suited to warfare that would become increasingly mobile. Clandestine development of a new gun led to the MG. 13, known during development as 'Gerät 13' to disguise its true purpose. Introduced in 1928 as the work of Simson & Co. of Suhl – the only gunmaker the Allies trusted to produce automatic weapons – the MG. 13 had been designed by Rheinmetall, and was being built secretly in the Sömmerda factory where Rheinmetall's predecessor, Rheinische Metallwaaren- & Maschinenfabrik, had built the 'Dreyse' rifles, pistols and machine-guns.

It has even been suggested that MG. 13 were rebuilt from pre-1918 Dreyse air-cooled guns, but the meagre output of the latter undermines such claims. What *is* undeniable, however, is that the MG. 13 was a minor adaptation of the older Dreyse design, sharing a recoil-operated breech-lock in which a pivoting bar in the receiver (above the trigger/pistol-grip assembly) locked the bolt securely behind the chambered cartridge. The bar was placed under considerable compressive stress at the instant of firing and could not compare with the strength of the interrupted-screw lock of the MG. 34 or the pivoting rollers of the MG. 42.

The MG. 13 had a bulky square-contoured receiver and a long barrel within a comparatively small-diameter casing that was pierced with holes to improve the circulation of air. The trigger, presaging that of the MG. 34, activated a hammer that struck a long firing pin running longitudinally through the bolt body. Pressing the upper segment of the trigger, marked 'E' for *Einzelfeuer*, gave single shots; pressing the lower portion, marked 'D' for *Dauerfeuer*, allowed fire to continue automatically until pressure was released.

The MG. 13 was very much lighter than the old water-cooled MG. 08, but could not sustain fire as effectively. An overheating barrel could be replaced only after partially dismantling the gun, unlatching the base of the receiver (which was then swung downward), removing the bolt unit, then withdrawing the barrel – possibly red-hot – backward and out of the receiver.

An attempt was made to mount the MG. 13 on a Danish Madsen tripod, for assessment as a medium machine-gun, but feed from 25-round box magazines and the unduly complicated barrel-change system doomed the experiments to fail. A special twin-drum 75-round *Patronentrommel 13* was developed in the mid 1930s, but proved to be heavy, difficult to load, and hung awkwardly on the left side of the breech.

The MG. 13 was usually mounted on a bipod, the *Zweibein 13*, which could be fixed either at the muzzle or the rear of the barrel casing ahead of the carrying handle. Most guns were fitted with flash-hiders, and had a tubular metal-frame butt with a clamshell-type shoulder pad. The butt could be swung back along the right side of the receiver to reduce overall length. Guns could be attached to the *Dreifuss 08/15*, necessitating a special adaptor or *Kupplungstück*, or directly to the *Dreifuss 34*. Pedestal mounts for use in pillboxes and strongpoints were also made.

A short-barrel MG. 13k was made in comparatively small numbers for use in tanks, vehicles and some aircraft prior to the advent of the MG. 34 and MG. 15. Once sufficient new guns had been issued, however, most surviving Dreyse-type guns were sold to Spain during the Civil War (1936–9) or to become the Portuguese 'Metralhadora M/938'.

The MG. 13 was efficient enough to remain in limited front-line service into the early years of the war; indeed, a few lasted in second-line, training, police and Volkssturm service until May 1945. But it was no more than a temporary solution to the Einheitsmaschinengewehr ('universal machine-gun') problems that had been exercising the minds of German small-arms designers since the First World War. The goal was to replace all the service guns at a single stroke, but although several promising prototypes had been made prior to 1930 – including one by Mauser and another in the 'Swiss' Solothurn factory partly owned by Rheinmetall – none had proved to be ideal.

Rheinische Metallwaaren- & Maschinenfabrik, known by 1927 as Rheinmetall AG, had been a leading producer of small arms and munitions during the First World War – so prominent, indeed, that the Allies forbade the company to make anything but artillery. Keen to evade these restraints, Rheinmetall had participated in the formation of Hollandsche Artillerie-Industrie en Handelsmaatschappij ('HAIHA') in the Netherlands in the early 1920s and, when this enterprise failed to prosper, had created Waffenfabrik Solothurn AG (effectively a Swiss subsidiary) before reaching an arrangement with Steyr-Daimler-Puch.

The perfected Rheinmetall Rh. 29 light machine-gun prototype, the work of Louis Stange, soon metamorphosed into the Solothurn S2-200. Offered for sale in a variety of chamberings, this gun initially generated little interest commercially except an isolated small-scale purchase by El Salvador in 1932. However, tests were impressive enough to convince the Austrian and Hungarian armies of its merits, and mass-production of the S2-200 began in the factories of Steyr-Daimler-Puch and Fegyvergyar ('FÉG'). The original Austrian M1930 and Hungarian 31.M machine-guns chambered the rimmed 8×56mm cartridge, but the later Hungarian 43.M shared the German 7.9×57mm rimless cartridge and an MG. 13-pattern box magazine.

The principal novelty in Stange's design was the method of locking. As the barrel, barrel extension and bolt recoiled, a rotating collar on the barrel extension was cammed out of engagement with an interrupted screw on the bolt. When the barrel and barrel extension stopped, the bolt reciprocated alone. It was then returned by the recoil spring and stripped another cartridge into the breech.

The Solothurn gun was efficient enough to serve the Austrian and Hungarian armies for many years, survivors of the Austrian issue being impressed into the German armies after the Anschluss and ex-Hungarian guns being added after the Germano-Hungarian Front collapsed in

1944. The principal drawbacks of the S2-200 were much the same as those of the MG. 13: detachable box magazines and a barrel-change system that limited its ability to undertake a fire-support role effectively. However, the efficient Stange collar-lock mechanism was perpetuated in the Rheinmetall-developed aircraft guns, the MG. 15, MG. 17 and MG. 131.

The prototype Mauser machine-guns were designated MV-1931 and MG. 32. Developed covertly through Metallwarenfabrik Kreuzlingen AG, a clandestine subsidiary in Switzerland, the MV-1931 shared the magazine, trigger mechanism and recoil-operated lock of the MG. 13. The improved MG. 32, generally credited to Ernst Altenburger, had a rotating bolt head that locked directly into the barrel rather than the barrel extension. Trials failed to demonstrate sufficient superiority over the MG. 13, and the Mauser design lay dormant until resurrected in 1934 to become the MG. 81 aircraft gun.

Rifles.   Little was done to the Gewehre 98 that had been retained for the Reichswehr, though experience gained from trench warfare had suggested improvements. The first changes were concerned more with finish than construction – the receivers were to be browned, and the bolts were to be greyed instead of bright-polished[1] – but a new tangent-leaf back sight, graduated down to 100 metres to facilitate close combat, was adopted in October 1924, and the width of the lower band was increased from 10mm to 18mm in June 1925.[2] The guns, though still full-length rifles, were subsequently redesignated 'Karabiner 98b'. The old Klammerfuss under the butt had been replaced with a lateral sling slot, and the bolt handles were turned down into a recess in the stock.

No substantial physical changes had been made to the Kar. 98 AZ retained for the Reichswehr and police, though nomenclature was changed to 'Karabiner 98a' to distinguish them from the full-length 'Kar. 98b'.[3] Rifles were also converted for instructional purposes (*Lehrgewehre*), for shooting practice (*Übungsgewehre*) or for drill-training purposes.

Field-service revealed a range of minor problems with the Mausers, and a variety of alterations were made in the late 1920s. These included the replacement of the spring controlling the bolt-release catch and ejector with two separate springs (1927); alterations to the bolt face to ensure that the magazine follower held the action open reliably after the last spent case had been ejected (1929); and alterations to the receiver and the extractor to cure failures of extraction caused when the extractor claw closed against the case-head instead of snapping over the rim (1931).[4]

The issue of sniping rifles was expressly forbidden in the Reichswehr, though not in the police units. Once the Allied inspection teams had withdrawn in 1926, after the signing of the Treaty of Locarno, attitudes changed. Though veterans of trench combat suggested that experienced men could fire as accurately over open sights as they could with the optical sights of the day, arguing that the extremely limited field of view obtained with a telescope sight blinded the sniper to threats that would have been obvious with the naked eye, the authorities demurred.

Accepting that the sights were comparatively delicate and a logistical complication, the Heeres-Leitung introduced the 'Zielvier' ('4×') in September 1927, then published details of an improved lateral adjustment in December 1927, and alterations to the bolt handle of the Kar. 98b to clear the barrel of the large-diameter sights that had been obtained from commercial production in September 1929.[5]

Service experience soon showed that the issue of optical sights was not particularly successful, forcing the army authorities into a change of heart. Consequently, sniping rifles were withdrawn in December 1931.[6] The guns and sights that had been placed in store were offered for sale during the early years of the Third Reich (q.v.).

There is little doubt that the police units – in Prussia at least – followed an independent course, and that Kar. 98a and Kar. 98b fitted with commercial 4× sights in conventional two-ring mounts were retained until the advent of the Kar. 98k. Usually these will have had distinctive police inspection marks somewhere on the gun.

Though the Allies had endeavoured to restrict the size of the Reichswehr, and to hamstring the development of an officer corps by insisting on unusually long service periods, the Germans soon found ways of camouflaging training. This was achieved partly by enlarging the police, and by creating a range of veterans organisations, 'sport clubs' and youth movements. Particularly valuable were the sports-flying and

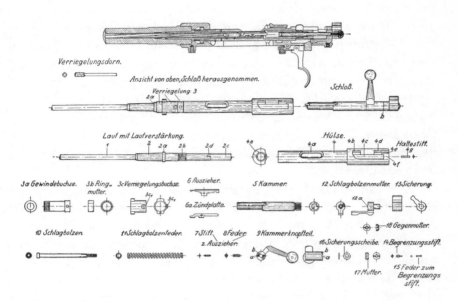

2. The components of the standard 5.6mm sub-calibre trainer for the Kar. 98k, the
EL. 24, from Fischer's *Waffen- und schiesstechnischer Leitfadung für die
Ordnungspolizei* (1943 edition).

sailing clubs, which enabled pilots and sailors to be trained at a time
when Germany had practically no air force and a navy that had been
reduced to the status of a token coast-defence force. In addition, the
paramilitary formations promoted by the N.S.D.A.P., initially small,
were greatly enlarged during the early 1930s.

Most of the basic firearms training was originally undertaken with
barrel-insert units (*Ziellaufchen*) chambered for 4mm Zielmunition 20,
tiny primer-propelled cartridges that were of no use at distances greater
than 25 metres. Realising that this prevented realistic training on
outdoor ranges, the army high command accepted the *Einstecklauf
24* ('EL. 24') on 29 June 1927.[7] Designed and made by Erfurter
Maschinenfabrik, subsequently known better as 'Erma-Werke', this
single-shot insert was similar to the preceding Ziellaufchen but fired
5.6mm lfb (.22 Long Rifle rimfire) ammunition with an effective range
of 100 metres.

Experience soon showed that the EL. 24 was a great improvement on its single-shot predecessor, but the inability to fire more than one shot compromised its value as a combat trainer. The answer was provided by a detachable five-round box magazine that projected down into the magazine well of the standard Kar. 98b. Known as the 'Einstecklauf 24 mit Mehrladeeinrichtung' ('EL. 24 m. M.'), the improved design was accepted in January 1932[8] and modified in 1936 (see Chapter Three). The magazine-fed barrel insert was so successful that many of the earlier single-shot examples were subsequently adapted to accept magazines.[9]

The Einsteckläufe were designed specifically for use in the standard rifles, the short-barrelled Kar. 98a and long-barrelled Kar. 98b (the modified Gew. 98), and could fit the perfected Kar. 98k with virtually no alterations. However, there were other solutions to the training problem. Mauser-type rifles, the so-called 'Wehrmanngewehre' or 'Wehrmannbüchsen', had been made in large quantities prior to 1918, chambering a special rimmed 8.15×46 cartridge designed in the 1890s by a gunsmith named Fröhn. This could be loaded to give good short-range performance, and was much better suited to practice in clubs and urban firing ranges where the power of the regulation 7.9mm rifle cartridge would have been a handicap. The 8.15mm rifles were virtually indistinguishable from the service issues, except in the design and graduation of the back sights.

A later solution was the introduction of purpose-built 5.6mm-calibre training rifles known as 'Kleinkaliberkarabiner' (KKK.') or, more commonly, 'Kleinkalibergewehre' ('KK. Gew.'). Derived from the rimfire sporting rifles that were being made by many of the leading German gunmaking companies, KK. Gew. usually had simple bolt mechanisms that relied on the base of the bolt handle to lock the action closed, but were stocked in much the same way as the Kar. 98k . . . complete with bayonet bar and military-style sling fittings. The design of the back sight and the safety catch also deliberately mirrored those of the Kar. 98k to facilitate training.

KK. Gew. were made in large numbers by many of the same gunmakers that had made the sporting guns, and who, in many instances, were also offering *Deutsches Sport-Modelle* ('D.S.M.') to the paramilitary

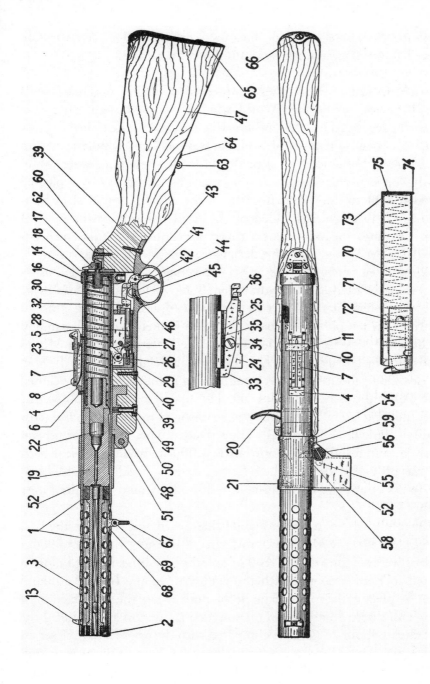

3. Sectional drawings of the MP. 28, from Fischer's *Waffen- und schiesstechnischer Leitfaden für die Ordnungspolizei* (1943 edition).

organisations. These guns all measured about 110–111cm overall, weighed about 3kg, and had five-round box magazines.

Submachine-guns.   The Allies confiscated surviving Bergmann MP. 18,I. at the end of the First World War. However, though some were apparently destroyed in 1920, others were reissued to the police to facilitate control of a civilian population that was increasingly polarising into armed camps. Designed to accept the TM. 08, these guns were subsequently converted to accept conventional box magazines by replacing the feedway block and removing part of the wooden fore-end. A bolt-blocking safety catch was added to the front left side of the receiver behind the magazine unit. Guns of this type are now sometimes misleadingly called 'MP.18,II.', but this designation has no official status.

A modified version of the MP. 18 developed in the late 1920s by C.G. Haenel Waffen- & Fahrradfabrik of Suhl was licensed to S.A. Belge Anciens Établissements Pieper of Herstal-lèz-Liége, allowing guns to serve the German police and be exported to China, Bolivia, Japan and elsewhere in 1928–35 without attracting Allied interference. The MP. 28 was adopted by Portugal as the Mo. 929, and in Belgium as the 'Mi. Mle. 34'. Measuring about 812mm overall, with a 200mm barrel, it weighed about 4kg without its magazine and had a selector button above the trigger, moving laterally, that allowed semi- or fully-automatic fire (customarily marked 'E' and 'D' respectively). The main spring was improved, and a ludicrously optimistic 1,000-metre tangent-leaf back sight was provided. Turning the retracted cocking handle up into a separate recess above the cocking-handle slot constituted the only safety feature.

Once the drive towards clandestine rearmament intensified, it became clear that the MP. 28 was not particularly noteworthy and better weapons were sought. The S1-100 or Solothurn submachine-gun, often credited to Louis Stange of Rheinmetall, refined the basic Bergmann system by placing the mainspring in the butt, where the bolt acted on it through an intermediary rod. This softened the action and reduced the cyclic rate by about 25 per cent compared with the original MP. 18 series. A sliding lever-type fire selector was let into the left side of the fore-end, and the receiver-top was machined from a solid block rather than a simple drawn tube. This allowed the top cover, hinged immediately behind the magazine feedway block, to swing upward to give access to the action.

A typical S1-100 was about 775mm long, with a 200mm barrel, and weighed 4kg empty. A loaded 32-round magazine added an additional 1.1kg. Cyclic rate was about 550–600 rds/min.

Waffenfabrik Solothurn A.G., the Swiss-based metalworking company created by Rheinmetall in April 1929 with the co-operation of Steyr, made a series of these guns in a number of differing guises, with barrels of varying length, bayonet lugs, and even a special light tripod mount. Small deliveries went to countries as disparate as Bolivia and Japan, in calibres ranging from 7.63mm Mauser to 9mm Steyr. A variant of the S1-100 was subsequently adopted by the Austrian army as the MP. 34, many being assimilated into the Wehrmacht after the 1938 Anschluss.

Handguns.   Parabellum pistols issued to the Reichswehr were marked '1920' to show that they had been inventoried in accordance with the restrictions imposed by the Treaty of Versailles. Most of them were standard Pistolen 1908, though a few navy pistols were kept for the Reichsmarine. Some of these were subsequently marked with '1920', and, when in need of repair, were customarily fitted with 10cm barrels.

D.W.M., by then renamed Berlin-Karlsruher Industrie-Werke (B.K.I.W.) began production again in the 1920s. Output was restricted to commercial and export markets, as the supply and refurbishment of German military and police pistols was the prerogative of Simson & Co. of Suhl. Simson habitually marked guns and rifles simply with 'S', the code allotted by the Allies after the Treaty of Versailles had been ratified to distinguish the prime contractor for 'Schusswaffen'.

Though the Allies had sold Simson & Co the production machinery having been taken from the Prussian government factory in Erfurt, most of the military and police Parabellums of this era were either 'reworks' of pre-1918 weapons or assembled from leftover components. However, three thousand new guns were delivered in 1925, followed by a similar quantity in 1926. Theoretically replacements for guns that had been 'worn out' in field service, but possibly also a way of returning the production line to working order, these pistols were marked 'SIMSON & Co.' over 'SUHL' on the toggles. Details of Parabellums used by the Reichswehr and the police, including a description of the Schiwy sear-safety system, can be found in Chapter Eleven of my book *The Luger Story* and some of the others listed in the Bibliography.

Signal pistols.   During the Reichsmarine period (1921–35), the navy, very short of signal pistols, had simply copied the standard pre-1918 pattern. Made in the naval workshops in Wilhelmshaven, largely of bronze (with some steel parts), this had a tipping-barrel block that was locked by a catch on top of the breech. Opening the barrel block cocked the internal strikers, but the safety lever on the left side of the frame – immediately behind the trigger – had to be rotated to expose the word 'FEUER' before firing.

The breech latch of post-1921 guns was enlarged, and was chequered instead of ribbed as on the original; grips were red or red-brown Bakelite instead of wood. The double-barrel type measured 215mm overall, had 113mm barrels and weighed about 1,225gm.

The standard army signal pistol was the Walther *Heeresmodell* or *Heeres-Leuchtpistole*, a vast improvement on preceding designs that showed Fritz Walther's genius for combining several functions in a single component. Patented in August 1930 (German Patent 506,011, sought on 22 December 1926), the single-action tipping-barrel breech was locked by an underlever. Adopted by the Reichswehr in 1928, the Heeresmodell was 245mm long, had a 155mm smoothbore barrel, and weighed about 1,275gm with the original steel frame. The calibre was '4-bore', nominally 26.65mm but actually nearer 26.9mm.

Substantial quantities of Heeresmodelle were delivered to the Reichswehr, but the rearmament programmes of the mid 1930s forced a reappraisal. Walther was asked to lighten the signal pistol by substituting a black-anodised duraluminum frame for steel, and Bakelite grips replaced chequered wood. Alloy-frame guns weighed only a little more than half as much as their steel-frame predecessors.

Small quantities of the 'Lauflose Fliegerpistole System Eisfeld', made by J.G. Anschütz of Zella-Mehlis ('J.G.A.'), satisfied the pre-1935 air force and paramilitary sports-flying agencies. Distinguished by its apparent lack of a barrel, the pistol had an 11mm-calibre laterally hinged breech unit into which the stem of a fixed flare could be placed once the side-latch had been unlocked. The breech unit was then closed, locked, and a pull on the double-action trigger ignited the charge.

Eisfeld pistols were about 145mm long, weighed merely 600gm, and accepted special ammunition.

3

The Third Reich, 1933–38

The death of President Hindenburg in August 1934 removed the last obstacle to Hitler's ambitions. The armed forces, realizing that a return to pre-1918 prominence was virtually guaranteed, immediately consented to Hitler assuming duties of commander-in-chief as well as head of state. Conscription was introduced in March 1935; the Saarland, which had been separated from Germany since 1918, voted to return to the Reich; and the last remnants of the Treaty of Versailles were effectively cast away.

Britain, Italy and France were sufficiently alarmed to confer, but Germany had gambled that the principal Allies would be split. Fascist Italy was already gazing covetously at Abyssinia; Britain and France remained unable to reach mutual agreement. In June 1935, Britain and Germany had even signed a naval agreement in which the former effectively condoned the latter's abrogation of the limitations imposed by Versailles. Civil war loomed in Spain. The gamble had paid off.

On 7 March 1936, German troops marched into the demilitarized Rheinland. No more than token Allied reaction had been forthcoming. The commencement of the Spanish Civil War in the summer of 1936 then diverted attention from potential confrontation between Germany and France to another theatre, in which rebels led by Franco ('Nationalists') endeavoured to wrest control from the Republican government.

The Civil War is best remembered for political events and the affairs of the International Brigade. However, many arms makers saw it as a heaven-sent testing ground for weapons and equipment. Italo-German aid was speedily forthcoming for the neo-Fascist Nationalists; Russia backed the Republicans, but propaganda skilfully obscured the true extent of foreign aid. Cleverly doctored photographs of American Martin aircraft were substituted for Russian Tupolev bombers, and excesses such as the bombing of Guernica by the Condor Legion – a test-bed for German warplanes, often flown by German pilots – tended to distract public gaze from the real advances in weapons technology. Though Spain proved to be the drain into which many obsolescent weapons could be poured, it was also the proving ground for Messerschmitt, Dornier, Heinkel and other warplanes that would grace a far greater stage within a few months.

Among the most important political changes made in Germany in this period was the abolition of the post of 'Minister of War', with the dismissal of the disgraced Werner von Blomberg. This allowed Hitler to assume a supreme power exercised through the *Oberkommando der Wehrmacht* (O.K.W.), the armed forces high command.

In the period of comparative calm between the wars, the Germans had collected copious details of foreign matériel and published it in 'Kennblätter fremden Geräts'. Huge numbers of captured rifles were taken into service during the Second World War; though the most important received German designations such as 'Gew. 29/40', most were known simply by their *fremd Gerät* number. The 'Gewehr 261 (b)', therefore, was the Belgian Mle. 89 Mauser rifle. The suffix letter merely identified the country of origin. Neither was the system restricted to small arms: the Soviet T-34 tank was the 'Pz. Kpfw. 747 (r)' and the British 25-pdr Mark I field gun was the '8.76cm FK. 281 (e)' if it had a box trail or '282 (e)' with a split trail.

By 1943, *Waffen- und schiesstechnischer Leitfaden für die Ordnungspolizei* was still listing a variety of captured weapons that had been impressed into police service. Belgium had provided the Gewehre 261 (b), 262 (b) and 263 (b) – Mle 89, 35 and 89/36 Mausers – while the Gewehr 211 (h) and Karabiner 413 (h), the M1895 Mannlicher rifle and No.3 (O.M. and N.M.) carbines, had been taken from the Dutch.

The French had contributed a variety of long arms, including the Gewehr 241 (f), the Mle 07/15 M 34 Berthier; the Gewehre 301 (f) and 303 (f), Mle 86/93 and 86/93 R 35 Lebels; the Gewehr 304 (f), the Mle 16 Berthier; and the Gewehr 361 (f), which was the venerable single-shot Mle 74 Gras. The Karabiner 552 (f) and 553 (f) were French Mle 90 and Mle 92/16 Berthier carbines respectively, and the Karabiner 561 (f) was the single-shot Mle 74 Gras pattern.

Norway had been comparatively unproductive, yielding only the Gewehr 214 (n), the Norwegian M/1894 Krag-Jørgensen, but Russia had provided the Gewehre 252 (r), 253 (r) and 254 (r) – obr.1891g Mosin-Nagant infantry, dragoon and cossack rifles – and the Selbstladegewehr 259 (r), the SVT40 Tokarev, plus Karabiner 453 (r) and 454 (r). The latter were the obr.1910g and 'M1924/27' (obr.1938g?) Mosin-Nagant carbines.

Regulation weapons

Machine-guns.   Just as progress with the Einheitsmaschinengewehr ('universal machine-gun') concept seemed to be stagnating, the Heereswaffenamt decided to amalgamate the best features of the competing weapons. Issued for troop trials in 1936–7 and formally approved on 24 January 1939, the *Maschinengewehr 34* ('MG. 34') had been perfected in Sömmerda under the supervision of Louis Stange and Major Dipl.-Ing. Ritter von Weber. It perpetuated features of the MG. 13 within the general appearance of the Solothurn (Rheinmetall) S2-200, but the breech lock combined Stange's interrupted-screw with the cam-and-roller rotation of the Mauser. Unlike the Solothurn S2-200, however, the MG. 34 bolt rotates; the Solothurn bolt moves straight back.

A recoil booster was fitted to the muzzle of the MG. 34 to increase the cyclic rate and improve reliability. The result was undoubtedly the most impressive gun of its day, as it had been equipped with mounts to suit every possible occasion. By the end of the Second World War, the MG. 34 had been issued with the *Zweibein 34* (bipod), *Dreifuss 34* (tripod), *MG-Lafette 34* (buffered quadrupod), *Fliegerdrehstütze 36* (pedestal), *Zwillingssockel 36* (twin anti-aircraft mount) and the *MG-*

Sockel 41. The breadth of the MG-Gerät 34, or 'machine-gun system', was one of the wonders of pre-1939 ordnance.

Unfortunately, such incredible complexity – the Solothurn-inspired buffered mount alone had more than two hundred parts – proved to be a terrible production handicap. The MG. 34 could not be made in large enough quantities to satisfy wartime demand, when quantity rather than quality was needed. The complex bolt system required particularly careful machining. Combat experience in Russia and North Africa soon showed that key tolerances were much too fine, and that mud, sand or grit often jammed the action. When clean, the MG. 34 was extremely efficient; when dirty, or in extremes of temperature, it was scarcely a match for the Degtyarev DP, even though the Russian gun lacked its German rival's capacity for sustained fire.

There were several versions of the MG. 34, the basic gun being made by Gustloff-Werke in Suhl (formerly Simson & Co.); Maget in Berlin; Mauser-Werke A.G. in Berlin-Borsigwalde; Steyr-Daimler-Puch A.G. in Steyr/Oberdonau; and Waffenwerke Brünn A.G. in Brno in Reichsprotektorat Böhmen-Mahren. From September 1939 until the end of the war, 345,109 guns were accepted by the H.WaA., peak production occurring in 1941 (81,467) with an additional surge in 1944. Guns were also supplied to Portugal, where they served into the 1970s as 'Metralhadora Mo. 944', while production continued in the Brno factory to equip the postwar Czechoslovakian army.

The first two series of semi-experimental guns, numbered between 1 and about 2300, had distinctively machined feed covers, rate reducers built into the action to vary the cyclic rate (700–1,000 rds/min), and wooden butts. The production variant abandoned the rate reducer, which was a superfluous complication, and was ultimately made with a plain stamped feed cover and a synthetic butt.

During the development phase, the *Oberkommando der Luftwaffe* (O.K.L.) had considered adapting the MG. 34 for airborne use. However, the weight of the gun, and land service-inspired features such as the selective-fire trigger and readily exchangeable barrel, prevented a satisfactory transformation. The O.K.L. subsequently purchased the Rheinmetall-developed MG. 15 and, when this was found wanting, then turned to the Mauser MG. 81.

The MG. 34 machine-gun was easily adaptable for tank and vehicle use. An armoured barrel jacket, solid for two-thirds of its length, replaced the standard pierced-sheet pattern in most vehicle roles. The butt, bipod-retaining stud and anti-aircraft sights could be removed to allow the guns to be clamped in special vehicle mounts. However, spare-parts kits comprising a butt, a bipod and a special clamp-mount for the anti-aircraft sight were carried aboard most vehicles to enable the guns to be dismounted for field service.

The standard MG. 34, which was 1,220mm long and weighed a little over 12kg with its bipod, could feed from a belt (*Patronengurt 34*) or a detachable 75-round saddle drum (*Patronentrommel 34*). Cyclic rate was reckoned to be about 800–900 rds/min, depending on the individual gun and the feed system; friction and weight slowed the belt-feed rate compared with spring-feed from the drum. Barrel life, originally about 6,000 rounds, was greatly prolonged by chrome-plating the bore and chamber during the war.

The comparatively leisurely development of the new Einheitsmaschinengewehr meant that virtually all guns made before 1940 went straight to the army. Consequently, the Luftwaffe eventually asked Rheinmetall to produce a refinement of the Solothurn S2-200, which eventually entered service as the MG. 15. The comparative failure of this gun, which fired too slowly, then forced the Luftwaffe authorities to turn to Mauser – still piqued by the choice of Rheinmetall to develop the MG. 34 – to transform the dormant MG. 32 into the MG. 81.

The Waffen-SS, which was still regarded as politicians playing at soldiery, also wished to acquire machine-guns of its own, preferably outside regular procurement channels where the Wehrmacht was generally accorded priority. Unfortunately, most of the major machine-gun manufacturers (especially Mauser and Rheinmetall) were already involved with the MG. 34 and MG. 81. Krieghoff, which had unsuccessfully tried to interest the Luftwaffe in a machine-gun in the mid-1930s, was also unable to proceed. It seemed that only Knorr-Bremse of Berlin, an automotive-brake manufacturing company with no previous experience of small-arms production, had spare production capacity.

Knorr-Bremse had acquired the rights to a German-financed light machine gun designed in Sweden by Lauf & Przikalla and patented in

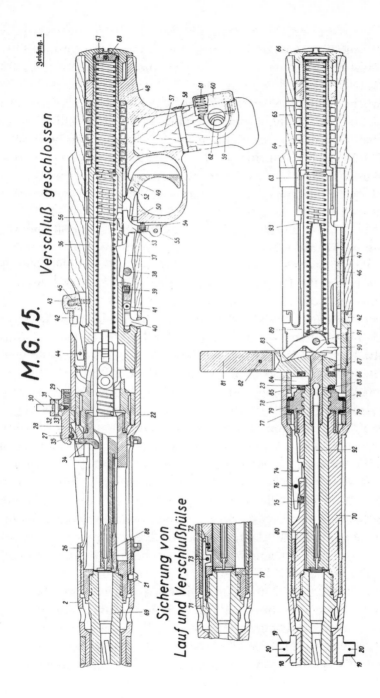

4. Sectional drawings of the breech of the MG. 15, the standard hand-held German aircraft machine-gun of the 1930s. From the official manual.

1933–4. Prototypes of the 6.5mm LH/33 had been unsuccessfully offered to Scandinavian governments, and improved 7.9mm-calibre LH/35 and LH/36 variants were hawked around Germany once Lauf's patents had been assigned to Knorr-Bremse. The Knorr-Bremse LH/36 was subsequently purchased by the Waffen-SS, but was speedily replaced by vz. 26 and vz. 30 light machine-guns after the occupation of Czechoslovakia. Surviving Knorr-Bremse guns were apparently shipped to Finland and expended during the Winter War. Not much was wrong with their basic design but, as the manufacturer had no experience of gunmaking or the demands of military service, some of the components were simply not robust enough.

The LH/36 was a very distinctive lightweight weapon, with a notable gap between the barrel and the gas port/piston-tube assembly above it. A prominent combination carrying/barrel-changing handle hung down below the feed aperture, into which a detachable twenty-round box magazine could be inserted.

The principal aircraft guns of the mid-1930s had been the MG. 15 and MG. 17, Rheinmetall designs intended for flexible and fixed mounts respectively. Developed from the Solothurn S2-200 land-service gun, they were designated T6-200 or S6-200 by their manufacturer. They had Stange-pattern breech arrangements and locking systems; the MG. 15 (T6-200) also had a wooden butt/spring tube that supported the trigger unit. Capable only of automatic fire at rates as much as 1,200 rds/min, the MG. 15 was usually encountered with anti-aircraft ring sights, a ball mount and an integral canvas bag to receive ejected cases. The saddle-pattern magazine held 150 rounds, feeding alternately from its two drums. The MG. 15 needed a suitable bipod for the ground role, though some were adapted for the Norwegian m/29 Browning tripod. The official Luftwaffe ground-role adaptations were created from a kit comprising a purpose-built bipod, a new mainspring tube and an extension butt similar to that of the MG. 13.

The belt-fed MG. 17 (S6-200), intended for fixed installations, could also be adapted to improvised tripod mounts, but the enlargement of the basic system, the 13mm-calibre MG. 131, was rarely encountered on ground mounts until the end of the Second World War. The MG. 131 existed in several versions – designated 'A'–'H', depending on features such as the method of charging, the design of the trigger system and the direction of belt-feed.

A typical MG. 131D was charged pneumatically, had an electro-magnetic trigger, and fed from the left side of the breech. Two guns in the series (subvariants 'G' and 'H', with right- and left-side feed respectively) were adapted to fire ammunition that was ignited electrically. However, virtually all MG. 131 emplaced in a ground role, even if they were confined to static defences, were observers' guns with pistol grips and special cocking handles. Fed from the Gurt 131, the MG. 131 embodied a modified Stange lock and an accelerator similar to that of the MG. 13.

Though the MG. 15 and MG. 17 were ordered into full production, proving effective enough to fulfil immediate needs, the Luftwaffe was satisfied by neither the double-drum magazine nor the comparatively low rate of fire. The army had offered participation in the development of a genuinely universal machine-gun, but the perfected MG. 34 had a cyclic rate that was too low for airborne combat where volume of fire could be decisive. The Oberkommando der Luftwaffe asked Mauser-Werke, still smarting from the army's rejection of the MG. 32, to develop an improved aircraft gun, and the *Maschinengewehr 81* (MG. 81) was adopted in 1936. It shared the basic rotating-lug locking system and several other features with the MG. 34, but was shorter, lighter and cheaper to make. The earliest guns had a 60cm barrel similar to that of the MG. 15, but this gave so much drag in the slipstream that the observer was unable to train the gun effectively; aircraft speeds had considerably increased since 1930. The barrels were shortened to about 475mm after 1938, increasing the fire-rate and paradoxically improving accuracy.

The MG. 81 shared a selectively distintegrating-link Gürt 17/81 with the MG. 17. By using a special plier-like tool, the belt could be converted to non-distintegrating form, or to ensure that it parted only in short link-sections. The recoil-operated MG. 81 had a cyclic rate of about 1,600 rds/min, which could be increased to nearly 3,000 by pairing otherwise identical left- and right-feed guns. Actuated by a single central pistol-grip unit, the MG. 81 Z. (*Zwilling*, 'twin') ejected spent cases into the space between the two receivers, to travel around chutes that curved up and over the receivers and be expelled on the side of the gun from which they had been fed into the breech.

The MG. 81 soon proved to be very efficient, especially the compact 'Z.' model. It was issued to the Kriegsmarine for short-range anti-aircraft defence – even though the lightweight barrel was unsuitable – and, late in the war, on rudimentary bipods for field service. Ground guns usually had simple butts that extended rearward from the pistol grip assembly, but several differing patterns are known.

MG. 81 were originally made only in the Mauser factory in Oberndorf; however, demand escalated until four other major contractors participated: L.O. Dietrich of Altenburg, Heinrich Krieghoff of Suhl, I.C. Wagner of Mühlhausen, and Norddeutsche Maschinenfabrik of Wittenberge.

The 15mm MG. 151 was another recoil-operated Mauser design, locked by a rotating bolt. Capable of firing 750 rds/min from the selectively distintegrating Gurt 151, the MG. 151 relied on a pinion on the return-spring tube in the receiver cover to engage a rack on top of the feed slide; the tube reciprocated during the firing cycle, presenting the next round to the breech. By exchanging tubes and a few minor parts in the mechanism, the feed direction could be reversed.

Most versions of the MG. 151 fired conventional percussion-ignition ammunition, though the MG. 151E was electrically primed. Towards the end of the war, when many had been displaced by the MG. 151/20 – a 2cm-calibre enlargement of the basic design firing more powerful ammunition – a few 15mm-calibre machine-guns were adapted for rudimentary tubular steel wheeled carriages, apparently for the Volkssturm in Thüringen. Others were impressed as anti-aircraft weapons.

Mention should also be made of the standard 2cm anti-aircraft gun, the Flak. 38, developed by Mauser to replace the comparatively unsuccessful Rheinmetall Flak. 30. Fed semi-automatically from a 25-round box magazine inserted in the left side of the receiver, the recoil-operated Flak. 38 was locked by a rotating bolt. In addition to its original role, which declined in importance as heavier weapons appeared, the Flak. 38 was regularly impressed into maritime and ground service. Some had been mounted on the lightweight purpose-built *Gebirgsjäger-Flaklafette 38*, with detachable pneumatic-tyred wheels; others appeared on rudimentary tubular-steel carriages with simple tyreless wheels. These were usually provided with crude butts supporting sizeable shoulder-pads. Owing to the diversity of 2cm ammunition, which included armour-piercing and high-explosive rounds, the converted anti-aircraft guns proved useful against lorries, half-tracks and lightly armoured vehicles.

Rifles.   Though the Karabiner 98a and 98b had remained the principal service weapons of the Reichswehr for the duration of the Weimar Republic, the army continually agitated for a purpose-designed short rifle that would combine the general characteristics of the Kar. 98b (the modified Gew. 98) with the general handiness of the Kar. 98a.

Waffenfabrik Mauser, renamed 'Mauser-Werke A.G.' in 1922, had introduced a 'Standard Modell' rifle in 1924, in long or short forms, to compete with essentially similar Mauser-type rifles being touted commercially by Fabrique Nationale d'Armes de Guerre and Československá Zbrojovka. Mauser had also been making the so-called 'Deutsches Reichspost' rifle from 1933 onward. These guns allied the standard 55cm short-rifle barrel with the fittings and furniture of the Kar. 98b, and led to a series of field trials with short rifles submitted by Mauser and Sauer. Differing principally in the design of the barrel bands and the way in which the bands were retained, these guns bore number-group makers' codes in addition to the coded date 'K' for 1934.

The Mauser prototype was preferred, and, with a few minor adjustments, was accepted for service. The introduction of the Karabiner 98k was announced in June 1935[1], together with a muzzle protector and a new sling. Series production began immediately, though some time elapsed before the first deliveries were made.

Measuring 111cm overall and weighing 3.9kg, according to the official specification, the Kar. 98k superficially resembled the Kar. 98b in most respects (except length) and accepted the Seitengewehr 84/98. The standard cartridge remained the 8mm S.-Patrone (redesignated '7.9mm'), together with the heavyweight s.S.-Patrone introduced principally for machine-gun use in 1918.

Field service revealed a variety of minor problems, which were discussed in the pages of *Heeres-Verordnungsblatt* and *Allgemeine Heeresmitteilungen* in the late 1930s. They ranged from a reduction in the size of the slider button on the 98k back sight and an alteration of the bolt-release catch housing to accept a stronger spring to the substitution of a more robust back-sight slider.[2] An improved muzzle protector appeared in February 1939, followed in December 1939 by a front-sight protector (Kar. 98k only) and a muzzle cap (all '98'-type guns).

Improvements to the standard sub-calibre trainer, the EL. 24 m. M., were approved in December 1936. Examples delivered into store after March 1937 had an improved magazine, a better magazine catch, and changes to the striker nut and the safety-catch assembly.[3] Production continued virtually until the end of the Second World War. Sub-calibre trainers were also used with the standard 3.7cm anti-tank gun. The authorities announced the 'Einspannvorrichtung für Karabiner zur Tak.' in June 1935, followed by the introduction of the perfected 'Schiessgerät 35 für 3.7 cm Tak.' in May 1936. The Gerät 35 was a modified Karabiner 98a in a special clamping that allowed it to be positioned inside the bore of the anti-tank gun.[4] It was soon supplemented by a 5.6mm rimfire barrel insert.[5]

Sniping rifles, which had been withdrawn from army service in 1931, continued to lack favour. Indeed, periodic attempts were made to sell sights that had been kept in store (the rifles had presumably been returned to service).[6] A typical entry in *Allgemeine Heeresmitteilungen* in 1935 stated that all telescope sights '×4 and all other types of sight [for the Kar. 98b], being stored by the ordnance office in Spandau, are to be set aside as they will no longer be required for military purposes . . .' In March 1938, however, the disposal of sights was stopped.[7] Official opinion, influenced by the tension that was rising in Europe, had had another change of mind.

Most of the earliest sniping rifles were fitted with the 'Zielvier' or 'four-power' type, acquired from manufacturers such as Zeiss of Jena and Hensoldt of Wetzlar. The sights varied considerably in detail, depending on the source. Some had adjustable ocular lenses, other did not; adjust-ments for elevation and windage varied; and there were differences in the rings that were used to attach the telescope-barrels to the mounts. The standard reticle was a 'picket post' – a thick vertical half-height taper-tipped post with a thin horizontal bar – but crosshair, crosshair-and-dot, and a variety of composite designs were tolerated.

A rail attached to the left side of the Kar. 98k receiver, with three short threaded bolts, accepted the base of the one-piece sight mount. A clamping lever on the mount locked over a pin projecting from the front of the rail, but the meagre proportions of the rail and the curved side of the receiver wall compromised stability. The rail loosened too easily, often after only a few shots had been fired, and could rarely be re-zeroed in such a way that the same mark could be hit without adjusting the sight itself. The problem was so serious that lock-screws and pins projecting into the receiver were tried, without notable success, until a perfected version with two lateral pins and an additional vertical clamp (which pressed a bar downward into the top surface of the rail) was proposed.

Assault rifles.   One of the most interesting developments in this period, but not obvious at the time, concerned the development of an 'intermediate' cartridge. The Germans had realized during the First World War that the standard 7.9mm rifle cartridge was too powerful. The Bergmann MP. 18,I. submachine-gun, despite its badly designed Trommelmagazin and excessive weight, promised great utility during close-quarter assaults. It was handy, simple to use, easily maintained, and had a good rate of fire. But the 9mm Pistolenpatrone 1908 prevented the MP. 18 replacing infantry rifles and standard carbines.

Experiments to define an optimal 'all-purpose' cartridge had commenced in 1915–16; however, as the First World War had bogged down at Verdun and the Somme, there was little opportunity to introduce a weapon at such a critical moment. Whether the G.P.K. would have progressed to hybrid cartridges after 1918 is an open question, as all experimentation was stopped by the Treaty of Versailles.

Trials were taking place at this time in Switzerland, where small numbers of 7.65×27mm cartridges had been made by the Eidgenössische Munitionsfabrik, Thun, under the direction of Oberst Eduard Rubin. Rubin's death in 1920 then opened the way for Adolf Fürrer. Best known for his complicated toggle-lock machine-carbines, Fürrer developed a 'Pistolengewehr' chambering 7.65×35mm cartridges in 1921 and a 'Maschinengewehrpistole' followed in 1922.

The ballistics of the short-case 7.65mm cartridges did not impress the Swiss authorities strongly enough, and the Fürrer-inspired l. MG. 25 subsequently chambered standard full-length Ordonnanzpatrone.

Experiments with the intermediate cartridges continued in Switzerland into the 1930s, when copies of the drawings apparently passed into German hands through the intermediacy of Waffenfabrik Solothurn. Wehrmacht experts accepted that no change in the 7.9mm service cartridge was likely prior to 1935, but nevertheless continued work on 'intermediate' patterns. Gradually, therefore, a vague requirement arose for a light automatic carbine developing appreciably greater power than a submachine-gun firing pistol ammunition.

In the early 1930s, Rheinisch-Westfälische Sprengstoff A.G. ('R.W.S.') and Gustav Genschow & Co. A.G. ('Geco') began trials with intermediate cartridges, initially adapted from '8×46R' or '8.15×46R' sporting pattern, developed in the 1890s, that had been widely used for training in Germany. The cartridge case, initially 45–46mm and then 40mm long, lost its rim and gained a jacketed spitzer bullet weighing about 4.9gm; the 57mm-long case of the standard 7.9mm round was loaded with bullets weighing about 12gm. The Heereswaffenamt, sufficiently impressed, awarded Geco a development contract. The name 'Winter' – Hans-Georg Winter, Director of the Genschow factory in Durlach bei Karlsruhe – is now generally attached to these experimental cartridges.

Genschow experimented with cartridges throughout the mid-1930s, their cases measuring 37–46mm and the bullets weighing 4.9–5.3gm. However, no acceptable results had been obtained by 1937, owing to inconsistent H.WaA. directives and the absence of a definitive specification. From this period, only the Vollmer A 35/I (1935) and A 35/II (1938) have been conclusively identified; these carbines, about 960mm long and weighing 4.25kg, chambered a 7.75mm cartridge with a 40mm case from which a 9gm spitzer bullet could attain nearly 700 m/sec.

Rheinmetall-Borsig's short-case round, designed by Fritz Herlach, crystallized as a 7mm bullet in a 36.5mm bottleneck case; the competing D.W.M. version, developed by research facilities in Lübeck-Schlutup, initially had a 39mm case. Neither was adjudged wholly successful, though the latter could develop muzzle velocities in excess of 960 m/sec. D.W.M. was still doggedly championing its 7mm cartridge as late as 1942, when the base diameter had been reduced to that of the standard 7.9mm pattern – enabling conventional ammunition belts to be retained.

Failure of the short-case cartridges was largely due to worries about power. The H.WaA. then recruited Polte-Werke of Magdeburg and progress was made, even though the first Polte cartridge had a minuscule 30mm case loaded with a bullet weighing a mere 3.7gm. Only high velocity made this combination any more effective than the 9mm Pist. Patr. 08.

By April 1938, the research and development bureau of the Heereswaffenamt, Wa.-Prüf. 2, had placed a contract with C.G. Haenel Waffenfabrik A.G. of Suhl to develop a selective-fire carbine for Polte's newest intermediate cartridge. The new firearm was termed 'Maschinenkarabiner' (MKb.) to distinguish it from 'Maschinenpistolen' (MP.), and was expected to replace infantry rifles, submachine-guns and possibly even the light machine-guns. Development took longer than expected, and the first trials were not undertaken until 1940. Details will be found in Chapter Four.

Anti-tank rifles.   The rifles of the First World War (T-Gewehre) were unwieldy and universally disliked on account of their ferocious recoil. After the end of the First World War, however, they excited much interest. By the mid-1930s, however, few countries had improved greatly on the T-Gewehr and a 13mm cartridge that had inspired the development of both the 0.5 Browning cartridge in the USA and the 0.55 belted Boys anti-tank rifle pattern in Britain. Various attempts had been made to accelerate rifle-calibre projectiles to prodigious speeds – notably by Gerlich in Germany and Janeček in Czechoslovakia – but these had been achieved by tapering the entire bore or adding a 'squeeze muzzle'. Additional penalties included excessive barrel wear and the expense of tungsten-cored shot.

Rifle-calibre ammunition, which could spare very little space for explosive payloads, was doomed to failure; 2cm cannon such as the Becker, tested by the Germans during the First World War and subsequently developed into the Oerlikon, held much greater promise.

When the campaigns in Poland began, the standard German anti-tank rifle was the 7.9mm *Panzerbüchse 38* ('PzB. 38'). Designed by

Dipl.-Ing. Brauer of the Heereswaffenamt – though often now credited to Rheinmetall – most surviving examples seem to have been made by Havelwerk ('cpj') or Gustloff-Werke ('dfb').

The PzB. 38 was an interesting single-shot auto-ejector with a wedge pattern breechblock sliding vertically in the breech. When the gun fired, the barrel, receiver and breech ran back together in the stock; at the end of the stroke, the return spring pushed the components back to their initial position, but cammed open the breech-block to eject the spent case. The firer then inserted a new cartridge manually, tripping the breech latch and allowing the action to close automatically.

The standard cartridge was the Patr. 318 – an 8mm bullet inserted in a 13mm case, the designation being the numbers reversed. This fired a 7.9mm projectile at more than 1,200 m/sec, but 30mm armour penetration at a distance of 200 metres was no great improvement on the T-Gewehr. Despite the inclusion of a tear-gas capsule in the original cartridge, this capability was so unimportant that it was discovered only by examining captured ammunition.

Submachine-guns.   The Austrian police service was sufficiently impressed by progress being made in Solothurn to adopt a variant of the S1-100 as the '9mm Maschinenpistole M. 30', and the Austrian army then approved a modified 'M. 34' variant; made under licence in the Steyr-Daimler-Puch factory, these chambered the 9mm Mauser 'Export' (army guns) or 9mm Steyr cartridges (police guns). The standard M. 95 knife bayonet would slip over the exposed muzzle and latch onto a lug on the right side of the perforated barrel jacket.

The 1930 police guns had an odd-looking butt with a concave comb, though the M. 34 military examples had a conventional butt with a distinctively pointed pistol grip. Tangent-leaf back sights on the receiver cover were graduated from 50 to 500 metres. An interesting feature rarely found on guns in this class was the charger guide milled into the top surface of the magazine feedway. The magazine could be inserted vertically underneath this to facilitate reloading, then removed and inserted horizontally to permit firing to begin.

The beautifully made MP. M. 34 was 810mm long, had a 205mm barrel, and weighed about 4kg empty; the loaded 32-round magazine

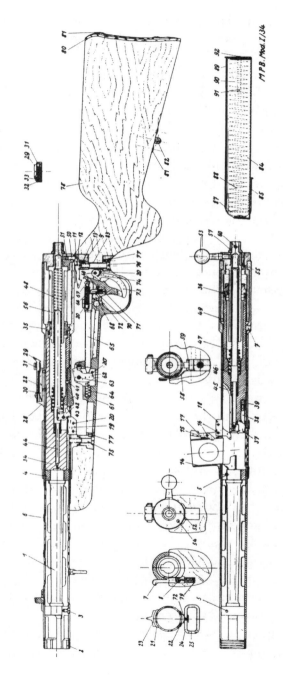

5. Drawings of the Bergmann MP. 35/I, from Fischer's *Waffen- und schiesstechnischer Leitfaden für die Ordnungspolizei* (1943 edition).

added another 600gm. Cyclic rate was 400–450 rds/min. Steyr-made guns were sold to Portugal, where they served as the Pistola-Metralhadora Mo. 937 (7.65mm) and Mo. 942 (9mm); others went to Spain, where they served in the Civil War, and to South America.

Bergmann & Müller developed several submachine-guns in Denmark in the early 1930s, where the 'Model 1932' (the application for a German patent being dated 6 July 1932) was manufactured by Schulz & Larsen Geværfabrik of Otterup. This gun had an unusually long barrel with the tangent-leaf back sight immediately above the magazine aperture, and a separate non-reciprocating bolt-type cocking handle on the right rear side of the action. A bolt-locking catch lay on the left side of the receiver.

Fitted with sling swivels, and with a lug for the standard Danish service bayonet attached to the right side of the perforated barrel jacket, the Schulz & Larsen/Bergmann guns were offered for export in chamberings ranging from 7.63mm Mauser to .45 ACP.

Once the influence of the Treaty of Versailles had waned appreciably in the mid-1930s, work reverted to Germany where Theodor Emil Bergmann and Dietrich Stahl had formed 'Theodor Bergmann & Co. G.m.b.H.' in Berlin. The company did not have its own gunmaking facilities and work was initially subcontracted to Carl Walther Waffenfabrik of Zella-Mehlis.

Two versions of the MP. 34 Bgm. have been identified, one with a long 1932-type barrel and the other with a short barrel enclosing the compensator. Chamberings available included 9mm Parabellum and 9mm Bergmann-Bayard. The short gun was 840mm overall, with a barrel measuring 200mm, and weighed about 4.1kg; its cyclic rate, about 700 rds/min, was appreciably higher than most other German submachine-guns. The back sight was normally placed on the receiver above the fore-end grasping groove, instead of on top of the magazine feedway block. A bolt-locking catch lay on the left side of the receiver behind the back sight. The barrel jacket had longitudinal slots, and a most distinctive automatic safety blade projected into the trigger guard immediately behind the trigger lever. When the trigger was pressed, the safety was pushed backward to disengage.

Unlike the earlier MP. 18 or MP. 28, which fed from the left, the MP. 34 Bgm. fed from the right. Consequently, spent cases were ejected, disconcertingly, across the body of the firer. Only about two thousand guns were made in 1934–6, some for export to Bolivia, but most went to the German police.

The MP. 35 Bgm. was a minor modification of its predecessors, originally made by Walther prior to 1939 for the German police and limited exports to Ethiopia, Sweden, Denmark and Spain. In 1940, however, the SS approached Stahl – then the sole proprietor of 'Theodor Bergmann K.G.' – hoping to acquire submachine-guns, as the army had priority for the new MP. 38. Work on the MP. 35 Bgm. recommenced towards the end of 1940, though production was switched from Walther (where facilities were occupied with the P. 38) to an SS appointee, Junker & Ruh of Karlsruhe.

The mainspring and the bolt of the MP. 35 differed from those of the MP. 34 Bgm., though the changes were undetectable externally. Production continued well into the Second World War, guns being encountered with laminated fir or beech stocks, no bolt-blocking safety, simplified machining, and the maker's code 'ajf' rather than the standard 'JRK' commercial monogram. The Bergmanns were apparently well liked, being sturdy and generally reliable, but the cocking mechanism was prone to break and the butt proved to be weak across the pistol-grip. Total production is estimated as five thousand by Walther and 40,000 by Junker & Ruh.

The submachine-guns designed by Heinrich Vollmer were generally made by ERMA–Erfurter Maschinenfabrik B. Geipel G.m.b.H. of Erfurt, Thüringen. Development began in the late 1920s and, by 1932, small-scale production was being undertaken in Switzerland or possibly even France. Though these early guns were simple blowbacks, they often featured telescoping monopods in the front pistol grip (beneath and immediately behind the magazine feedway). However, these were speedily eliminated. Chamberings were restricted to 7.63mm Mauser, 7.65mm Parabellum or 9mm Parabellum, and attempts were made to establish an export market. Guns are known to have sold in Mexico and China, and were doubtless used in small numbers elsewhere.

The standard Vollmer design, the *Maschinenpistole Erma* or 'MP. E', proved to be popular with the police and paramilitary units, though taken into German army service only when other weapons ran short. It was exported to Spain during the Civil War of 1936–9, where guns were made – perhaps under licence – in the Fábrica de Armas 'La Coruña'. Small batches were also sold to the French army and police. These were withdrawn, from the army at least, when sufficient examples of the 7.65mm SE-MAS 35 and the later MAS 38 became available, and were given to the Milice (the pro-Vichy paramilitary police force) or taken by the German occupation forces.

The MP. E was a simple blowback, cocked by a reciprocating handle on the right side of the receiver. It was 892mm long, had a 250mm barrel, and weighed about 4.15kg without its magazine; cyclic rate was about 500 rds/min. A radial lever-type fire selector lay in the cut-out in the right side of the stock above the trigger, being marked 'E' and 'D' for *Einzelfeuer* and *Dauerfeuer* (semi- and fully-automatic operation respectively). The magazine fed from the left, the barrel had a slotted barrel jacket, and most guns had a distinctive auxiliary pistol grip pinned and glued beneath the fore-end. A few, however, probably dating from the end of production, had straight MP. 28-type fore-ends with a longitudinal flute.

Early MP. E often had tangent-leaf sights graduated from 50m or 100m to 1,000m, but later ones, especially those used in German service, had standing-block back sights set for 100m with a small auxiliary leaf, for 200m, pivoting on the block body. The MP. E was one of the first attempts to simplify production, representing an intermediate stage between guns based on the MP. 18 and the later MP. 38.

The obsolescence of the original Bergmann-Schmeisser design, which dated from the First World War, persuaded the authorities to undertake a variety of experiments during the 1930s. Trials were undertaken with Vollmer and Bergmann designs (described previously), and the Schmeisser-designed Maschinenkarabiner submitted by Haenel of Suhl. The Schmeissers culminated in the MK. 36/III., which was a simple 9mm-calibre blowback designed specifically to incorporate as many Kar. 98k parts as possible in the stock and furniture. Consequently, the carbine had a cut-down rifle stock, a barrel band, and a nosecap that accepted the standard knife bayonet. It also had a small tangent-leaf sight, but was much too cumbersome to justify its existence. The MK. 36/III., with a Vollmer-type telescoping mainspring, was 1,130mm long, with a

502mm barrel and weighed 4.77kg without its magazine. Cyclic rate is estimated to have been about 500 rds/min, and a detachable 20- or 32-round magazine protruded centrally beneath the action.

Unfortunately, the gun was far too large and the power of the 9mm Pist. Patr. 08 justified neither the excessive weight nor the optimistic sighting arrangements. The Mk 36/III. was a developmental dead-end. Had it fired an intermediate cartridge, the first examples of which were then being tested experimentally in the Vollmer A. 35, the MK. 36 might have been a great success. Instead, it was rapidly consigned to the scrapheap.

The principal German submachine-guns of the Second World War, generically but wrongly known as 'Schmeissers', were designed largely by Heinrich Vollmer and Berthold Geipel of Erma-Werke and embodied Vollmer's patented telescoping mainspring. They are really little more than the MP. E refined for series production and advanced fabricating techniques.

Developed for paratroops and armoured-vehicle crews, the *Maschinenpistole 38* (MP. 38) had a main-spring assembly adapted from the MP. E allied with a receiver/magazine housing unit that had been formed from two large pressings; the durable grip units were made from resin-impregnated paper fibres; the barrel jacket was omitted; and a folding metal stock replaced the cumbersome wooden pattern. The cocking handle was moved to the left of the receiver, permitting the firer to cock the gun without moving his firing finger far from the trigger.

Adopted in the summer of 1938[8], the perfected submachine-gun measured 835mm overall with the stock extended, or merely 630mm when folded; the barrel was 250mm long, rifled with six clockwise-twisting grooves. The first guns weighed 4.1kg, plus 665gm for the loaded staggered-column box magazine. Capacity was supposedly 32 rounds, though experienced servicemen rarely loaded more than 27; not only were the last five difficult to force into the magazine, but constantly carrying the gun with a fully-loaded magazine could weaken the magazine-follower spring and compromise reliability. Restricting the magazine capacity prolonged the effective life of the spring by reducing the load.

Production of the MP. 38 began in the Erma factory in the summer of 1938 and, perhaps helped by Haenel, continued into mid-1940.

Guns generally display the manufacturer's code '27', though a few assembled concurrently with the earliest MP. 40 are coded 'ayf'. Some MP. 38 may also be encountered with the auxiliary cocking-handle safety introduced with the perfected MP. 40, which allowed the bolt to be locked into the receiver in its forward position. These were known as 'MP. 38/40'.

Handguns.   When Hitler gained power in 1933, the service pistol of the German armed forces was still the 9mm Pistole 08 (Parabellum or 'Luger'), which had been adopted in August 1908. The gun was unusually accurate, but difficult and expensive to mass-produce. Nor was it always as reliable as some of its leading competitors.

The Parabellum was recoil-operated, relying on a distinctive strut-and-pivot toggle-lock system described in the previous chapter. However, though a masterpiece of engineering physics, the gun was notoriously difficult to make. Commercial examples were made by Deutsche Waffen- und Munitionsfabriken ('D.W.M.') and its successor, Berlin-Karlsruher Industrie-Werk, until the production line was transferred from Berlin to the Mauser-Werke factory in Oberndorf am Neckar in 1930. At this time, military guns were being refurbished and assembled exclusively by Simson & Co. of Suhl – nationalised in 1934 as 'Berlin-Suhler-Werke' and finally named 'Gustloff-Werke' – but only a few thousand 'new' pistols appeared in the late 1920s.

Refurbishment continued into the mid-1930s, much of it hidden from prying Allied eyes, until the advent of conscription on 16 March 1935 heralded overt militarism. The production of all small arms was accelerated from 1 October 1935, the immediate goal being fivefold enlargement of the seven-division army!

Mauser-Werke was supplying the army with as many Parabellums as it could make; by the end of 1935, monthly production was exceeding 10,000 guns. As the Kriegsmarine's needs were comparatively small, the navy authorities simply waited for the army's initial needs to be satisfied before acquiring additional Pistolen 08. The Luftwaffe was less patient, immediately negotiating a contract with Heinrich Krieghoff of Suhl. Krieghoff subsequently acquired the ageing ex-Erfurt equipment once owned by Simson & Co., by then nationalised by the N.S.D.A.P.

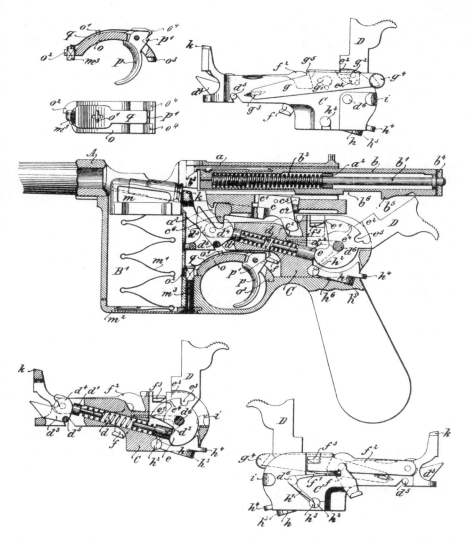

6. Drawings of the action of the Mauser C/96 pistol, from the patent of 1895. This shows the original design, with a single locking recess on the underside of the bolt ('b⁶'). The locking block, 'c', is cammed down and slightly backwards to release the bolt immediately after firing.

However, appreciable machining differences suggest that very little of the original equipment was used for anything other than to guide re-tooling.

Though the Krieghoff P. 08 offered excellent quality, only a little over 13,000 were made between 1936 and the end of the Second World War. The company had obtained a solitary 10,000-gun contract, and the remaining Luftwaffe needs were satisfied by Mauser. To put the importance of Krieghoff into proper context, Mauser-Werke supplied the O.K.L. with more than 130,000 Pistolen 08 in 1939–42.

Mauser-Parabellums, all of which emanated from the Oberndorf factory, initially bore a coded date in the form of 'K' (1934) or 'G' (1935) before the last shackles of the Versailles Treaty were openly rejected. Thereafter, the guns were dated in full ('1936') and then with only the last two digits (e.g., '41' for 1941). The manufacturer's code was successively 'S/42', '42' and 'byf'.

The Mauser C/96 was another nineteenth-century design, ironically making use of the cartridge originally designed by Hugo Borchardt, the inventor of the Parabellum's immediate predecessor. An elegantly engineered gun, though externally somewhat clumsy, the Mauser C/96 embodied a recoil-operated action locked by a rising block beneath the breech-bolt. It could not be mistaken for anything other than a Mauser (apart from a Spanish copy), as it had a distinctive integral charger-loaded magazine immediately ahead of the trigger aperture.

After an uncertain start, and an unwanted reputation for persistent jamming, the C/96 had been developed into a powerful battle-worthy weapon let down only by its clumsiness. It even made a passable light semi-automatic carbine when attached to its convertible wooden holster/shoulder stock. Large numbers of C/96 had been purchased during the First World War, chambered for the regulation 9mm Parabellum cartridge, and many guns, 7.63mm and 9mm alike, survived to serve the Reichsmarine and Weimar-period police.

By 1930 the standard 7.63mm-calibre C/96 was being offered with grooved walnut grips, a 50m–1,000m tangent-leaf sight on top of the receiver, and a ten-round magazine that could be loaded with a charger or single rounds. Small quantities were also being made for the 9mm Mauser Export round, which was perceptibly more powerful than the

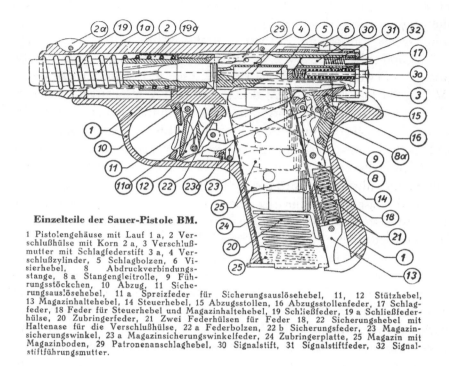

Einzelteile der Sauer-Pistole BM.

1 Pistolengehäuse mit Lauf 1 a, 2 Verschlußhülse mit Korn 2 a, 3 Verschluß-
mutter mit Schlagfederstift 3 a, 4 Ver-
schlußzylinder, 5 Schlagbolzen, 6 Vi-
sierhebel,   8   Abdruckverbindungs-
stange, 8 a Stangengleitrolle, 9 Füh-
rungsstöckchen, 10 Abzug, 11 Siche-
rungsauslösehebel, 11 a Spreizfeder für Sicherungsauslösehebel, 11, 12 Stützhebel,
13 Magazinhaltehebel, 14 Steuerhebel, 15 Abzugsstollen, 16 Abzugsstollenfeder, 17 Schlag-
feder, 18 Feder für Steuerhebel und Magazinhaltehebel, 19 Schließfeder, 19 a Schließfeder-
hülse, 20 Zubringerfeder, 21 Zwei Federhülsen für Feder 18, 22 Sicherungshebel mit
Haltenase für die Verschlußhülse, 22 a Federbolzen, 22 b Sicherungsfeder, 23 Magazin-
sicherungswinkel, 23 a Magazinsicherungswinkelfeder, 24 Zubringerplatte, 25 Magazin mit
Magazinboden, 29 Patronenanschlaghebel, 30 Signalstift, 31 Signalstiftfeder, 32 Signal-
stiftführungsmutter.

7. A longitudinal section of the Sauer & Sohn Behörden-Modell pistol, from Fischer's *Waffen- und schiesstechnischer Leitfadung für die Ordnungspolizei* (1943 edition).

9mm Pist. Patr. 08 and proved the durability of the basic Mauser design. Most post-1930 guns had a small ring hammer and the so-called Universal Safety, protruding from the rear left side of the frame, that allowed the hammer to drop safely onto a loaded chamber by blocking the firing pin.

Though the police had appreciable numbers of Pistolen 08, many had passed into the hands of the army when the Landespolizei had been absorbed in August 1935. And though occasional deliveries of P. 08 and P. 38 were made in 1943–5, quantities were minuscule. As a result, the police and the paramilitary – together with officers in the armed forces – relied on small blowbacks and captured equipment. In the period

1939–42, the Wehrmacht alone took 140,427 Walther, Mauser and Sauer blowbacks.

The most important of these were the Walthers, the *Polizei-Pistole* or 'PP' and the shorter *Kriminalpolizei-Pistole* ('PPK'), patented in 1929 and introduced commercially in 1930–2. They were known to the police as 'Walther-Pistole PP' and 'Walther-Pistole PPK' respectively, generally abbreviated as 'P. W. PP.' and 'P. W. PPK'. The PPK had also been officially adopted by the Sturm-Abteilung as the 'Ehrenwaffe des politischen Leiters' in 1936. Total procurement for the Wehrmacht and the police has been estimated as about 100,000 PP and 72,000 PPK, but many others were purchased by the paramilitary.

The Walthers were the first personal-defence guns to incorporate an effectual double-action trigger system, allowing them to be carried in perfect safety even though a live round had been chambered. This was rarely practicable in single-action designs and, consquently, a great sales asset.

The success of the PP/PPK series forced Walther's leading rivals, Mauser-Werke of Oberndorf and Sauer & Sohn of Suhl, to develop competitive designs. The standard Mauser personal-defence pistol in the mid-1930s was the Modell 1934, a conventional single-action blowback developed from the original Modell 1914. Known to the police as the 'Pistole Mauser' (or simply 'P. M.'), it had a lengthy pedigree but little to commend it other than good quality; consequently, procurement was minimal – possibly 8,000 for the Wehrmacht, 4,500 for the police and an unknown quantity for the paramilitary. Sauer offered the standard Modell 1913 ('Pistole Sauer & Sohn' or 'P. S.& S.') and the cosmetically improved Behörden-Modell ('P. S.& S. BM.'), 7.65mm blowbacks with origins early in the twentieth century. Like the Mauser M34, the single-action 7.65mm Sauers were well made and efficient enough, but lacked stopping power.

In the late 1930s, after a series of false starts, Mauser perfected the HSc (*Hahn-Selbstladepistole, Modell C,* or 'third pattern self-loading pistol with hammer'). Known to the police as the 'Mauser-Pistole neuer Art' or 'P. M. n.A.', this presented a more streamlined appearance than the Walthers, a double-action trigger system and comparable safety arrangements. Interestingly, military procurement of the HSc never reached the heights of the Walther and Sauer guns; it is suspected that the bulk of the guns went to the police (perhaps 22,500 of them) and the paramilitary.

The Sauer & Sohn M. 38 double-action personal-defence pistol ('P. S.& S. M. 38'), which appeared contemporaneously with the Second World War, had an internal hammer and a separate cocking lever protruding from the left grip immediately behind the trigger aperture. It proved to be very popular, even though manufacturing quality declined greatly as the war progressed. Purchases are variously estimated as about 50,000 for the Wehrmacht and 70,000 for the police, but much larger quantities clearly went to the paramilitary.

Signal pistols.   In 1938, with rearmament in full swing, the standard Walther-made Heeresmodell signal pistol was simplified in an attempt to accelerate production. Components that had been machined from solid forgings and bar-stock were replaced with stampings; the operating spring that had once been enclosed in a double cylinder was simplified; the lanyard ring was retained by rivets instead of bolts; and a plain-faced extractor was fitted. A signal pin was added to indicate when cartridges were chambered.

Walther's *Doppelläufige Signal- & Leuchtpistole* ('SLD'), intended to replace the previous navy guns, was among the first signal pistols to be made of corrosion-resisting stainless steel. Designed in 1935 and adopted by the Kriegsmarine a year later, it was a masterpiece that mated the dropping-barrel action of its predecessor with an enclosed double-action trigger mechanism adapted from the Polizei-Pistole. The interlocking parts were self-retaining and a radial safety lever appeared on the left rear of the frame, where it could be thumbed down to expose 'SICHER' ('safe') or horizontally to display 'FEUER' ('fire').

The breech was latched by an underlever beneath the trigger guard, and a lever-type selector on top of the breech fired either barrel, or both together if placed centrally. A distinctive wooden fore-end was attached beneath the barrels. The earliest guns bore Walther's banner mark and the date on the left side of the breech below the barrel-block, together with the serial number; post-1940 guns were simply marked '1940 ac

1833'. Production of the stainless-steel SLD ceased at the end of 1943, after about four thousand had been made.

The *Einzelläufige Signal- & Leuchtpistole* ('SL' or 'SLE') was simply a single-barrelled SLD lacking the selector. Production began in the mid-1930s and continued until the end of 1944. The first guns bore the Walther name and banner trademark on the left side of the frame below the barrel-block, until an 'ac' code was substituted in the autumn of 1940.

The Luftwaffe adopted the 'Modell L' or *Fliegerleuchtpistole* ('FL'), which was complicated, light (weighing less than a kilogram) and singularly unpleasant to fire. It was designed on behalf of the Oberkommando der Luftwaffe by amalgamating the basic features of the best contemporary designs.

The barrels tipped downward after a finger-lever resting against the front of the trigger guard had been pushed forward. A radial lever-type selector on the breech behind two cocking indicators could fire either or both barrels, and there was a safety lever on the left side of the frame.

The aluminium frames of the original guns were anodised black or dark grey. Most of the screws were nickel-plated; the finger lever, the trigger and the firing mechanism were usually steel; and the selector and the safety catch generally proved to be brass (early guns) or light alloy (later examples). The grips, originally chequered walnut, eventually became Bakelite. Overall length of the 165mm-barrel Modell L varied between 275 and 280mm. Weight was 1,210–1,275gm.

The guns were made by Emil Eckholdt of Suhl (marked 'ECKO' in an oval, later 'ojr'); Heinrich Krieghoff of Suhl (an encircled 'HK' monogram, 'fzs'); Gustav Bittner of Weipert ('GBW' on a triangle, 'gpt'); and August Menz of Suhl (an enwreathed 'AM' monogram). Menz ceased work prior to the Second World War, while Eckholdt made the 105mm-barrelled 'Hahnlos Doppelläufige Leuchtpistole' for commercial sale under the designation 'Modell K'. Most survivors will also display the Luftwaffe inventory number 'FL.24483' – later 'LN.24483' – on the left side of the frame above the finger-lever.

4

The Road to War

Any union between Germany and Austria had been expressly forbidden by the Treaty of Versailles. However, there were strong movements in both countries for something that would impose the right-wing politics that many Austrians still craved. A vocal right-wing minority was being so effectively orchestrated by the N.S.D.A.P. that Schussnigg, the Austrian chancellor, was forced to announce a plebiscite. Well aware that this could provide a substantial pro-independence majority, Hitler was forced to act.

Austrian resistance was clearly signalled when the country's president refused to accept pro-N.S.D.A.P. puppet Artur Seyss-Inquart as chancellor in place of Schussnigg, who had resigned. At 8.45pm on 11 March 1938, therefore, the order to invade Austria was given; two days later, Seyss-Inquart announced the voluntary incorporation ('Anschluss') of the Austrian state into Greater Germany.

The changing fortunes of Germans in Austria spurred three million inhabitants of western Czechoslovakia (who had been Germans prior to 1918) to demand autonomy. These Sudeten Germans had never settled in artifically created Czechoslovakia, where even Czechs and Slovaks mingled uneasily; encouraged by the N.S.D.A.P., they now worked tirelessly in support of their cause. Eventually, in a clear-sighted effort to avoid trouble, Czechoslovakian president Beneš agreed to grant each and every Sudeten-German demand. If he had hoped for Allied support, he was wrong; meetings between Britain's Neville Chamberlain, France's Daladier and Hitler in Munich in September 1938 ended with Anglo-French appeasement. Any districts in the provinces of Bohemia and Moravia that had a *Volksdeutsche* population exceeding fifty per cent of the total would then be incorporated in the Deutsches Reich. The deadline for compliance was set for 10 October 1938. A later 'Vienna Agreement', 2 November 1938, then gave parts of Slovakia and Ruthenia to Hungary, and allowed Poland to seize Teschen.

The Czechoslovakian government – not even represented at the proceedings – had no option but to accept such strongly-backed terms, and the British Prime Minister Neville Chamberlain returned to London promising 'peace in our time'. Yet the road to war was steepening rapidly.

Demands for autonomy led to the creation of a state of three components: the Czech Lands, Slovakia and Ruthenia, but Czechoslovakia then broke up; the Slovak national assembly voted to secede on 14 March 1939 and Hitler seized the opportunity to annex Bohemia and Moravia. These provinces became the 'Reichsprotektorat Böhmen-Mahren'. On 15 March, German troops marched into Prague.

Not only had Hitler eliminated one of the most efficient armies in Europe (albeit comparatively small), but he had also gained control of the giant Skoda arms-making business and also Československá Zbrojovka, one of the most important small-arms factories in Europe. Tens of thousands of pistols, rifles and machine-guns – and the (then) modern vz. 38 tank – plugged an important gap in the Wehrmacht inventory.

Captured and non-standard weapons

1) AUSTRIAN
Much of the Austrian army was immediately absorbed into the Wehrmacht. Though the frontline units were speedily re-armed with German weapons, Austrian patterns remained in the hands of second-line and reserve units. The Germans also gained access to the great arms-making centre of Steyr. Steyr-Daimler-Puch hankered for a return to the halcyon pre-1918 days of its predecessor, Österreichische Waffenfabriks-

Gesellschaft, and immediately declared a willingness to work for its new masters. Though Steyr's contributions to the German automotive industry were important, however, its value as a small-arms producer was primarily as a subcontractor for the standard Kar. 98k and MG. 34, preparation for which began immediately. MP. 40 submachine-guns and MG. 42 machine-guns were to be made during the Second World War, while small numbers of Polish 'Radom' (VIS wz. 35) pistols were assembled in the last desperate days of 1945.

Machine-guns. The standard heavy machine-gun was the Schwarzlose M 07/12, a pre-First World War German design chambered for the old 8×50mm Austro-Hungarian service cartridge. There were also substantial numbers of the light 8×56mm M. 30S (Solothurn S2-200) pattern. However, the Austrian army was not particularly large; most of the men inducted into the Wehrmacht immediately re-armed with standard German guns, and the Austrian guns were either handed to the police or placed in store.

Rifles. Large quantities of 1895-type Mannlicher rifles, short rifles (*Stutzen*) and carbines were taken from the Austrian army and police. Many were reissued to police forces, not just in Austria but also throughout Germany to free Kar. 98k for military service. However, some of the guns were eventually handed back to the armed forces as the tide of war gradually turned against the Third Reich. For example, the Chef der Heeresausrüstung approved test-firing procedures as late as 1943.[1]

The Mannlichers were operated simply by pulling back on the bolt handle that protruded horizontally behind the receiver bridge. A combination of the backward movement and cam tracks revolved locking lugs on the separate bolt head out of engagement with recesses in the receiver, and allowed a spent case to be extracted and then ejected. Pushing the bolt handle forwards stripped a new round into the chamber and revolved the bolt head back to its original position.

The mechanism could be operated very rapidly, as long as it was kept clean, but primary extraction was very poor and the Mannlichers had attained a reputation for jamming with the poor-quality ammunition that had been made during the First World War. The clip-loaded magazine was another poor feature, as it prevented loose rounds being used in an emergency. The M. 95 short rifles issued to German police units fell into two patterns: the original design, chambered for the 8×50R cartridge, and those that had been modified in the early 1930s for the more powerful 8×56R. Modified guns had a 12mm-high 'S' above the chamber; known as '8 mm M. 95 "S"-Stutzen' in German service, they were initially confined to what had been Austrian territory.[2] Manuals give overall length as 1,005mm with a 498mm barel, and an empty weight of 3.4kg. Attaching the standard Austrian knife bayonet increased length to 1,251mm and weight to 3.8kg. The M. 30S cartridge obtained a muzzle velocity of 695 m/sec with a fired 13.4gm bullet, compared with 15.8gm and 580 m/sec for original 8×50R ball ammunition.

Submachine-guns.   After the Anschluss, when the remnants of the Austrian army were assimilated into the Wehrmacht and suitably re-equipped, surviving MP. 34 were re-issued to the Luftwaffe as 'Maschinenpistole 34 (ö)'. The relevant manual, L.Dv. 258, is dated 30 October 1939. Other guns were issued to the German police forces under the designation 'MP. 34'; most of these chambered the 9mm Steyr cartridge (Pist. Patr. M. 12 [ö]), and would thus have been taken from the Austrian police. Some were converted for the Pist. Patr. 08 in the early 1940s. The Austrian guns were much liked, being reliable and superbly made.

Austrian-type MP. 34 (ö) bear the normal commercial Steyr marks. However, production of modified 9mm Parabellum guns continued under H.WaA. supervision. These lacked the original bayonet lug and bore the coded maker's mark '660'. Production appears to have stopped in 1940, when the Steyr factory was ordered to tool for the standard MP. 40 (q.v.).

Handguns.   The most important pistol was the 9mm-calibre Steyr-Pistole M. 12, an interesting recoil-operated rotating-barrel design developed by Österreichische Waffenfabriks-Gesellschaft from the Repetierpistole M. 7 ('Roth-Steyr') and adopted by Romania shortly before the First World War. When hostilities began in 1914, the M. 12 was successfully impressed into Austrian service and vast numbers had been made prior to the Armistice. Small quantities had even been purchased by the Bavarian army in 1916–18 to eke out supplies of the P. 08.

Many M. 12 pistols were still serving with the Austrian forces in 1938, virtually all the 60,000-plus survivors finding their way into the hands of the German police forces in Ostmark and Böhmen-Mahren. They were originally designated 'Pistolen M. 12 (ö)' ('P. M. 12 [ö]') and issued with the standard Austrian 9mm cartridges, which were longer than the Pist. Patr. 08 and could not be interchanged. Ammunition supplies soon ran short, however, and selected M. 12 pistols were converted for the 9mm Pist. Patr. 08, becoming 'Pistolen M. 12 (ö) umg.' (*umgeändert*, 'modified'). A distinguishing '08' was struck into the left side of the slide.

The charger-loaded Steyr M. 12 pistols could not be confused with any others, as their butts were virtually perpendicular to the bore. The Steyr-Pistole M. 34 was a less impressive product. Chambering the popular (but ineffective) 7.65mm Auto cartridge, it was based on a Warnant-Pieper blowback design dating back to 1905. The tipping barrel facilitated cleaning, but also permitted single shots to be fired manually. Until the chaotic days of 1944–5, the M. 34 was restricted to what had become the Ostmark region of Greater Germany.

2) CZECHOSLOVAKIAN

Among the most important result of the occupation of Bohemia and Moravia was the seizure of the arms-making factories, Česká Zbrojovka ('C.Z.') and Československá Zbrojovka ('Z.B.'), which were making vast quantities of pistols, rifles and machine-guns.

As the standard Czechoslovakian vz. 24 service rifles were essentially similar to the Kar. 98k, little difficulty was found in re-issuing them to German forces. Most of the machine-guns could also be impressed immediately, as they chambered a cartridge that was identical in all but the most minor tolerances with the German 7.9mm cartridge. However, though the machine-guns were well made and efficient, they had no long-term future within the arms procurement programmes; the production facilities had soon been converted to make parts for the MG. 34 Einheitsmaschinengewehre.

The Czechoslovakian weapons were highly regarded by the German authorities, and were often encountered in front-line service. The light machine-guns were particularly popular with the police and the Waffen-SS, owing to their portability and the convenience of the box-magazine feed system. Unlike many other impressed weapons, they were never designated by *fremd Gerät* numbers.[3]

Machine-guns.   Czechoslovakia had made machine-guns not only for indigenous troops but also for export. Large numbers of them, therefore, were in store or awaiting despatch when the Germans invaded.

After an uncertain start, the eminent designer Václav Holek, assisted by his brother Emanuel, had produced the recoil-operated Praga I-23 light machine-gun, locked by a vertically tipping breech-bolt. The belt-fed Praga proved effectual, but clearly needed refinement. The Ruční Kulomet 'Praga' vz. 24 (Praga light machine-gun, model 1924) subsequently amalgamated a top-mounted box magazine with the basic I-23 action. Its mainspring ran back through the butt, and a specially sprung butt-plate was intended to absorb some of the recoil forces generated during prolonged firing.

By the time the prototypes had been perfected, a shoulder-support had been added to the butt, a drum sight had replaced the previous leaf, and the barrel had been partially finned to improve cooling. Successful tests against a Hotchkiss and a lightened Schwarzlose allowed the vz. 24 to be approved as the 'lehký kulomet Z.B. vz. 26' in the summer of 1927. The first production guns appeared in 1928–9 and it soon became clear that the vz. 26 was very efficient; by 1938, guns had been exported in quantity to Brazil, China, Ecuador, Iran, Japan, Lithuania and Yugoslavia. Eleven had also gone to Chile. All the guns were chambered for the Czechoslovakian 7.92mm round, identical with the 7.9×57mm German type, except those sold to Brazil and Chile in 7×57mm.

The Romanians had indicated a willingness to make the basic Z.B. machine-gun under licence, but had requested changes. The resulting Z.B. 30 was similar externally to the Z.B. 26, but had a seven-position adjustable gas-port assembly and markedly different bolt/piston extension construction. By 1938, it had been exported in quantity to Afghanistan, Bolivia, Ecuador, Ethiopia, Peru, Romania and Turkey;

Guatemala, Latvia, Nicaragua and Uruguay had also purchased a few guns. More than fifteen thousand 'M30' light machine-guns (Z.B. 30/J) were supplied to Yugoslavia in 1931–6, to be joined by 'M37' guns made in the government manufactory at Kragujevač, principally for the armed forces but also for limited export.

Most of the Z.B. 30 were chambered for the 7.92mm cartridge, exceptions being the 7×57mm guns supplied to Guatemala and Uruguay, and the 7.65×53mm Bolivian and Peruvian purchases.

Brno also made the 'ZGB' sub-variant, adapted to feed rimmed cartridges. Though the project was created to participate in trials in Britain, the ZGB 33 being the last of a series of guns offered in the early 1930s as a replacement for the Lewis Gun, sales were also made to Bulgaria, Egypt, Iraq and Latvia. The Bulgarian guns were chambered for the 8×50R Austro-Hungarian round, but the others accepted the British .303 (7.7×56R)

The ZGB 33 was refined by the substitution of a plain-surface barrel and adopted for British service as the 'Bren'. While production lines were being readied in the small-arms factory at Enfield, however, Československá Zbrojovka also made Bren-type guns for commercial sale.

The box-magazine Z.B. patterns were generally considered as light machine-guns, though attempts were made to adapt them for support fire. Though several impressive-looking tripod and quadrupod mounts were offered, and despite a readily exchangeable barrel, limitations imposed by the box magazine restricted the volume of fire the Z.B. could produce.

When the Germans invaded Czechoslovakia, they seized existing guns (Z.B. 26, Z.B. 30, Z.B. 30/J, ZGB/Bren) and immediately reissued them to the Wehrmacht. Modifications were rarely necessary, as most already chambered the standard German 7.9mm service cartridge. Z.B. machine-guns were well made, very accurate, and their box magazines were easier to handle than the belt-feed or saddle-drums associated with the MG. 13 and MG. 34; tactically handier than either German gun, the Z.B. patterns were greatly favoured by Fallschirmjäger, police and paramilitary units such as the SS, whose procurement was normally subordinated to army needs.

The guns were known as 'leichte Maschinengewehre 26 (t) und 30 (t)' in German service, the small number of Bren-type weapons apparently being considered as le. MG. 30 (t). Production continued for some years after the German invasion, though greatly reduced after a decision to concentrate on the MG. 34 had been taken in the summer of 1940. However, an attempt had been made to adapt the 26 (t) pattern for potential anti-aircraft use, consisting of the issue of an anti-aircraft sight, a pillar mount, and an adaptor allowing the gun to be attached to the pillar.[4]

In addition to the guns that had been found in Czechoslovakia, the Germans eventually retrieved substantial numbers from Yugoslavia and Romania. The Romanian M30 was similar to the Yugsolavian guns, chambering the same 7.92mm cartridge; 17,131 were made in Brno and about 10,000 by CMC in Cugir. Small quantities of these weapons entered German service by way of Romanian units serving on the Eastern Front, and were assimilated with the ex-Czechoslovakian guns serving the police.

The standard Czech heavy machine-gun had originally been the ex-Austrian Schwarzlose, small quantities of the 07/12 model being converted to 'vz. 07/24' standards (and the 7.92mm cartridge) by the Janeček factory in 1924–5. These were produced for several years, permitting a small export market to be created, but were clearly antiquated. As the Schwarzlose blowback system was only marginally strong enough for the 7.9mm cartridge, attempts were made to transform the Holek Praga I-23 design into a suitable heavy machine-gun. The first stage was the Z.B. 50, developed by Václav Holek and Miroslav Ročik, which progressed to the Z.B. 52 and Z.B. 53. The Z.B. 53 was perfected in 1934 and adopted tentatively as the 'tezhký kulomet vz. 35', and then finalized as the 'vz. 37' once field trials had suggested some minor modifications. Zbrojovka Brno made both types concurrently, rapidly establishing an impressive export market and persuading the British to adopt the Z.B. 53 as the 'Besa'.

The Germans also seized quantities of the vz. 35 and vz. 37, production continuing for some time under H.WaA. supervision. The guns were known as 'schwere Maschinengewehre 37 (t)'; some were issued to the Wehrmacht, particularly when production of the MG. 34 was lagging and the MG. 42 had yet to appear. By 1944, most had found their way into the hands of the police forces to supplement ageing Maxims. They were generally issued with Czech-made Z.B. 308 tripods,

Platzpatronenzerleger 26 (t)

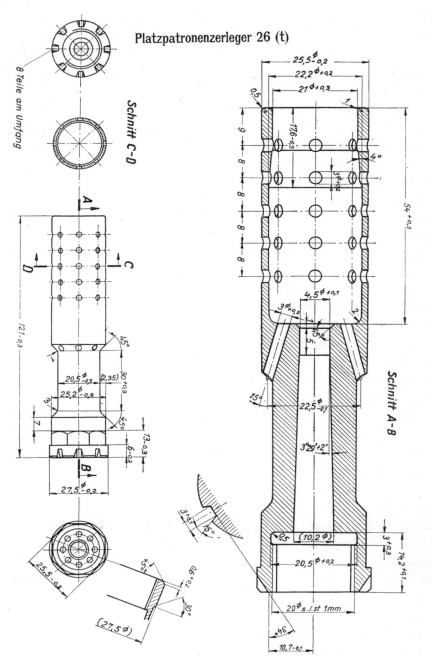

8. The blank-firing attachment for the le. MG. 26 (t), from *Heerestechnisches Verordnungsblatt*, 1943.

but may sometimes be encountered adapted for standard German mounts.

The Czechoslovakian machine-guns served until the end of the Second World War, though the inventory declined towards the end of hostilities. Production had stopped, and it is assumed that supplies of spare parts had also been run down. Instructions for test-firing procedures for the Czechoslovak rifles and machine-guns (light and heavy patterns alike) were published in November 1939[5], using German 7.9mm s.S. ball ammunition, and a special blank-firing attachment was introduced in 1940[6] to allow le. MG. 26 (t), s. MG. 35 (t) and s. MG. 37 (t) to fire the standard 7.9mm German blank round, the Platzpatrone 33, instead of original Czechoslovakian ammunition that was in short supply.

The fixture (which replaced the flash-hider) consisted of a tubular flash-suppressor/booster unit or *Platzpatronenlager*, with a series of circular vents around the periphery and a small-diameter 'barrel' designed to ensure that sufficient gas left the bore through the gas port instead of venting weakly through the muzzle. However, the differences in operating characteristics forced the Germans to issue two differing non-interchangeable blank-firing units, one for the le. MG. 26 (t), with a bore diameter of 4.5mm, and another for the s. MG. 35 and 37, with a diameter of only 3.3mm.

Further experience showed that the Platzpatrone 33 caused problems in the rechambered Schwarzlose guns, and its use was subsequently banned in the s. MG.07/24 (t) – in addition to the Polish variations of the Browning Automatic Rifle (le. MG. 28 [p]) and water-cooled M1917 Browning machine-gun (s. MG. 30 [p]).

Rifles.   The principal contribution Czechoslovakia could make to the German arms inventory was the 'Gewehr 24 (t)', a designation that covered the Kar. 98k-type vz. 24 and vz. 24/30 short rifles being made in Brno by Československá Zbrojovka. There were also smaller quantities of vz. 98/22 and vz. 98/29 long rifles, which approximated to the Karabiner 98b, and the vz. 33 short rifle issued to gendarmerie and treasury guards. The short rifles were issued as 'Gewehre 33 (t)', providing the basis for the Gewehr 33/40 described below.

It has often been claimed that no more '24 (t)' and '33 (t)' rifles were made in Brno after the German occupation, but published figures ascribed to the Heereswaffenamt indicate that the truth was very different. Prior to 1942, when instructions were given to transform the production facilities to make the Kar. 98k Kriegsmodell, Československá Zbrojovka – renamed 'Böhmische Waffenfabrik' – had delivered a little over 330,000 Gew. 24 (t) and about 131,500 Gew. 33/40.

Comparatively few changes were made to the rifles in German service, though some butts were altered to accept German sling fittings after August 1940; changes were introduced in January 1942 so that the bayonet scabbards would fit German frogs; and the muzzle rings of surviving Czechoslovakian 'Seitengewehre 24 (t)' were removed from August 1942 onward to allow the standard Kar. 98k-type muzzle protector to fit the *Gewehr* 24 (t).[7]

Submachine-guns. Czechoslovakia provided small quantities of the 9mm ZK 383, a sturdy if conventional gun that had entered limited paramilitary service in 1937. Patented by Josef and František Koucký in 1933 and made in Brno, the ZK 383 was an interesting selective-fire blowback, firing from an open breech, with an optional bolt-weight that could reduce the cyclic rate from 700 to 500 rds/min. The standard ZK 383 (though not the police ZK 383P) had a folding bipod that swung back into the fore-end. As the barrel could be exchanged very easily, the provision of the bipod was not the anachronism it initially seemed; the ZK 383 could deliver a greater volume of fire than most comparable guns, as long as spare barrels were accessible. The gun measured about 875mm overall, had a 325mm barrel and weighed 4.83kg with a laden 30-round box magazine. Feed was horizontally from the left. Quality was excellent and the gun was popular with the pro-German Czechoslovakian SS units it equipped. Remaining guns from seized Czechoslovak stores were passed to Bulgaria.

Handguns. The first indigenous Czechoslovakian handguns had been the vz. 22 and vz. 24, recoil-operated and locked by rotating the barrel into engagement with the slide; however, these guns had proved to be temperamental and too complicated even though the vz. 24 remained the standard service weapon for some years. Production was approaching 200,000 when work stopped in 1938, and many guns survived to be seized by the Germans – some even being assembled from the copious stocks of unused components. They were all known as 'Pistolen 24(t)' in the Wehrmacht.

The vz. 27 police/paramilitary blowback, derived from the vz. 24, was a much simpler proposition. About 16,000 guns had been made prior to 1939, and 5,000 were assembled from existing parts under H.WaA. supervision; these all had standard ČZ marks. The factory was then renamed 'Böhmische Waffenfabrik', the marking dies changed and production resumed until the 'fnh' code was approved in June. Output was considerable, 105,500 being acquired in 1939–42 alone. Many of the guns were used by the army and the Luftwaffe as 'Pistolen 27(t)', but most went to the police as 'Pistolen Modell 27' ('P. M. 27'). It has been estimated that about 465,000 pistols were made during the German occupation.

Shortly before the German invasion of Czechoslovakia, the vz. 24 had been replaced by the quirky ČZ vz. 38, designed by František Myška. This gun contained a conventional 9mm blowback action in a far from conventional exterior, and had a double-action trigger with a particularly knuckle-whitening pull. The first 41,000 guns had all been completed before the Germans seized Československá Zbrojovka, but the basic design had so little to offer that only a few additional guns were assembled from existing components. All but the three thousand guns retained for the Kriegsmarine went straight to the army under the designation 'Pistole 39 (t)'.

Regulation weapons

An ammunition-compatibility chart published by the Oberkommando des Heeres in April 1940 indicated that the regulation army-service weapons were considered to be the Maschinengewehre 08/15, 08, 13 and 34; the Maschinenpistolen 18, 38 and 40; the Karabiner 98k, the Gewehr 33/40, and the Pistolen 08 and 38.

Machine-guns, submachine-guns and handguns.   Most of these are described in detail in the preceding chapter. Work was concentrating on series production of the MG. 34, the other machine-guns, regarded as obsolescent, being relegated to second-line use or training. The MP. 38 had only just entered service in substantial numbers, and the field trials of the perfected P. 38 (Walther) pistol – destined to replace the P. 08 (Parabellum) – were only just finishing.

Rifles.   The ever-increasing chance of war was reflected in the haste with which the Kar. 98k was introduced, and the way in which production was allocated.

The successful campaigns in Austria and Czechoslovakia were accompanied by a reintroduction of the sniper rifle, accompanied by a new 4× sight developed by the Heereswaffenamt. The Zf. 39 (a modified 'Zielvier') was attached to Kar. 98k specially selected by the Heereszeugämter in Hannover, Königsberg in Preussen, and Spandau on the basis of 'best bores'. There is no evidence that they were selected on the basis of test-firing, which would have been a better arbiter of accuracy.

The original short-rail mount was abandoned in favour of a tower-and-post design (usually known to Anglo-American collectors as the 'turret mount'). The bases, which were permanently attached to the gun, consisted of a turret above the chamber and a short transverse rail, which could be adjusted laterally, above the bridge. A post attached to the front telescope-retaining ring was inserted in the turret, which had a hollow centre with a circumferential groove, at right angles to the bore. This allowed diametrically-opposed lugs on the post to enter vertical channels inside the turret walls, and a ninety-degree turn of the sight allowed a lug on the underside of the rear retaining ring to slide onto the rail on the rear mount. A radial latch on the left side of the rear base then locked the sight in place. The retaining rings were soldered onto the telescope barrel to prevent movement, but the fixture was still not as rigid as the recoil of the 7.9mm cartridge demanded, and difficulties in keeping the 'zero' remained.

Rifles of this type were customarily confined to the army, though a few examples with commercial-type double-claw mounts are said to have been acquired for the Waffen-*SS*.

The snipers' *Zielfernrohr-Karabiner 98k* (Zf.-Kar. 98k) was standard apart from its optical sight, though the guns were specially selected for their quality. The earliest combinations used the 4× Zf. 39 made by Zeiss, Leitz, Goerz, Hensoldt and others; during the war, however, the smaller 1.5× Zf. 41 became increasingly common.

5

Lightning Strikes

Many of the commentators of the day saw Anglo-French connivance in dismantling Czechoslovakia as the only way of avoiding a European war. The governments of Chamberlain and Daladier were prepared to allow Hitler to acquire the *Lebensraum* – 'living space' – that Germany demanded, as long as that space came from the eastern margins of Europe.

The policy of appeasement cloaked a sudden about-face by the British government, which allowed Chamberlain, backed uneasily by France, to guarantee assistance to Poland if the Germans invaded. This uncharacteristically partisan move is now seen as the catalyst for war. Britain and France had failed to seek the views of the U.S.S.R., smarting from exclusion from the Munich conference, and valued the Polish army much too highly. Realising that the situation had changed, and that conquering Poland had to be completed before the autumn rains turned many areas into marshland, Hitler and Stalin concluded a mutual non-aggression pact that secretly divided Poland between them. This historic document was signed in Moscow on 23 August 1939. Stalin was keen to encourage Hitler to strike westward, reducing the threat to the U.S.S.R., directly or indirectly, that Britain and France would attack.

The Germans had always looked to Poland as an ideal way of gaining territory, and to reclaim land that had been lost in 1919. Still dominated by the *Volksdeutsche* population, this included the Silesian coalfields and many important industrial centres. Invading Poland also allowed Danzig (Gdansk) to be retrieved, and a link with Ostpreussen to be re-established. The extreme eastern portions of Prussia had been cut off from the rest of Germany by the 'Polish Corridor'.

Where the Czechs had been forced to capitulate comparatively easily, the Poles were expected to resist. In the late spring of 1939, therefore, Wehrmacht planners were ordered to prepare for the invasion of Poland later in the summer; to clear the way politically, the five-year-old Germano-Polish non-aggression pact was repudiated and a formal alliance, the 'Pact of Steel', was signed between Germany and Italy.

Italy informed her one-time Allies, Britain and France, that her troops would side with Germany if the Polish crisis escalated to war. Protracted diplomatic manoeuvring failed to resolve the problems until, finally, Hitler made his move. Determined to invade Poland but needing justification to do so, he approved a plan mooted by the SS for Germans dressed in Polish uniforms to attack the radio station at Gleiwitz, a few kilometres from the Germano-Polish border. To hoodwink the world, corpses of internment-camp victims dressed in German uniforms would be 'killed' during the raid to prove 'Polish provocation'.

At 4.45 in the morning of Friday 1 September 1939, war with Poland commenced with air attacks on airfields, bridges and key railway junctions, terrifying the population of the largest cities in the process.

The two German army groups, commanded by Bock in the north and Rundstedt in the south, swept over the borders an hour after the Luftwaffe had softened Polish defences with precision dive-bombing. The antiquated warplanes of the Polish air force had simply been brushed aside by escorting fighters.

Crucially relying on the empty promises of support from the Western Allies, the Polish high command had formed its primary defensive line westward of the diagonal formed by the river Vistula and its principal tributary, the San. The Poles also had complete faith in their army, which was very large and could call on two million reservists. However, the confidence was misplaced. Over-confident leadership had placed a dangerous faith in cavalry at the expense of mechanised units and artillery, and an absence of an arms industry (for anything other than small arms) had limited the reserves of munitions.

The open nature of the Polish Plain, despite a dearth of good roads, allowed the numerically inferior German mechanised divisions to out-flank the Poles with unforeseen ease, then turn to prevent the latter, penned westward of the Vistula, from falling back on their prepared defences.

Cut off by Germans in front and behind, separated into small pockets by intelligent thrusts and menaced by the Russians from the east, the Polish forces fought bravely until they could do nothing but capitulate. A general retreat was ordered on 10 September; Warsaw fell on 28 September; and, by 5 October, the last sizable remnants of the Polish army had surrendered.

German gains in Poland were immense. It has been estimated that about 694,000 of the 800,000 men under arms had been captured, together with about 16,500 machine-guns, 1,700 mortars, a vast number of rifles (mostly Mausers) and a stupendous quantity of ammunition.

France and Britain had actually declared war against Germany on 3 September 1939, but the rapid demise of Poland – and their own unpreparedness – resulted in western Allied inaction. The French army had ventured into Germany, but the first attacks were not made until 17 September; mobility had been exceptionally slow, and, with few exceptions, the French commanders still saw campaigns in First World War terms. Progress came to a halt on the minefields that had been sown in front of the Siegfried Line.

Hitler proposed peace on 6 October, asking that the seizure of Poland be approved, but neither Britain nor France could agree if credibility were to be retained. Vacillation and bad weather prevented an escalation of hostilities in the west until after the 'Phoney War' of 1940, but the Germans, in particular, made use of the lull to revise their long-term plans. This was due to the loss of a full set of original invasion plans when a navigational error forced a Luftwaffe plane to crash-land in Belgium.

Norway and Denmark were the first to be overrun and conquered by the audacious Operation 'Weserübung', beginning on 9 April 1940, and the upward spiral began. More than 20,000 British troops were landed in Åndalsnes, Namsos and Narvik in a forlorn attempt to isolate

German troops in northern Norway from stronger contingents in the south, but the well-trained Gebirgsjäger, reinforced by Kriegsmarine personnel in an infantry role, proved superior to British units.

Unable to make headway, the last British troops withdrew on 7 June 1940 and the Norwegian authorities formally surrendered on 9 June. Operation 'Weserübung' had cost the Germans a little over five thousand men, many with the cruiser *Blücher*, sunk in Oslofjord by torpedoes launched from the Oscarborg fortress. But while the Norwegian campaign gained the Kriegsmarine valuable naval bases on the West Atlantic coast, it contributed little directly to the Wehrmacht's small-arms arsenal.

War in the West

The German plans had been revised in an attempt to gain surprise. Though moves would be made all along the expected defensive line envisaged by the Allies, who had not bothered to alter their response to the expected German attacks in anything other than detail, the main thrust would be made by mechanised units through the Ardennes in southern Belgium. Known more for its dense woodlands and forest, this was not an area that was suitable for tank warfare. Consequently, the Franco-British forces left only weak forces along the frontier bordering the Ardennes, allowing the strengthened left wing to pivot up through Belgium and the Netherlands.

War came to Belgium, the Netherlands and Luxembourg on the morning of 10 May 1940. Commanded by Bock, the northern German army group soon overran the Netherlands by a combination of daring paratroop attacks, terror bombing and sheer weight of numbers. The Royal Dutch Army surrendered on 14 May, having lost a quarter of its strength in four days; Belgium sought an armistice on 26 May, despite the brave resistance of its army. France was also caught by surprise as the German southern army group, commanded by Rundstedt, surged out of the Ardennes rather than more northerly parts of Belgium.

By outflanking the Maginot Line and pitting combat-hardened veterans against weak French units, the Wehrmacht made great gains. The Allies, conversely, had made a fatal strategic mistake, allowing the

Germans access to the broad plains of northern France before they could be checked. Racing ahead of the main army – often too quickly for Hitler and the High Command to bear – Guderian and his armoured forces swept aside opposition along the Somme valley to reach the Channel coast by 20 May.

Almost the entire British Expeditionary Force, and substantial portions of the French army, had been enveloped in a gigantic pincer that threatened to push them back into the sea.

The fall of Calais on 26 May persuaded the British Commander-in-Chief, Lord Gort, to order the commencement of Operation 'Dynamo' – evacuation from the channel ports. The miracle of Dunkirk, completed on 4 June 1940, saw the rescue of more than 330,000 British and French troops at minimal cost, but virtually all their equipment had been lost and thousands of French troops to the south had been unable to gain safety.

The French military blamed the 'cowardly' British to gloss over an inability to mount a concerted riposte to the invasion. Unfortunately, severe damage had been done to Franco-British relations and enthusiasm for war in France, with the nightmare of Verdun fresh in mind, weakened perceptibly. The French government fled from Paris to Bordeaux on 12 June, Premier Reynaud resigned four days later and his successor, Pétain, immediately requested an armistice. On 22 June 1940, the French government accepted swingeing German terms at Compiègne . . . in the same railway carriage that had seen German representatives sign the armistice in 1918.

The campaign had been exceptionally successful, allowing the numerically inferior German units to defeat the two leading armies in western Europe almost at will. But it also contributed too much to the mythology of *Blitzkrieg*, 'lightning war'. Surprise had clearly been an important factor in the success, implicit in the unexpected advances through the Ardennes and, on a more personal scale, the subjugation and ultimate capture of the 1200-man garrison of the Belgian Fort Eben-Emael by 78 Germans who had been parachuted onto the roof of the fort – where no significant defensive gunfire could be brought to bear on them. Yet the Wehrmacht was not unstoppable. The mechanised forces represented only a fraction of the total establishment; the tanks were weakly armed and poorly armoured; many of the infantry units were inexperienced; and surprising reliance was still placed on horse-traction.

An important factor in the conquest of France was the inability of the French to provide a concerted defence. Mobilisation was ponderous; the development of the *Armée de l'Air* had been ignored, preventing French pilots gaining air superiority; and the best French tanks, more powerful than their German rivals, were frittered away in classic pre-1918 infantry-support roles instead of grouped together to face the German advance. On the few occasions when British or French armoured units were able to attack the Panzers, they were surprisingly successful. The problem was simply that there were never enough of them to turn the tide.

The unexpectedly speedy collapse of Western Europe allowed the myth of German supremacy to salve the consciences of ineffectual governments and high-ranking soldiers whose grasp of tactics was twenty-years-old. As Captain Sir Basil Liddell Hart observed in his classic work, *History of the Second World War* (Cassell, 1970), 'The dazzling effect of what the new elements achieved has obscured not only their relatively small scale but the narrow margin by which success was gained. Their success could easily have been prevented but for the opportunities presented to them by Allied blunders – blunders that were largely due to the prevalence of out-of-date ideas. Even as it was . . . the success of the invasion [of France] turned on a lucky series of long-odds chances . . .'

The capitulation of the Netherlands, Belgium and France provided a considerable haul of weapons. As far as small arms were concerned, however, there was little to offer other than the production facilities of Fabrique Nationale d'Armes de Guerre in Herstal-lèz-Liége in Belgium, where, as 'D.W.M. Werk Lüttich', many hundreds of thousands of pistols and rifle components were made until September 1944. The Netherlands had only the comparatively small-scale Hembrug factory, and though the French government had appreciable manufacturing capacity, the standard small arms were unacceptable.

Procurement was subsequently limited to handguns, particularly from commercial operations in Bayonne and Hendaye, though small numbers of rifles were taken back to Germany for the police. Large numbers of Mle. 24/29 ('Châtellerault') and Mle. 31 machine-guns were eventually emplaced in the Atlantic Wall fortifications, but the necessity to arm the pro-German Vichy forces restricted supplies to the Wehrmacht.

The experiences in Western Europe in 1940 had practically no effect on the development of German small arms. With the fall of France, attention switched to the air war on Britain, and attempts to close the sea-lanes by U-boat warfare. Not until the invasion of Russia in 1941 would the performance of German small arms – and the ability of industry to maintain supplies in the face of unexpectedly high losses – come under scrutiny.

Captured and non-standard weapons

1) POLISH
An ammunition-compatibility list published in April 1940 noted that the vanquished Polish army had contributed a range of small arms to the German inventory: the Pistole 35 (p) or 'Radom'; the Gewehre 98 (p) and 29 (p); and the Maschinengewehre 28 (p) and 30 (p). There were also some refurbished MG. 08 Maxims, most of which were old German guns given to emergent Poland as war reparations in 1920–1.

Large numbers of sporting rifles were also confiscated from the Polish civilian population. In the spring of 1940, 'by order of Reichsmarschall Göring', these and the guns taken in Czechoslovakia were handed back to the Volksdeutsche (ethnic Germans) and hunting-licence holders in the Sudetenland and the 'Polnischer Gebiet'.[1]

But this does not seem to have rid the authorities of all these unwanted weapons, which existed in an infinite variety of calibres and conditions. In April 1941, therefore, the O.K.H. offered all the guns that remained in the hands of the 'military authorities in the occupied territories' for sale commercially, with the proviso that any remaining on hand at the end of May would be scrapped. Prices ranged from 10 Reichmarks (RM) for a telescope sight and 12 RM for a hammer shotgun to 16 RM for a hunting rifle and 25 RM for a *Drilling* (a typically German three-barrelled rifle-shotgun), the buyers being asked to gamble with the condition and desirability of their 'unseen' purchases.[2]

Machine-guns.   The Maxims were simply assimilated into the German inventory as 'MG. 08', which, having been made in Germany prior to 1918, was exactly what they were. The Poles also had a variety of Browning Automatic Rifles, including the survivors of 10,000 guns ordered from Fabrique Nationale d'Armes de Guerre in December 1927. These were issued as the wz. 28 ('le. MG. 28 [p]' to the Germans). The 'wz. 30' was a water-cooled 1917-type Browning chambered for the 7.9mm rifle cartridge.

The Germans issued the 's. MG. 30 (p)' in small numbers. Manual D 132/1, published in October 1942, referred to the 'Maschinengewehr 30 (p)' and two differing tripod mounts – 'Dreifuss 34 (p)' and 'Dreifuss 36 (p)' – and instructions were published in September 1944 to guide the manufacture of new piston-head extensions for the le. MG. 28 (p), pinned to the remnants of the original piston rod to repair oxidation damage.[3]

Rifles.   Poland provided the Germans with large quantities of indigenous Mauser rifles, made on machinery that had once equipped the Imperial German rifle factory in Danzig. The standard service rifles were the Karabiner wz. 98 and wz. 29, the former being a near facsimile of the German Kar. 98 AZ. (but with a uniquely squared stacking rod and sling swivels) and the latter being essentially similar to the Czech vz. 24 short rifle. As the Karabiner chambered the German 7.9mm cartridge, the Wehrmacht easily assimilated large numbers of ex-Polish weapons.

The Poles also had small numbers of wz. 25 rifles (or 'wz. 91/98/25'), which were shortened ex-Russian obr. 1891g Mosin-Nagants, modified for the rimless 7.9mm cartridge. Unlike the original Russian rifles, however, they accepted standard knife bayonets.

However, German test-firing instructions, dating from May 1940, were concerned only with the full-length Gewehr 98 (p) and the short rifles, Gewehr 29 (p) and Karabiner 98 (p), which were to be tried with Patr. s.S. Stahlhülse.[4]

It is sometimes claimed that production of wz. 29-type rifles in the Radom factory ceased almost immediately after the collapse of Polish resistance, and that the factory was then put to making components for the essentially similar Kar. 98k. However, wartime Heereswaffenamt procurement data indicates that nearly 370,000 'Gewehre 29 (p)' were delivered in 1940–2.

Experience soon showed that the tips of the strikers in Polish rifles had a tendency to fail, and, in June 1941, the O.K.H. ordered that regimental armourers should replace them with the Kar. 98k pattern when the old guns were returned for repair.[5] Finally, the muzzle rings were removed from ex-Polish bayonets after May 1942.[6]

Handguns. The Polish army had had a particularly traumatic 1920s, when a licence to build Russian Nagant gas-seal revolvers had been acquired and a decision to build the Czech vz. 24 was only narrowly averted. Finally, however, Wilniewczyc and Skrzpinski had perfected a locked-breech Colt-Browning variant chambering the standard 9mm Parabellum cartridge. Officially known as the 'VIS wz. 35', this first-class weapon remained in production throughout the war, even though the design was simplified and quality declined appreciably as the Russians drew inexorably nearer to Fabryka Bronie w Radomiu.

The first deliveries of the 'Pistole 35 (p)' – excepting those that had simply been seized – were made in 1941. By the end of 1942, nearly 74,000 had been delivered to the army and 10,500 to the Kriegsmarine. German-controlled production totalled about 289,000 guns in three differing patterns; the earliest had a high-polish finish and a stock-slot on the butt; the second had a military-grade finish and lacked the slot; while the last and worst type, generally lacking the dismantling catch, often displayed wood grips, riveted-in lockwork and notably poor finish.

The Radom factory was evacuated in January 1945, and many tons of components were sent to Steyr-Daimler-Puch, where approximately 22,000 poor-quality guns were assembled from a mixture of Steyr and Radom parts in 1945.

2) DANISH AND NORWEGIAN

Denmark and Norway were both small countries with armed forces that reflected their populations of just a few million people each. However, Denmark was the home of the DISA-Madsen arms-making business, and both had sufficient government-owned small arms and munitions factories to make a significant contribution to the Wehrmacht inventory.

Machine-guns.   Denmark and Norway provided a few Madsens and Maxims respectively, together with a number of Browning automatic rifles. The only guns that were important enough to show on the German inventories were 'le. MG. 158 (d)', described in the lists of foreign equipment as '8mm Madsen 03/04'. These were retained for garrison use in Denmark and for training, an appropriate manual, D 101/6, being published by the Heereswaffenamt (Wa.Z.-4) in July 1943.

Rifles.   Denmark and Norway both used the Krag-Jørgensen, which was popular with pro-German defence forces and, it is said, Norwegian SS volunteers. The principal Norwegian rifle was the bolt-action 6.5mm-calibre m/1894, a sturdy gun with an unusually smooth action and an odd lateral magazine beneath the bolt. Unlike the Mausers, the Krag could be loaded with loose cartridges even when a round had been chambered. The Norwegians had also issued several carbines, but most were retained for the 'loyal' units of the Norwegian army.

Handguns.   The invasion of Denmark and Norway provided small numbers of two distinctive pistol designs, the Danish Bergmann-Bayard, m/10-21, and the Norwegian M/1912 and M/1914 Colt-Brownings (Pistolen 657 [n]). In addition to 22,211 M/1914 guns made in the Kongsberg arsenal prior to the German invasion of Norway, 7,288 were made in 1941–2 and a final batch of 935 followed in 1945. These are also said to have been issued largely to Norwegian Waffen-SS volunteers, but output of Norwegian Colts was not great enough to affect the pistol-procuring programme.

3) BELGIAN AND DUTCH

Belgium had a centuries-old tradition of gunmaking, concentrated in Liége. By 1940, however, Fabrique Nationale d'Armes de Guerre of Herstal (near Liége) had a mass-production monopoly. F.N., once substantially German-owned, had enjoyed a particularly chequered history prior to the First World War. Though the factory had returned to indigenous control in 1918, it was immediately sequestered when the Germans invaded Belgium in 1940 and placed under the control of Deutsche Waffen- & Munitionsfabriken A.G. – with which, irony of ironies, Fabrique Nationale had participated in the pre-1914 Mauser rifle-making cartel. Operated as 'D.W.M. Werk Lüttich' until recaptured by the Allies in September 1944, the Herstal plant made hundreds of thousands of small arms for the Wehrmacht.

The Netherlands, conversely, had comparatively little recent gun-making history. Production of small arms was concentrated in the government-owned factory in Hembrug, where Mannlicher rifles, Schwarzlose and Lewis machine-guns had all been made, but handguns had usually been purchased in Germany or Belgium.

Machine-guns. Belgium provided Browning aircraft guns made by F.N. and Fabrique d'Armes de l'État in Liége. The Netherlands contributed the M. 08/13 Schwarzlose and M. 20 Lewis Guns, known to the Germans as the 's. MG. 242 (h)' and 'le. MG. 100 (h)' respectively. Manual D 101/9 for the Schwarzlose and its tripod mount was published in May 1943, and Manual D 101/8 for the Lewis Gun and its tripod followed in September. The Netherlands also issued substantial quantities of 6.5mm-calibre Madsen light machine-guns, in a variety of patterns that included some for colonial service with the Netherlands Indies army (K.N.I.L.). There is no evidence that any of these entered German service.

Automatic rifles. Mle. 30 Browning automatic rifles ('le. MG. 127 [b]') were obtained from Belgium, where they had been made under licence by Fabrique Nationale d'Armes de Guerre in Herstal.

Rifles. Chambering a 7.65mm rimless cartridge, the Belgian Mle. 89, or Gewehr 261 (b), could be distinguished by its projecting magazine casing and jacketed barrel. By the Second World War, however, most surviving pre-1918 Mle. 89 rifles had been shortened to 'Mle. 89/36' standards and their barrel jackets were removed – an expedient while supplies of the 7.65mm Kar. 98k-type Mle. 35 short rifle had been assured. Issue of the latter was not universal by 1940. The Germans designated the 89/36 as the 'Gewehr 262 (b)' and the Mle. 35 as the 'Gewehr 263 (b)';

there were also two carbines, the Karabiner 451 (b) and 453 (b). However, few Belgian rifles were used by the Wehrmacht, being issued to police and gendarmerie keeping order in occupied territory.

The Belgian guns embodied a primitive form of the locking system that had been perfected in the Gew. 98, and, in particular, had a simpler safety arrangement. This gave problems in German service, and, in November 1941, the O.K.H. was forced to remind the field army how to operate guns of this type safely. A few of the carbines subsequently had their slings altered to conform with German practice, undertaken by unit armourers from September 1942 onwards.[7]

Mannlichers were captured in quantity after the invasion of the Netherlands, but were generally retained for reserve, gendarmerie and police units serving in the Low Countries. The principal rifle was the 6.5mm M. 1895 ('Gewehr 211 [h]'), and there were a handful of 6.5mm No. 3 Old and New Model carbines ('Karabiner 413 [h]'). The turning-bolt rifles had distinctively-shaped projecting box magazines beneath their split-bridge receivers and a unique bayonet fixing system. Many of the bayonets were shortened after September 1942, contemporaneously with the French designs (see below).

Submachine-guns.   The Belgian 'Mi. Schmeisser-Bayard Mle. 34', a facsimile of the MP. 28 chambering 9mm Pist. Patr. 08, was assimilated into German service as 'MP. 740 (b)'.

Handguns.   The Belgian Pistolen 626 (b) and 641 (b) were simple single-action Mle. 10/22 blowbacks deriving directly from designs John Browning had perfected early in the twentieth century. Chambering the 7.65mm Auto and 9mm Short cartridges respectively, they offered excellent quality but no great knockdown capability. Production of the 626 (b) was initially diverted almost exclusively to the Luftwaffe, which received a little over 100,000 by the end of 1942; deliveries of the 9mm 641 (b) to the army, however, had been less than 3,500 in the same period owing to an H.WaA. decision to make no new 9mm components once Belgian supplies had been exhausted. Total Mle. 10/22 production prior to the evacuation of Herstal in September 1944, threatened by the Allied advance, amounted to about 363,200 guns.

Additional F.N.-made Mle. 10/22 Brownings were retrieved from the Royal Netherlands Army (which designated them 'M1925') and also from Yugoslavia, where 60,000 had been sold in 1923–5. These are practically identical with the guns made in Herstal for the Germans, but have recognisably different markings.

The Pistole 640 (b) was quite different from the other Brownings: a powerful 9mm locked-breech recoil-operated design, better known as the Mle. 35 G.P. ('Pistolet à Grande Puissance' or 'High Power'). Developed from the U.S. Army .45 Colt-Browning M1911 in the early 1920s, the G.P. had been completed by F.N. technicians after Browning's unexpected death in Liége in December 1925.

The crash of Wall Street in 1929 and subsequent worldwide depression deferred mass-production of the new gun until 1935, when the Belgian army had immediately adopted it. Substantial quantities were soon exported to China, Estonia, Finland, France, Lithuania, Peru and Sweden; about 69,000 High Powers had been made prior to the German invasion, followed by another 319,000 in 1940–4.[8]

Excepting guns that were assembled from Belgian-made parts, with butts cut to receive shoulder stocks, the Germans concentrated on a stockless tangent-sight pattern; and then, when manufacture proved unnecessarily time-consuming, on a simpler pattern with a fixed back sight. The finish deteriorated visibly in 1943–4, though the material remained sound.

The G.P. was at least the equal of the P. 08 and P. 38; though it lacked the former's accuracy and the latter's double-action trigger, it was more durable than the Parabellum and offered a thirteen-round staggered-column magazine instead of the Walther's eight. The first deliveries reached the Wehrmacht in the summer of 1940; 153,464 had been delivered by the end of 1942, exclusively to the army. In later years, however, guns began to reach the Waffen-SS as well.

The Dutch Brownings, which were made in Belgium, have already been mentioned. Many of the 1906-type 9mm Parabellums used by the Royal Netherlands Indies Army (K.N.I.L.) fell into the hands of the Japense in 1942, but supplies of the 9mm 1908-type 'Pistool Automatisch No. 1 (Parabellum)' issued to the Royal Netherlands Navy (*Koninklijke Marine*, 'K.M.') prior to 1939 were seized by the Germans.

The earliest of these guns, which were practically indistinguishable from the German P. 08, were bought from Berlin-Karlsruher Industrie-Werke in 1928–30, distinguished by the 'DWM' monogram on their toggles, '*GELADEN*' on both sides of the extractor instead of merely the left, and an arrow and '*RUST*' in the safety-lever recess on the left rear side of the frame. A few near-identical guns delivered by Mauser-Werke in 1930–6, though still bearing the 'DWM' banner, had 'crown/crown/U' proof marks instead of the previous 'crown/N'.

The last batches were delivered by Mauser in 1937–9, taken from commercial production and distinguished by 'v'-suffix numbers beginning at 2330v. Six hundred guns were awaiting delivery in September 1939, but were immediately diverted to German troops. Consequently, they had Dutch 'arrow/RUST' marks in the safety recesses and German military inspectors' marks on the major components. The remaining 400 guns were never assembled, though the parts (which included frames with the unmistakeable safety markings) had soon been incorporated in the standard Wehrmacht-issue P. 08.

4) FRENCH

In view of the size of the armed forces and a healthy state-owned small-arms manufacturing industry based on the factories in Châtellerault, Saint-Étienne and Tulle, France proved another arms-procuring disappointment. This was partly due to the way in which the capitulation had been arranged, with the partition of the country into occupied and 'free' or 'Vichy' zones. The need to maintain not just a small French standing army but also police units strong enough to retain control of the population persuaded the Germans to leave most of the small arms where they had been. In addition, the French weapons were obsolescent, except for some of the machine-guns, comparatively meagre supplies of the new 7.5mm MAS 36 and MAS 36 CR 39 rifles, the SE MAS 35 submachine-gun; and the 1935-type SACM and MAS pistols.

Machine-guns.   Vichy forces retained most of the quirky French designs apart from those that armed captured tanks and many 7.5mm Mle. 24/29 'Châtellerault' light machine-guns, similar externally to the Z.B./Bren series. Most of the surviving 7.5mm Mle. 31 *Mitrailleuses de*

Fortresse, with their extraordinary side-mounted drum magazines, were eventually sent to equip the Atlantic Wall.

A manual for the Saint-Étienne Mle. 07/15 machine-gun, 's. MG. 256 (f)' was published in 1942, together with manual D 101/5 for the '8mm s. MG. 257 (f)' – the Mle. 14 Hotchkiss and its Mle. 16 tripod.

German manuals, and Fischer's *Leitfaden für die Ordnungspolizei*, suggest that small numbers of the Chauchat or C.S.R.G. machine rifle, 'le. MG. 156 (f)', were issued to the police in small numbers. It is suspected that these were restricted to training, or held in reserve in the hope that they would never be needed!

Rifles. Though substantial quantities of French service rifles were captured in 1940, most were subsequently returned to the Vichy Government. Known to the Germans as 'Gewehr 361 (f)', the Mle. 74 (Gras) was an obsolescent 11mm single-shot bolt-action rifle; the 8mm Mle. 86/93 (Lebel) or 'Gewehr 301 (f)', had been the world's first successful small-bore rifle firing a cartridge loaded with smokeless propellant, but its under-barrel tube magazine was anachronistic by 1940. An attempt had been made to shorten the Lebel, resulting in the Mle. 86/93 R 35 ('Gewehr 303 [f]'), but only a few thousand of these conversions had been completed when the fighting began.

The 8mm-calibre Berthier was a much better design. Though its complicated bolt resembled the Lebel's, the magazine was a clip-loaded box. A series of successful *Carabines* and *Mosquetons* (Mle. 90 and Mle. 92), plus the Mle. 02 and Mle. 07 colonial rifles, had persuaded the French authorities to standardise the Berthier for univeral issue as the Mle. 15. The Germans recognised the 'Karabiner 552 (f)' and '553 (f)' among the weapons that had been seized, these being the Mle. 90 carbine or Mle. 92 short rifles ('552') and the Mle. 90/16 carbine or Mle. 92/16 short rifle ('553').[9]

The French had realised that their rifles lagged behind those of potential rivals, and the charger-loaded 7.5mm MAS 36 was a much more battleworthy weapon. Unfortunately, the new rifles were only beginning to reach the army when the Germans invaded France and had few chances to show their merits.

Problems with Berthier Mle.16 rifles ('Gewehr 304 [f]') in German service were addressed in July 1942, owing, it is assumed, to accidents.[10] A manual for this particular rifle, D 121/1, appeared at the end of October. Most of the pre-1918 French designs lacked any form of applied safety system other than a half-cock notch, and were a liability in the hands of troops who had been trained with the Kar. 98k.

In addition, many French Mle. 86 and 86/15 *épée* bayonets, 'Seitengewehre 102 (f) u. 103 (f)', were shortened by unit armourers after September 1942 (along with comparable Belgian and Dutch designs).[11]

Submachine-guns.   France was intending to re-equip with the 7.65mm MAS 38, but this gun – an interesting 'straight line' blowback design with the barrel set at an angle to the axis of the receiver – had been adopted only on 9 May 1940. However, production of 19,500 SE-MAS 35 (a prototype form of the MAS 38) had been sanctioned in January 1939, owing to the deteriorating political situation in Europe, but only six guns had been delivered by the beginning of June 1940. When the armistice was signed later the same month, the Saint-Étienne factory had completed fewer than two thousand. Only a few hundred had been issued, mostly to tank- and motorised anti-tank gun units.

However, after the partition of France, Saint-Étienne was included in the *Zone Libre* ('Vichy France') and the SE-MAS 35 was abandoned in favour of the MAS 38. The new gun continued the 'F'-suffix serial numbers of the SE-MAS 35. About 14,000 submachine-guns had been made when the Germans took control of Vichy arms-making factories. Most had been sent to French colonial units in North Africa. The MAS 38 was about 630mm long, with a 220mm barrel, and had a detachable 32-round magazine. It weighed about 3.4kg loaded. The barrel was angled upward in relation to the receiver-top at an angle of about six degrees, giving a distinctive appearance, and the trigger lever could be pushed forward to serve as a safety catch.

Production subsequently continued under German control, but at an exceptionally leisurely pace that was often interrupted by surreptitious acts of sabotage and 'go-slow' working. Consequently, by the time the Germans evacuated Saint-Étienne in the summer of 1944, only about 15,000 guns had been made. Distinguished by German military proof and inspectors' marks, many of these were then sent to units stationed in and around Vienna. Work began again after the end of the Second World War, initially for French colonial units, output peaking at about 39,000 in 1945. The use of 'F'-suffix numbers continued until August 1947 (when 'G' was substituted); consequently, only the guns with numbers below about 32,000 can be associated legitimately with German use.[12]

The German police received small quantities of ex-French 'P.M. Vollmer Erma' (virtually identical with the German MP. E), which served as 'Maschinenpistolen 704 (f)'.

Handguns.　　The French had been largely revolver-orientated prior to 1918, though there is no evidence that the Mle. 92 ('Lebel' or 'Modèle d'Ordonnance') was ever issued in Germany. Guns of this type were simply left with the Vichy forces and police.

When the Franco-German armistice was agreed on 22 June 1940, cunning partition ensured that the Pyrenean arms-making centres of Hendaye and Bayonne lay in the German occupation zone. Manufacture of 7.65mm-calibre seven-shot Unique Mle. 16 and nine-shot Mle. 17 pistols continued, about 2,000 of the former and 30,000 of the latter being accepted by the Wehrmacht. The first of about twenty thousand Unique *Kriegsmodelle*, a German-inspired modification of the Mle. 17, then began to leave the Hendaye factory. Unlike their predecessors, these had exposed hammers and rounded backstraps. Production continued until the Hendaye area was recaptured in September 1944.

Handguns were also acquired from Manufacture d'Armes de Bayonne ('MAB'), about 1,130 6.35mm MAB Mle. A, 2,600 7.65mm MAB Mle. C and possibly 51,160 7.65mm Mle. D being delivered in 1940–4.

Throughout the inter-war period, the French army had experimented with a variety of blowback pistol designs, until a locked-breech Colt-Browning clone appeared. Patented in 1934 by Charles Petter, who claimed novelty only in the lockwork, this was promoted by *Société Alsacienne de Constructions Mécanique* ('S.A.C.M.'), unexpectedly won the army trials, and was adopted as the 'Pistolet Mle. 35A' – apparently as an expedient while the government arsenal at Saint-Étienne adapted the design for series production. However, only about 9,500 Mle. 35A pistols had been made prior to the German invasion, numbered from

A001A, together with less than 2,000 of the improved Mle. 35S. Work on the Mle. 35A (or 'Pistole 625 [f]') recommenced under German supervision in October 1940 and continued until April 1944, though only 23,850 guns were satisfactorily completed.

The Mle. 35A was an efficient design, though the position of the safety catch was poor (but not as bad as some ill-informed writers now claim). Its worst feature was the comparatively weak and uniquely French 7.65mm Longue cartridge. Had the Mle. 35A chambered the 9mm Parabellum, for example, it would have been regarded among the best of the impressed guns; the action undoubtedly had sufficient inherent strength to handle higher pressures than generated by the original 7.65mm chambering.

5) OTHERS
Note: Guns made in occupied territories to German designs and under German supervision are considered to be regulation patterns, and are included in the appropriate section.

Spain remained neutral throughout the Second World War, cheerfully supplying weapons to both sides. The German purchases were restricted to Unceta y Cia ('Astra') of Guernica and Bonifacio Echeverria y Cia ('Star') of Eibar. Initially imported through Sudost-Handelsgesellschaft von Ramin of Berlin, without H.WaA. marks, the Astras were either based on the Mauser C/96 or the uniquely tube-slide blowbacks that had been adapted from the Campo-Giro.

The Mauser-type guns included the Astra Mo. 903 machine pistol, the best of the Spanish Mauser copies. This deviated internally from the German prototype in several important details; the locking block was pinned to the barrel extension – unlike the free-floating Mauser pattern – and a unique flat-surface detachable sideplate gained access to the lock components. 'Astra-Mausers' purchased on behalf of the H.WaA. bore nothing other than standard Spanish markings and could only be identified by their serial numbers. They included 1,004 delivered to the German authorities in Hendaye, France, in November 1940. A second consignment of a thousand followed in March 1943, accompanied by 1,050 standard Astra Mo. 900 pistols.

Purchases of the tube-slide blowbacks included 1,510 6.35mm-calibre Astra 200 (all but ten in January 1943); 85,390 examples of the Astra 300 (7.65mm Auto and 9mm Short) delivered in 1941–4; and six thousand 9mm Largo service-pattern Astra 400 acquired in 1941.

The Astra 600/43 was an adaptation of the Astra 400 chambering the 9mm Pist. Patr. 08. After 10,450 had reached the Germans, a consignment of 28,000 was intercepted by the Allies in September 1944 and returned to Spain, where production ran on into 1945. Ironically, the guns made in 1945 were sold to West Germany in the early 1950s to equip the emerging Bundeswehr.

The Star Modelo B – another of the pistols that was sold to Allied and Axis purchasers alike – was a powerful recoil-operated Colt-Browning lookalike chambering the standard 9mm Parabellum cartridge, but only 25,000 were acquired in two large consignments; the bulk of the output appears to have been acquired by Britain.

Regulation weapons

Machine-guns.   The MG. 34 had been introduced in large numbers, and was performing well enough to persuade the authorities to continue production – even though trials with the prototypes of what was to become the MG. 42 had already begun. The shortages of light support weapons had been solved by issuing as many ex-Czechoslovakian Z.B. guns as could be obtained.

Rifles.   The Gewehr 29/40 (ö), often said to be a 'variation of the standard Austrian M1929 service rifle', was apparently created to supply the Luftwaffe with rifles at a time when the army was taking most of the new Kar. 98k. Made from Polish wz. 29 actions that had been moved from Radom to Steyr, the rifles also had distinctive nose-caps, handguards that stretched from the receiver ring to the nosecap, and stocks with pointed Austrian-style pistol grips. They also accepted the standard German SG. 84/98.

Production was never large; only three hundred guns show on surviving Heereswaffenamt procurement records, all delivered in 1940, but it is assumed that thousands more had been accepted by the OKL. At this date, the Luftwaffe was still acquiring small arms independently of the army.

Few changes were made to the standard German service rifles in this period, though the first supplies of the Zielfernrohr-Karabiner 98k to be fitted with the Zf. 39 reached the troops. The earliest known manual, *Das Zielfernrohr 39 (Zielvier) für den Karabiner 98k* (D 134), is dated 22 January 1940.

However, problems had arisen with the accuracy of the Kar. 98k, forcing the Oberkommando des Heeres to send instructions refining test-firing procedures to all the rifle manufacturers. The tests were undertaken with a special target, consisting of a solid rectangle with tapering edges at the lower corners, which provided an aiming point. The guns were checked to ensure that they had appropriate proof marks, and that the bores had been satisfactorily degreased. A couple of sighting rounds were fired to ensure that aim taken coincided approximately with the fall of shot at a distance of 100 metres, and then five rounds were then fired at a pristine target. Strict instructions were given to prevent experienced marksmen deliberately 'aiming off' to ensure that shots hit the target, camouflaging that the sights needed adjustment.

If the gun placed five rounds in a pre-defined rectangle measuring 8cm × 14cm, and all five rounds so that they could be covered by a 12cm-diameter disc, it was deemed to be acceptable. If it satisfied the first criterion but not the second, the barrel was allowed to cool and the test was repeated. If the rifle still failed to meet expectations, it was returned to the factory for attention. Though s.S. ball ammunition was used exclusively, separate sighting targets were provided for brass- or steel-case ammunition. Experience had shown that the latter tended to give a mean impact several centimetres higher than the former.

A new front-sight hood and disposable rubber 'Mipolam' muzzle caps were adopted in December 1939, replacing the original sheet-metal patterns, and a *Kolbenkappe* ('cupped butt plate') replaced the original flat-plate pattern early in 1940 to protect the edges of the butt.[13]

Officially adopted by the Wehrmacht on 16 November 1940,[14] the *Gewehr 33/40* had originally been introduced as the Krátká četniká puška vz. 33 pro čs. četnictvo a finační stráz', but only about

25,000 had been issued to the Czechoslovakian 'gendarmerie and treasury guards'. A handful of minor changes were made and production of the minuscule Gew. 33/40 continued under German supervision; intended for the Gebirgsjäger, most guns display a reinforcing plate on the left side of the butt. A short-lived variant even had a folding stock. The standard 33/40 had a German-style nosecap, but a full-length handguard ran from the front of the back sight to the nosecap. Unlike the original Czech vz. 33, the German version accepted the SG. 84/98.

Anti-tank rifles. The PzB. 38 proved to be a failure when tested in Poland, even though the armour of the Polish tanks was relatively thin. It had proved to be cumbersome, though lighter than the T-Gewehr, and the semi-automatic breech system was unreliable in adverse conditions. Dipl.-Ing. Bauer then produced the simplified PzB. 39. Externally similar to its predecessor (though notably slimmer), it had a simple dropping-breech action operated by unlatching and pushing down on the pistol-grip/trigger assembly.

The new rifle weighed merely 12.4kg which, with the omission of the recoil-absorbing springs, gave it a far heavier recoil than the PzB. 38. Tested in the campaigns in the Netherlands, Belgium and France, the PzB. 39 also proved a failure – not because it was any less efficient than the PzB.38, but simply because increasing tank-armour thickness was defeating all rifle-calibre weapons.

The Germans turned to the Gerlich-system *schwere Panzerbüchse 41* (s. PzB. 41), which squeezed a 28mm-diameter projectile to emerge as 21mm calibre at the muzzle, but shortages of tungsten soon forced this particular project to be abandoned.

Submachine-guns. The improved *Maschinenpistole 40* (MP. 40) appears to have been accepted in April 1940, shortly before the invasion of the Low Countries and France, but none would have been delivered in time to take part in the fighting and the 'Schmeissers' of the time would have been MP. 38. By the beginning of February 1941, however, most submachine-gun-carrying front-line personnel had received the improved design.[15]

Production of the MP. 38 had been relatively small, but sufficient experience had been gained to reveal serious problems. So many changes were being suggested that the H.WaA. was forced to adopt a 'new' pattern.

The ejector and the magazine-catch assembly had been substantially altered, fluting was omitted from the receiver, and the grip and sub-frame extension were pressed from steel rather than cast from aluminium. The barrel collar was modified; the barrel-stop was changed to formed steel from compressed fibre; and the recoil-spring unit was redesigned. The earliest magazine housings were smooth, but proved to be weak until five short horizontal ribs were added to increase rigidity.

Experience in Poland showed that the basic safety system needed to be modified so that the bolt could be locked forward in such a way that it no longer rested on the primer of a chambered round. In this case, a sudden blow (dropping the gun, for example) would fire the round accidentally. The new cocking handle simply engaged a semicircular cut-out in the front upper edge of the cocking slot, and many older guns were fitted with a leather interceptor to hold the cocking handle in its rearward (cocked) position.

The guns fitted with cocking handles that could be locked in their forward position were officially designated 'MP. 40/I', many older MP. 38 and MP. 40 subsequently being modified by exchanging the cocking handle and cutting the engagement notch in its slot.

Once mass production was underway, it was immediately evident that Erma ('27' and 'ayf') could not cope with demand. Steyr-Daimler-Puch was recruited to make the MP. 40 in the autumn of 1940 – its products being coded '660' or 'bnz' – while C.G. Haenel of Suhl ('fxo') joined in 1942. Production of the submachine-guns relied heavily on sub-contractors, particularly for the large pressings; consequently, the marks of Merz-Werke of Frankfurt am Main ('cos'), National Krupp Registrier-Kassen G.m.b.H. of Berlin-Neukölln ('cnd') and the Steyr-Daimler-Puch factory in Graz ('kur') may be found on the receivers.

Production of the MP. 40 continued until the end of the Second World War, though it was curtailed greatly in favour of the MP. 44 in July 1944. Erma continued to make a few thousand guns monthly until the end of April 1945, but the inventory of pistol-cartridge Maschinenpistolen was sustained by manufacturing the Beretta M38A/42 in Italy, by developing the MP. 3008, and even by attempting to copy the British Mk II Sten Gun. This story is related in greater detail in Chapter 8.

The MP. 40 was accompanied by a variety of accessories, including three-magazine pouches with belt-loops and a 'D'-ring for a stabilising strap. Most of the pouches made prior to 1943 were leather, either black or left 'natural', but later examples often had leather flaps and straps and fabric bodies. There was also a special six-magazine pouch that attached to a shoulder strap.[16]

Most pouches also have small pockets, originally on the spine but subsequently on the front of the body, which held a special magazine loader and the muzzle protector. After the summer of 1942, a magazine cleaner was also carried.

Handguns. Though the Parabellum had a good reputation, particularly outside Germany, time-and-motion studies had always shown that nineteenth-century origins scarcely suited the design to mass production. Exemplary accuracy excused neither excessive cost nor the waste of raw material.

Trials had been undertaken seriously even in Weimar days; by 1938, the enclosed-hammer Walther Armee-Pistole, which had been patented in Germany two years earlier, was performing well enough to overcome rivals promoted by Mauser-Werke and Berlin-Suhler-Werke. An exposed hammer was easily substituted for the enclosed pattern so heartily disliked by the H.WaA., and Walther Heeres-Pistolen underwent exhaustive troop trials that stretched on into the campaigns leading up to the Second World War. Once the problems inevitable in any untried design had been corrected, the Walther was approved for issue on 26 April 1940, as the *Pistole 38* ('P. 38').

When the gun fired, the barrel and slide recoiled through about 7mm, securely locked together; the barrel was then stopped by a shoulder on the frame and an actuating pin pushed the locking block down to release the slide. The slide reciprocated alone, stripping a new cartridge into the breech as it returned. As the slide and barrel ran back to their original position, the locking block beneath the breech was forced up onto its plateau; concurrently, 'wings' on the locking-block engaged recesses in the slide sides to lock the entire mechanism together.

Ironically, though the Walther pistol was much easier to make than the Parabellum, the design is still exceptionally complicated. This is partly due to the double-action trigger, the first of its type to be sturdy enough to withstand active service, which contains a proliferation of levers, pins and springs.

The P. 38 proved to be very successful; it was popular in German service and, like the Parabellum, was much prized by Allied servicemen. But while the P. 08 was regarded as a souvenir, the P. 38 was prized as a true combat weapon. British Army revolvers could not offer the same rate of fire, whereas the U.S. Colt-Browning lacked the double-action trigger that could fire the first shot so much faster than a conventional single-action automatic. It is usually much too dangerous to carry single-action guns with the hammer down on a loaded chamber, and the slide must otherwise be retracted manually before the first shot can be fired.

Though largely overlooked in Germany after the end of the First World War, the venerable Mauser C/96 was especially popular in Spain, where copies were made under the 'Astra', 'Azul' and 'Royal' brand-names. The Astras were by far the best finished of these, even though their material was sometimes soft; during the Second World War, there-fore, the Germans acquired several thousand Astras to supplement their genuine C/96.

During the 1920s, the Spanish manufacturers attempted to trans-form Mauser copies into light fully automatic carbines, a role to which the comparatively lightweight pistol was unsuited. Excessively high cyclic rates exhausted the magazines in a fraction of a second, and the guns became impossible to control. Yet despite what may seem to be important shortcomings, sales of the fully automatic guns were suffi-ciently buoyant to persuade Mauser to copy the Spanish lead.

Prototypes of the 1931-patent Nickl C/96 *Schnellfeuerpistole* appeared in 1932, but the perfected model was the work of Karl Westinger. His master patent was sought in 1933, but not granted for several years. Though basically identical to the standard C/96, the Schnellfeuerpistole had a detachable twenty-round box magazine and a selector switch on the left side of the frame immediately above the grip/trigger guard joint. This rotated to 'N' for single shots and 'R' for fully automatic operation. The guns were generally sold with wooden holster/stocks, supported in a leather harness.

Westinger-patent Mauser Schnellfeuerpistolen – introduced commercially in 1936 – proved to be popular in the Far East in addition to Central- and South America, though German purchases may have been limited to 7,800 guns purchased in 1940 for Luftwaffe Flakabteilung motorcyclists.

P. 08 and P. 38 were generally sent to front-line troops, particularly after reverses in Russia and North Africa forced the Germans into an increasingly defensive campaign. However, there were many servicemen, paramilitary-organisation members and policemen who also needed a handgun. The collection of huge quantities of pistols in the occupied territories explains why even some of the oddest, such as the Belgian Armand Gavage, may now be found with post-1940 German proof- or ownership marks.

Signal pistols. An aluminium-alloy frame version of the Doppelläufige Signal- & Leuchtpistole ('SLD'), originally the work of Walther, was made from c. 1942–3 by a local trade association – Lieferungsgemeinschaft westthüringisches Werkzeug- & Metallwaren-fabriken GmbH of Schmalkalden (code 'eeu') – until the end of the war. Despite black-anodised finish and light weight, it was virtually identical to the standard gun. The same agency contributed a variant of the Einzelläufige Signal- & Leuchtpistole ('SLE', single barrelled) with a black-anodised aluminium-alloy frame that reduced the weight from 1,785gm to 1,105gm.

6

The Great Adventure

For the Wehrmacht, at least in the beginning, the Balkan campaign proved to be a pleasant diversion from other theatres of war. Over in a few weeks, at a cost of merely five thousand casualties, the men looked forward to a pleasant sojourn in a backwater – until the Russian Front beckoned and Četnik partisan activity became widespread.

Hitler and his generals had not initially intended to conquer Greece, which was seen as an unwanted diversion from the meticulously pre-planned strike at the Soviet Union. But Benito Mussolini, desperate for success that would camouflage the reverses in North Africa, invaded the Greek mainland in October 1940 without warning his German allies. At first, Hitler made little response. Then the Italian army suffered a series of humiliating defeats that pushed the front line back into pro-Axis Albania, and the arrival of a small British force raised the spectre of an Allied push up through Salonika (as had been done during the First World War) to threaten the underbelly of the southernmost army group that would soon be attacking the U.S.S.R.

A more important catalyst concerned the political status of Yugoslavia. The Germans had no sooner negotiated a non-aggression pact with the government of the regent, Prince Paul, than a coup d'état led by General Simovich – commander of the air force – upset the balance. Angered by rejection of his terms, Hitler immediately decided to invade Yugoslavia, which could then be used as a springboard to attack Greece.

The invasion of Yugoslavia was launched on 6 April 1941, with major incursions from Austria and Hungary in the north-west, Romania in the east, and Bulgaria in the south-east, forming a giant pincer movement designed to snap shut on Belgrade. The poorly-armed Yugoslavs were unable to stop the irresistible advance of the German armoured units, and the first phase of the way had soon been won. Success allowed the Germans to make a rapid two-pronged advance into Greece, outflanking the major defensive positions. The Greek army capitulated on 28 April 1941, and the supporting British units were withdrawn to Crete.

The Germans then launched an audacious attack on Crete, relying on their parachutists to achieve what the British commander, fearing a seaborne invasion, believed to be impossible. Eventually, nearly 22,000 German troops, landed by parachute, glider and transport aircraft, overcame nearly twice the number of British, Australians, New Zealanders and Greeks. Many of the British and colonial troops were lifted from Crete by the Royal Navy (at great cost in ships and seamen), but the fall of the island was a disaster that threatened the British presence in the eastern Mediterranean. Fortunately, Hitler deemed the casualties among the parachutists to be unacceptably high, and refused to allow Student and other proponents of striking from the air to repeat what was a notable strategic victory.

By 31 May 1941, all of the Balkans were either pro-Axis or in German hands, but it has often been claimed that this campaign was a sideshow that delayed the invasion of the U.S.S.R., the implication being that the Germans would have defeated the Russians had an earlier start been made. This belief was supported by several high-ranking German generals, particularly Rundstedt, commander of Army Group South, whose armoured units could not be deployed effectively until reinforced with those that had fought in Yugoslavia and Greece. Many of the tanks that had been used in the Balkans were in need of maintenance and repairs, and weeks elapsed before they could be sent to Russia.

The truth of the situation is much more complicated. The proposed invasion of the Soviet Union, originally set for 15 May 1941, had been moved back by a month as early as March 1941 — after it had been decided to invade the northern part of Greece as a way of securing the advance into Russia but before Hitler's spur-of-the-moment decision to attack Yugsolavia, which was not taken until the coup d'état of 27 March. The other obvious reason was the weather. German strategists were well aware that eastern Poland would be exceptionally wet after the Spring thaw; indeed, the river Bug was still overflowing its banks only a week or two before the revised invasion date. The Pripyat marshes and the margins of the Beresina river were also largely impassable, particularly as few metalled roads travelled eastward.

The die is cast

The attack on Russia was no spur-of-the-moment decision, but a meticulously planned assault across a front line measuring a thousand miles. Work on 'Directive No. 21. Case Barbarossa' had begun in mid-December 1940, though the assault, originally scheduled for 15 May 1941, had been postponed for five weeks owing partly to the need to complete the conquest of the Balkans (not envisaged in the original schemes) and partly to a desire to let the flooding on the margins of the Russo-Polish frontier subside before risking the passage of armoured vehicles.

Finally, at 4.15am East European time, after a 6,000-gun bombardment that had enlivened the pre-dawn greyness of Sunday 22 June 1941 and the despatch of 'Code Dortmund', the commanders of three army groups sent their men surging over the borders separating European Russia from East Prussia and German-occupied Poland. Operation 'Barbarossa' had begun.

Army Group North sped northward; its goals were Leningrad, the Baltic and a link with the Finns. Army Group Centre, given the major role, was to envelop the defenders in a pincer movement, then rush for Minsk and Smolensk to encircle large sections of the Red Army. Army Group South was to drive from southern Poland to Kiev, seize the grain-rich Ukraine and then take the vital industrial basin of the Donets River.

Initially, the army command wished to push on through Group Centre and take Moscow, destroying the Communist Party hierarchy and the principal centre of communications. Unlike his generals, however, Hitler was obsessed with securing the Baltic States. Here he rightly foresaw that anti-Russian feeling could be exploited; but, as he also wished to seize the important agricultural and industrial regions in the south, the seeds of later doubt had been sown.

The Germans enjoyed immediate success. The Red Army had been caught totally unprepared; indeed, the first reports of the invasion were dismissed in Moscow simply as rumours or scaremongering. Massing of German troops on the Russo-German border had been noted, but virtually nothing had been done to prepare defences. Not until four hours after the invasion had begun was limited retaliation authorised.

By the time the messages were despatched, many addressees were long dead. Soviet troops sometimes rallied and fought to the death; but though slowed temporarily, particularly in the Ukraine, the Germans rolled on. At the end of the first week in July, Army Group South was less than a hundred kilometres from Kiev, the Ukrainian capital; in the middle of August, a trap had been sprung around twenty Soviet divisions near Uman and more than 100,000 prisoners taken. By August, the Red Army, withdrawing to the east bank of the Dnieper, had abandoned the garrisons of Kiev and Odessa to their fates.

On 15 July, Guderian's Group Centre Panzers had reached Smolensk while Hoth, after taking Minsk on 26 June, stood at Vitebsk in the north. The Smolensk pocket was completely encircled the following day, forcing two Soviet armies and countless smaller units – nearly 140,000 men – to capitulate. Group North had penetrated 250km inside Russia by 26 June, just four days after the invasion had begun. Dvinsk fell; Leningrad appeared to be there for the taking.

By the end of August, the Germans were ascendant. The Soviet Union had lost unbelievable numbers of men to death, incapacitation or capture. German Army Group North had pushed up through Dvinsk towards Leningrad, where it was being held at a makeshift defensive line running through Luga. Group Centre's advance had taken it to little more than 300km from Moscow. Group South occupied much of the Ukraine, and was ready to sweep over the Dnieper into the industrialised heartland of European Russia. The German commanders wanted victory, sensing that the road to Moscow lay open. But Hitler wanted Leningrad instead.

The overwhelming of the Red Army, so large and ostensibly properly equipped, was due to the sheer weight of the surprise attack and political interference that counselled attack instead of concerted defence. The Germans had invaded Russia with 135 infantry- and nineteen Panzer divisions, two motorised brigades and a motorised regiment; against these, the Russians should have been able to muster 197 divisions, but few were at full strength. The forces were fairly evenly balanced, as even the addition of Romanian, Italian and Slovakian troops (of somewhat doubtful quality) could not give the Germans numerical superiority.

However, the Luftwaffe obliterated the Russian air force in the invasion zone and denied the Red Army air cover. The prodigious losses of men and matériel to German advances soon tipped the balance; by the middle of July, therefore, the Wehrmacht and its allies had achieved even a numerical advantage.

The failure of the Red Army depended as much on self-inflicted wounds as on the Germans' performance. Despite pre-war fears that the wholesale enlargement of the German army had left no time for proper training, combat experience in Poland, the Western Front and the Balkans had turned raw recruits into seasoned veterans. From the humblest private virtually to the top of the military hierarchy, the Red Army could offer little by comparison; during the purges of 1937–8, three of the five marshals, thirteen of fifteen corps commanders and more than half the brigade commanders had been arrested, were murdered, had 'committed suicide' or simply disappeared.

As all but five members of the 80-strong Supreme Military Council had been imprisoned, together with the entire Vice-Commissariat of Defence, results were predictable. New commanders were acceptable politically, but lacked combat experience and did little but adhere strictly to Stalinist dogma. The Red Army could only suffer until survivors of the purges could be 'rehabilitated' from exile or the labour camps.

The 1917 revolution had severed the links with France, once a valuable collaborator, and no western assistance had been forthcoming until the late 1920s. Then Germany, hell-bent on developing a clandestine arms industry, began to court Soviet assistance, but the Germans were willing to co-operate only to suit their own needs. Many of their greatest advances remained hidden from the Red Army; production of others often proved more than Soviet industry could handle.

By the late 1930s, the U.S.S.R. was making vast numbers of tanks, aircraft and small arms. The Red Army ranked among the largest in the world; qualitatively, however, its deficiencies were clear. The Germans soon proved the pointlessness of thousands of slow, cumbersome and weakly armed aircraft; Panzers and anti-tank guns annihilated delicate medium tanks, under-armoured tankettes or impossibly cumbersome super-tanks alike; and Russian rifle divisions were simply hordes of rifle-men rather than the sophisticated mixture of rifles, automatic and support weapons that characterised Wehrmacht equivalents.

The swift advance of the Wehrmacht threatened the entire indus-trial basis of the Soviet economy. Though comparatively little of the arms industry fell to the invaders in the first few weeks of the campaign, towns such as Tula, Kalinin, Kharkov, Kursk, Orel and Stalingrad were soon all under threat. Tula held out, as did Stalingrad, but only after being reduced to smoking rubble. In desperation, the defenders evacuated whole factories and entrained them eastward piece by piece. This was undoubtedly assisted by the crude nature of much of Soviet industry, but it was also one of the greatest feats of organisation ever seen. By sheer determination and an acceptance of impossible hardship, the workers gradually rebuilt the factories hundreds of miles from their original sites and – slowly, laboriously – war production began again.

The winter of 1941–2, as severe as any Russian could have expected, greatly restricted the German advance. Germany had staked everything on a lightning strike, but even Blitzkrieg can fail in a Russian winter. Guns jammed; lubricants froze; the Luftwaffe could not take to the air when most needed. Even the Panzers' comparatively narrow tracks were at a disadvantage to the wide tracks of the Soviet tanks, which reduced ground loading appreciably and could support the vehicles on snow.

The German advance ground to a halt, continually at the mercy of partisan activity and Russian snipers. Generaloberst Franz Halder reported in his war diary that 'for once, our troops are compelled, by the stubborn Russian resistance, to fight according to their combat manuals. In Poland and in the west they could take liberties, but here they cannot get away with them . . .'[1]

The enthusiasm with which the Russians had embraced sniping con-trasted greatly with the German attitude, and was to cost the invaders dearly. Marksmanship training had always been an integral part of the activities of Komsomol, the Soviet youth movement, and the nature of the Soviet Union – and imperial Russia before it – had always encouraged hunting. By 1938, more than six million adults, men and women alike, had become 'Voroshilov Sharpshooters' and their ranks were swelled annually by graduates of the youth categories.

The Germans also discovered that the specially selected Mosin-Nagant sniping rifles were much more accurate than the Kar. 98k, and could virtually guarantee a successful 'head-shot' at 300 metres; German marksmen habitually struggled to emulate this performance at half the range. Attempts were made to impress captured Soviet rifles, but the unfamiliarity of operation restricted this to purely local initiatives. Attempts were also made to fit Soviet PE sights to the Kar. 98k; something of an irony, as the PE, stronger and better than the German Zf. 39, had originally been built in a factory equipped by Carl Zeiss of Jena.

Experience in the U.S.S.R. also persuaded the Germans to develop a sound-suppressor for the Kar. 98k to fire a special low-power cartridge design, the 'Nahpatrone s.S.'. Several prototypes were entered in the trials, including one from the Arado company (better known for its aircraft), but the winning design was credited to an army N.C.O. named Schalze. His 'Hub-23' suppressor considerably reduced the noise of firing, though the reduction of muzzle velocity to merely 220 m/sec also severely restricted the maximum effective range.

The period of comparative inactivity allowed the Soviet industries to recover the strength vital to meet the German challenge that would be renewed in the spring. The Red Army even counter-attacked in December 1941, when the index of industrial production had fallen to its all-time low. Caught unprepared in more than one zone, the Germans soon rallied; yet damage had been done for, despite predictably disastrous casualties, the Red Army had managed to halt the Wehrmacht for the winter. Flagging Soviet morale recovered sufficiently to stop the precipitate removal of industry eastwards.

As the Germans penetrated ever deeper into Soviet territory, their lines of communication were stretched to breaking point and the need to police the ever-growing territory that had been occupied grew alarmingly. A universal call-up in Germany at the end of 1941 netted nearly

300,000 men, but this had an unwanted effect: more than sixty per cent of the conscripts came from occupations that had previously been considered as 'reserved', including the munitions and armament industries, and the output of small arms suffered. The shortages were ultimately made good by the use of forced labour, but the seeds of disaster were there for those who cared to look.

Another major change occurred in February 1942, when Dr Fritz Todt, who had presented plans to centralise the German arms industry only a month previously, was killed in an air crash. He was replaced as armaments minister by Albert Speer, better known as Hitler's architect but keen to impose greater discipline on a notoriously fragmented system. Each of the armed services was still encouraging the development of weapons independently, and valuable resources were being frittered away. One result of this rationalisation was the abandonment of rifles such as the Czechoslovakian Gewehr 24 (t), the Polish Gewehr 29 (p) and the Gew. 33/40, to concentrate resources on the Kar. 98k. Helped by the recruitment of additional contractors, output virtually doubled in two years – from a total of 1.075 million Kar. 98k accepted by the H.WaA. in 1942 to 1.922 million in 1944.

By the end of 1941, the Germans were struggling to maintain control of occupied territories that covered a vast area. Sabotage and partisan activity distracted many rear-echelon units, making the task of supplying the front line increasingly difficult. Planting booby-trapped rifles on corpses or in captured arms dumps was just one of the harrying tactics used by the Red Army.

By February 1942, the situation had become so bad that the H.WaA. was forced to issue a warning about the Mosin-Nagant rifles, externally indistinguishable from thousands of others, that had had the barrel bored out ahead of an enlarged chamber. Firing a cartridge in these usually resulted in the barrel blowing apart at the breech, even though the Mosin-Nagant action was exceptionally strong. There had been so many casualties that instructions were given to prevent Soviet rifles being fired until they had been examined by qualified armourers.[2]

Other incidents involved sabotaged ammunition, dropped by Soviet pilots flying behind German lines, which gave the appearance of standard 7.9mm s.S. cartridges in standard packing. Internally, however, the propellant had been replaced with a small explosive charge and an initiator powerful enough to destroy a rifle and injure or even kill the firer.[3]

The summer of 1942 brought another German thrust – Operation 'Blau' – seeking to take land west of Stalingrad with a pincer movement and then seize the city itself, but the opening stages coincided with a poorly-planned Red Army counter-offensive optimistically intended to raise the investment of Leningrad, reconquer the Crimea and re-take Kharkov. The Germans, from the stronger position, dispersed the Russian threat. However, time had been lost and the winter of 1942 brought a Red Army offensive that smashed its way through the Romanian and Italian units, encircling the German Sixth Army in Stalingrad.

Continual probing along the German lines on the Eastern Front revealed a weakness through which Soviet forces cleared most of the Ukraine during 1943. In addition, Hitler's insistence on strongpoints known as 'hedgehogs' – against his generals' penchant for less restrictive linear defences – enabled the Russians to bypass these positions and then mop them up at leisure. The Germans had employed a similar system in the opening stages of Operation 'Barbarossa'.

North Africa and the Mediterranean

Elsewhere, the tide of battle had also begun to turn against Germany. British successes in North Africa – particularly immediately after El Alamein – began to tell on the Afrika Korps. The rupture of the Mareth line at the end of March 1943 was followed by near-rout of the Axis forces; and the German commander, Jürgen Sixt von Arnim, surrendered with approximately 290,000 men on 12 May. The stage had been cleared for Operation 'Husky', the invasion of Sicily on 10 June 1943 by the British 8th and U.S. 7th Armies. Events in Italy were precipitate: the Sicilian capital, Palermo, fell to US troops on 22 July; Mussolini was forced out of office on 25 July and the Italian fascist party was dissolved the following day. Italian armed forces surrendered on 8 September 1943, the day before the U.S. 5th Army under Mark Clark landed at Salerno and the British 1st Airborne Division landed at Taranto. The general northward advance through Italy then led to an armistice, signed on 29 September, and Italy declared war on her one-time ally, Germany, on 13 October.

In the north of the country, however, the Germans determined to resist. Overseen by Luftwaffe Generalfeldmarschall Kesselring, who proved a wily infantry commander, a counter-attack was mounted on the Allies in February 1944. A long, slow slog northwards ensued; the monastery at Cassino, which fell to Polish troops in May, became a symbol of German resistance. Not until August did the 8th Army reach Florence.

The Italian campaigns had practically no effect on Wehrmacht small arms, excepting that, in addition to unusually large numbers of Beretta Mo. 938A submachine-guns ('MP. 739 [i]'), the Germans obtained Beretta pistols, F.N.A.B. submachine-guns, and even some Mo. 938 rifles modified for the standard 7.9mm rifle cartridge.

Captured and non-standard weapons

1. YUGOSLAVIAN
The invasion of Yugoslavia provided the Germans with a large supply of Mauser short rifles, essentially similar to the Kar. 98k, and an efficient modern manufacturing plant in the town of Kragujevač. This was a legacy of co-operation with Fabrique Nationale d'Armes de Guerre, resulting from an order placed in July 1923 by the 'Kingdom of Serbs, Croats and Slovenes' – 'Yugoslavia' from 1929 – for 50,000 7.9mm-calibre Mauser rifles and 50 million rounds of ammunition. The order also required F.N. to install a factory capable of making 200 rifles and 200,000 cartridges daily, and though another 40,000 rifles and 60 million rounds were ordered from Belgium in February 1926, production in Kragujevač was in full swing by 1930.

Machine-guns.   Yugoslavia had been supplied with 1,500 vz. 26 light machine-guns, made by Československá Zbrojovka, to enable large-scale field trials to be undertaken in 1927. These had been followed by 15,500 Z.B. 30/J guns, all chambering the 7.92mm infantry-rifle cartridge. Many of these weapons survived to be confiscated by the Germans and assimilated into the Wehrmacht, the Waffen-SS and the police.

Rifles. The Germans acquired a variety of Mauser rifles, short rifles and carbines from Yugoslavia, including some ancient pre-1914 Serbian weapons and others that had been acquired as reparations at the end of the First World War. The most modern weapons were known as the M. 24, or, to the Germans, 'Gewehr 290 (j)' or 'Karabiner 491/1 (j)' depending on length. In January 1942, the O.K.H. published instructions to govern the test firing of these rifles with Yugoslavian M. 24 and M. 38 ball ammunition.[4]

Experience showed that Yugoslavian rifles jammed regularly with German ammunition, a fault that was traced to the fractionally smaller chambers. Orders were given in May 1942[5] to relieve the chambers, the work being undertaken by the Heeres-Zeugämter Waffenwerkstätte in Hannover, Ingolstadt, Konigsberg i. Pr., and Spandau.

Other alterations included the adaptation of the scabbards to fit German bayonet frogs, and the removal of the muzzle rings of the Seitengewehre 106 (j), 107 (j), 108 (j) and 109 (j) so that the standard Kar. 98k-type muzzle protector could be used.[6]

Handguns. These were mostly examples of the 9mm F.N.-Browning Mle 10/22, though a very few ex-Serbian Parabellums are said to have been among them. The most common Parabellum was the M. 1910, a 9mm 1908-type gun identical with the German P. 08 except for markings and a lanyard ring on the butt.

2) RUSSIAN

The success of the opening phases of Operation 'Barbarossa' netted the Germans colossal numbers of prisoners and huge quantities of war matériel, ranging from pistols and revolvers to field artillery and tanks. Not all of this unexpected windfall was useful, but some of the small arms were better than the German service weapons (especially under Russian conditions), and the 7.62cm field guns had soon been converted into excellent anti-tank weapons.

Machine-guns. The lightweight pan-fed D.P. ('le. MG. 120 [r]') was a true infantry weapon, designed for only a specific role but very easy to use. Persistent magazine jams and a badly placed mainspring contributed

ate 1. The formation of veterans associations, sports clubs and similar organisations allowed the ermans to keep militarism alive. This photograph, dating from 1926, shows the members of one such it. The rifles are pre-1918 7.9x57mm Gewehre 98, with Lange-pattern tangent back sights, instead of e 8.15x46R 'Wehrmannbüchsen' that were often used for short-range practice.

ate 2. Old Prussian colours are paraded on Volkstrauertag, national mourning day, 1932.

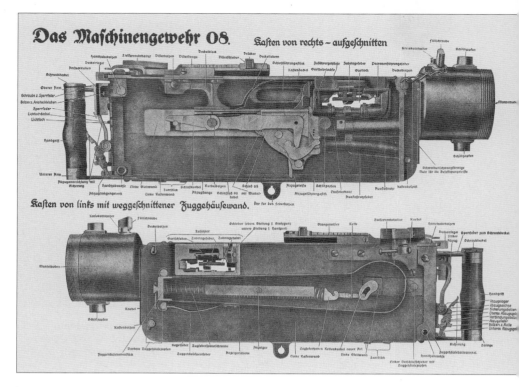

Plate 3. The parts of the Maxim-type MG. 08, from Fischer's *Waffen- und Schiesstechnische Leitfaden für die Ordnungspolizei* (1943 edition).

Plate 4. Taken from a picture-postcard published in the early 1930s, this picture shows two gunners armed with an MG. 13 ('Dreyse'). Machine-guns of this type are easily identified by their box-like receiver and long slender barrel casing.

The MG. 13 ('Dreyse'), the first new light machine-gun to be issued in the Reichswehr.

An MG. 15 aircraft machine-gun, with a pistol grip for observer's use.

The MG. 34, the 'first general purpose machine-gun' to be issued for general service in the German army.

This Danish Madsen machine-gun, originally a vehicle gun, was modified during the Second World War to serve the Germans in a ground role.

Plate 9. The crew of an MG. 34 pose for the camera, with the tripod extended and an anti-aircraft adaptor in place. The tricoloured shields on the helmets show that this picture dates from the mid 1930s.

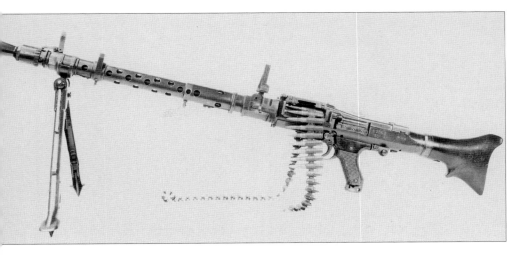

Plate 10. The MG. 34/41, an adaptation of the MG. 34, was made for extended trials. Shorter than its predecessor, it had been altered to fire much more rapidly. However, trials being undertaken contemporaneously with the MG. 42 gave better results. This is MG. 34/41 S., no. 501.

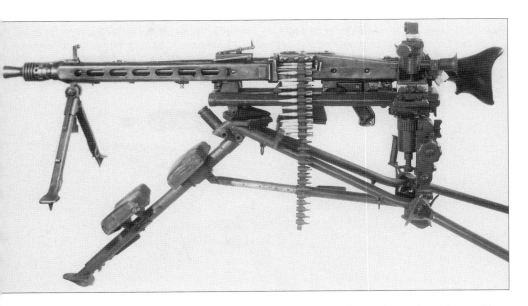

Plate 11. The MG. 42 was characterised by an exceptionally high rate of fire, and was almost impossible to control except when mounted on a tripod (though even this benefited from a few additional sandbags).

Plate 12. This experimental adaptation of a MG. 34 vehicle gun (note the lack of ventilating holes in the jacket) has been modified to accept a periscope sight. The idea was to protect the gunner, allowing him t fire without exposing the top of his head, but the high cyclic rate and the tendency of the recoil impulse t rotate the gun around the pivot point (the base of the grip) would make the unit very difficult to control.

Plate 13. The Czechoslovakian Z.B. vz. 37 heavy machine-gun was pressed into service in quantity as the 's. MG. 37 (t)'. This is example is mounted on the distinctive Z.B. 208 tripod.

Plates 14 – 17.

14. A Zf.-Kar. 98k, fitted with a 1.5xZf. 41 optical sight. These small sights were very disappointing in service, though many served until the end of the war. The gun is a pre-1940 example, with the old-style flat butt plate and a forged-steel nose cap.

15. A Czechoslovakian vz. 24 Mauser short rifle, used by the Wehrmacht in large numbers as the 'Gew. 24 (t)'. Note the design of the hand guard, which stretches forward to the nose cap, and the absence of a sling slot in the butt. The bolt handle is straight, and the band and nose cap are retained with separate springs.

16. A Kar. 98k 'Kriegsmodell'. Note the 'boot'-type butt plate, intended to protect the edges of the butt from damage, and the simple nose cap. The cleaning rod is absent.

17. The Gew. 41 (M) competed unsuccessfully against the Gew. 41 (W), undergoing extensive field trials in 1941-2. The separate cocking handle is shown ready to be drawn back; it was turned down horizontally at the end of the forward stroke.

Plate 18. Members of the Gebirgsjäger, or mountain troops, scale a snowy gully. These men are carrying the Kar. 98k, though the shorter Gew. 33/40, with a protective plate on the left side of the butt, was preferred for everything except its strong recoil.

Plates 19 – 22.

19. Soviet Tokarev rifles, or S.V.T., popular souvenirs of the Russian campaign, were often turned against their former owners. This is a 1940-type semi-automatic gun, with a sheet-steel hand guard ahead of the barrel band.

20. The MP. 43 was the first successful assault rifle, chambered for a short-case 'intermediate' 7.9mm cartridge. However, reliance on novel production techniques greatly restricted output, and the guns were never able to change the outcome of the war.

21. The Spanish Astra Model 'F', based on the Mauser C/96 pistol, was purchased in small quantities during the war. It was capable of firing automatically, but, despite a rate reducer built into the trigger system, emptied its magazine in a trice. This is an Astra 903 essentially simular to the 'F', but lacking the retarder mechanism.

22. The FG. 42, made only in small numbers, was one of the most influential (but numerically least successful) of German attempts to create an automatic rifle/light machine-gun chambering the 7.9mm rifle cartridge. This is an example of the so-called 'FG. 42 II.', made largely of carbon steel.

Plate 23. Testing the aim laid by trainee marksmen using the Kar. 98k, before progressing to the firing range. Note the wooden dolly being used by the instructor to ease the strain of crouching.

Plate 24. German soldiers pose for the camera. Note that they are armed with ex-Czechoslovakian Gew. 24 (1 the hand guards run forward to the nose cap, and sling swivels lie on the left side of the pistol grip.

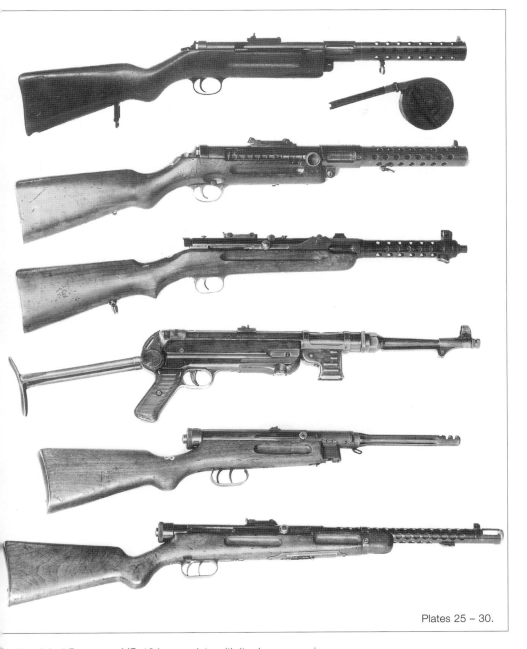

Plates 25 – 30.

25. An original Bergmann MP. 18,I., complete with its drum magazine.

26. An MP. 28, probably made for export. The cocking lever on the guns used by the German police forces was usually a spurred design.

27. The beautifully-made Steyr MP. 34 (ö). This is the standard Austrian military-issue pattern, chambered for the 9mm Mauser Export cartridge.

28. A standard MP. 40, without its detachable box magazine.

29. The Beretta Mo. 38/42, a simplified version of the Mo. 38 made during the Second World War.

30. The Beretta Mo. 38 was heavy for a gun of this class, but was accurate and unusually comfortable to fire.

Plates 31 – 35.

31. The P. 08 (Parabellum, 'Luger') was supplied to the Wehrmacht until 1942. This is a Luftwaffe-issue gun dating from c. 1938, with a distinctive inspector's mark on the front of the receiver.

32. The P. 38 (Walther) replaced the P. 08, and was made in quantity until the end of the war. This Spreewerke-made gun ('cyq') exhibits the rough machining that characterised guns made in 1945.

33. The FN-Browning G.P. Mle. 35, or 'Pistole 640 (b)' was made in German-occupied Belgium until the summer of 1944. This gun has a tangent-leaf back sight, but fixed-sight guns were easier to make and more common after 1942.

34. This Mauser HSc has a special slide, made of a sturdy pressing and representing one of the simplifications that were to lead to the Volkspistolen.

35. The Pistole 37 (ü) was a variant of the standard Hungarian service pistol, adapted for German service. Tens of thousands served the Wehrmacht.

ate 36. An employee of Deutsche Waffen- & Munitionsfabriken checks the dimensions of a cartridge-case n. The supply of ammunition was just as important as the supply of weapons.

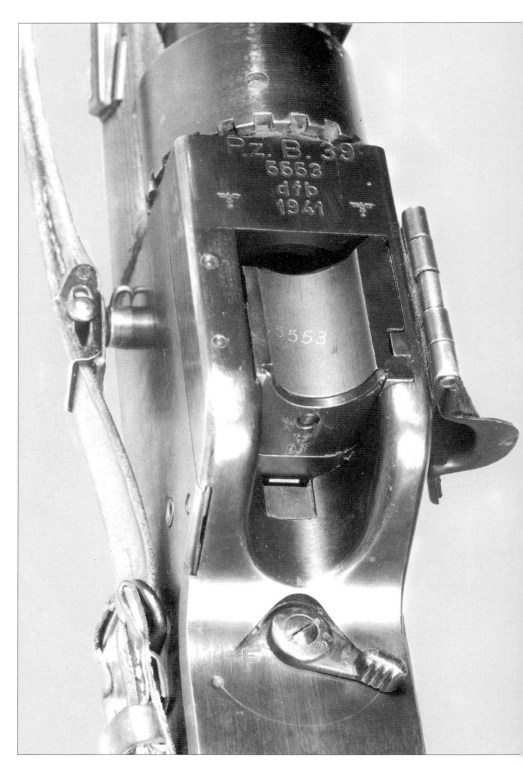

Plate 37. The breech of a Pz.B. 39, a single-shot anti-tank rifle firing a 7.9mm bullet from a greatly enlarged cartridge-case in search of hyper velocity. This gun was made by Gustloff-Werke ('dfb') in 1941. Most Pz.B. 39, ineffective against Soviet tanks, were subsequently converted to grenade launchers.

Plates 38 – 42.

38. The Heeresmodell, a Walther design, was the standard army-issue signal pistol at the start of the war. This gun was made by Berlin-Lübecker Maschinenfabrik ('237') in 1940.

39. The Walther SLE, a single-barrelled variant of the navy SLD, was a large, cumbersome but exceptionally well-made signal pistol. It lacked the barrel-selector customarily found on top of the SLD breech.

40. The Sturmpistole was a variant of the Heeresmodell adapted to fire hollow-charge grenades. It was heartily disliked, owing to its horrendous recoil.

41. A double-barrelled navy signal pistol made by the Artillerie-Werkstätten, Wilhelmshaven, in the 1920s. The barrel drops downward to expose the breech for loading.

42. This is an example of the Volkspistole, crudely made and poorly finished. Now usually attributed to Mauser-Werke (though once to Gustloff), it embodies a gas-delay system to slow the opening of the breech.

Plate 43. Even the hard-pressed Germans sometimes found time to smile. This cheerful Luftwaffe soldier, armed with an MG. 42, was pictured on 20 March 1945 – just a few weeks from the end of the war.

to operating problems, as did the broad metal-to-metal contact surfaces in the dusty Russian summer, but the D.P. was otherwise acceptably reliable.

Like the Germans, the Russians had no modern heavy support machine-guns when hostilities began and relied on the old Pulemet Maxima, or obr.1910g (P.M., 's. MG. 216 [r]'). Comparable with the German MG. 08, the water-cooled P.M. was solid, efficient and capable of sustaining fire for long periods, but was also heavy, awkward and obsolescent. The mobility of the wheeled Sokolov mount, however, conferred several advantages over the static German Schlitten 08 and MG-Lafette.

By 1941, neither of the modern Russian machine-guns, the 7.62mm D.S. ('s. MG. 218 [r]') and the 12.7mm D.Sh.K. had been developed satisfactorily. Indeed, the D.S. was subsequently abandoned entirely and manufacturing problems with the otherwise promising D.Sh.K. persisted into the post-war era. The few 7.62mm D.S. guns seized during Operation 'Barbarossa', playing no part in the H.WaA.'s schemes, were given to the police – though at least some of the sturdy D.Sh.K. were reissued to the German troops fighting on the Russian Front.

Oddly, the Germans never bothered with infantry machine-guns comparable to the .50 Browning or the D.Sh.K., preferring a perfected general-purpose machine-gun (the MG. 42) to supplement the MG. 34.

The Russian equivalent of the MG. 42 was the 7.62mm S.G. 43 or Goryunov machine-gun, the first prototypes appearing just as mass-production of the MG. 42 commenced. The S.G. 43 was a sturdy and reliable belt-fed medium machine-gun, intended to replace the Maxim, and could be mounted either on a tripod or a Sokolov-inspired wheeled carriage. Comparatively few Goryunov machine-guns were used by the Wehrmacht; by the time they reached service, the Germans were no longer ascendant, and far smaller amounts of war matériel were being captured than in the heady opening campaigns of Barbarossa.

Automatic rifles.   The exceptionally rapid advance of the German armies into the U.S.S.R., and the capture of huge numbers of Soviet troops, allowed the collection of substantial quantities of semi-automatic rifles. The Soviet designers had made much greater progress than the

Germans in this particular field, though manufacturing quality rarely matched the efficiency of the basic ideas; most of the pre-1941 German developments, conversely, had been very poor.

The first Soviet rifle to be manufactured in quantity had been the Simonov-designed A.V.S., a gas-operated selective-fire design known to the Germans as the 'Selbstladegewehr 257 (r)'. Officially adopted in 1937, after trials that had lasted for some years, the Simonov had only been made in small numbers and, as many had been lost during the Russo-Finnish 'Winter War', was comparatively rarely encountered by the Germans. However, survivors were pressed into service in the absence of anything better, and found their way into the German inventory.

Service experience had shown that the A.V.S. was too lightly built to withstand the strain of firing automatically, and that the design placed demands on manufacturing industry that could not be met. It had been replaced by the S.V.T. 38, a gas-operated Tokarev, with a tilting breech-block instead of the dropping hollow block of the A.V.S. The Tokarev S.V.T. 38 (or 'Selbstladegewehr 258 [r]') also proved to be too weak to withstand active service, and was almost immediately replaced by the sturdier S.V.T. 40 ('Selbstladegewehr 259 [r]'). More than a million were made in 1940–3, allowing substantial numbers to be taken into German service.

Though the Tokarevs were outwardly similar, the earlier gun had a wooden fore-end and a full-length cleaning rod set into the right side of the stock. The later version had a pressed-metal fore-end and a half-length cleaning rod beneath the barrel.

The Soviet auto-loading rifles fired the powerful-but-clumsy rimmed 7.62×54mm cartridge, which was far from ideal in automatic weapons and contributed greatly to jamming. However, the basic designs were excellent; despite the low standards of construction – and occasional problems with the material – the Tokarev was well liked by the Germans, as its detachable box magazine was preferable to the internal box of the Gew. 41 and the gas system was easier to maintain than a cumbersome muzzle chamber.

Snipers were also issued with autoloading rifles. A few A.V.S. have been reported with P.E. optical sights in conventional two-piece ring mounts, but most guns prove to be the purpose-built S.N.T. 40. This was fitted with the short-barrel P.U. sight in a special one-piece mount, attached to the rear of the receiver, which swept forward above the action. Experience showed that the S.N.T. was not ideal for a sniping role, partly owing to the mechanical noise of the autoloading action but also to the lack of rigidity in the sight-mounting system. There is also a suggestion that the tipping-block breech lock of the Tokarev failed to give the accuracy of the A.V.S., which had a bolt that ran back axially, and it was certainly inferior to the bolt-action Mosin-Nagant. Consequently, the S.N.T. had soon been replaced by the obr. 91/30, usually with the P.U. sight in a one-piece side mount.

The jam-prone Tokarev was too complicated for the average Soviet soldier's grasp of preventative maintenance, but performed much better in the hands of the better-trained Wehrmacht personnel. Test-firing instructions were issued in April 1942, followed by Manual D 199 in November.[7]

Rifles.   Bolt-action Mosin-Nagants were captured in huge quantities during the early phases of Operation 'Barbarossa'. Most were obr. 1891/30g, the Soviet derivative of the old Tsarist obr. 1891g, but obr. 1938g carbines were also collected. Smaller numbers of obr. 1871g Berdans were seized from partisans, together with old Mosin-Nagants – including a few obr. 1910g carbines. Though long, clumsy and poorly made, the Russian rifles were very sturdy and surprisingly tolerant of sloppy manufacturing tolerances. Though they chambered an awkward rimmed 7.62mm cartridge, a unique interruptor in the magazine-well assured an efficient feed.

There was little to choose between the Kar. 98k and the obr. 1891/30g Mosin-Nagant (known to the Germans as the 'Gewehr 254 [r]'). The Soviet rifle was a little longer and cruder, but had much the same performance. The Kar. 98k was better made prior to 1942, but production quality declined after the substitution of the Kriegsmodell and the guns made in 1945 were very poorly finished. After the initial dislocation of production, the quality of the Mosin-Nagant metallurgy, if not its finish, began to increase as the war ran its course.

Such large numbers of Mosin-Nagants were seized that attempts were undoubtedly made to alter them to chamber the standard rimless

German 7.9mm cartridge instead of the original rimmed 7.62mm Russian pattern. This echoed the First World War, when the Germans had converted some for 7.9mm ammunition, apparently re-boring the barrels to suit, and the Austro-Hungarians had altered many thousands for the 8×50mm rimmed round simply by altering the chamber and adding a 'forcing cone' between the chamber and the rifling to squeeze the larger Austrian bullet down to a size that suited the Russian bore. This was a testimony to the strength of the Mosin-Nagant, as chamber pressures rose considerably.

However, most of the conversions of Soviet weapons undertaken under German control concerned submachine-guns, altered for the 9mm Pist. Patr. 08, and machine-guns altered to 7.9×57mm (see Chapter Seven). The test-fire instructions issued by the O.K.H. in December 1942 were devoted exclusively to the standard guns: Gewehre 252 (r), 253 (r) and 254 (r), which were the old full-length obr. 1891, the obr. 1891 dragoon rifle (mostly dating from Tsarist era) and the Soviet obr. 1891/30 respectively.[8]

Anti-tank rifles.   The field-gun type anti-tank weapons of the protagonists were comparable, though neither army had a particularly efficient anti-tank rifle in June 1941. The Germans had issued a few 7.9mm PzB. 38 and PzB. 39, plus some awesome 20mm Steyr-Solothurn 'Kw. K. 35' cannon on shoulder mounts, but ever-increasing thickness of tank armour soon made such rifles valueless.

The Red Army, after making a few modified copies of the Mauser T-Gewehr and then standardising the semi-automatic P.T.R. in the autumn of 1939, discovered that neither was particularly useful. In desperation, they developed the 14.5mm-calibre P.T.R.D. (Degtyarev) and P.T.R.S. (Simonov) concurrently. Though the guns were useless against the frontal armour of the German medium tanks, Soviet gunners were taught to shoot at the thinly armoured flanks, undersides or rear of the Panzers. Fuel tanks, engine air intakes, gun-sights and visors were also favourite targets. As a bonus, the P.T.R.D. and P.T.R.S. were very useful against armoured cars, half-tracks and soft-skinned vehicles; unlike their German equivalents, they served until the end of the war.

Submachine-guns.   Russia proved to be the first major source of guns of this type. Though small numbers of the 7.62mm Degtyarev-designed P.P.D. 34/38 and P.P.D. 40 blowbacks were taken (known to the Wehrmacht as 'MP. 715 [r]' and 'MP. 716 [r]' respectively), the most important was the blowback P.P.Sh., or 'MP. 717 (r)'. Designed by Georgiy Shpagin and adopted prior to the German invasion in December 1940, engineering problems delayed production of the P.P.Sh. until the autumn of 1941. Total deliveries of submachine-guns in the year amounted to less than 100,000 (including 6,000 P.P.D. 40), but production accelerated rapidly; by 1945, annual production had reached 2.5 million and had far outstripped the ability of the German gunmaking industry to compete.

Many German units quickly seized on the P.P.Sh., particularly for re-issue to officers and senior NCOs who carried nothing more effective than a Parabellum or Walther pistol. The Soviets' guns were greatly appreciated for their 71-round drum magazines and a reliability that usually belied their crude appearance. The magazine was extremely heavy, but gave Russian soldiers an appreciable advantage over Germans armed with the MP. 38 or MP. 40.

So many P.P.Sh. were captured that the Germans converted many to fire 9mm Pist. Patr. 08, designating them 'MP. 717 (r) umg.' or 'MP. 41 (r) umg.' The feedways of these guns were altered for the standard MP. 38/MP. 40 box magazines.

Thompson M. 1928, Reising Models 50 and 55 and U.D. 42 submachine-guns, survivors of more than 112,000 supplied during the Second World War under Lend-Lease, were also seized from the Soviet forces.

The 1928-model Thompson ('MP. 760 [r]'), a complicated and expensive design incorporating the so-called 'Blish Principle' delay system, usually had a conventional wooden fore-end – with a grasping groove – and 50-round drum magazine. Designed by Eugene Reising, who had sought patent protection in the U.S.A. in June 1940, about 100,000 examples of the Models 50 and 55 were made by Harrington & Richardson in 1941-5. The selective-fire blowback system proved to be complex and unreliable under service conditions; the U.S. military authorities were unimpressed, and took the chance to get rid of the guns by sending them to the U.S.S.R. The Reisings had cocking slides under the fore-end, and sliding safety/selector levers on the right side of the receiver. They fired from a closed breech, measured 35.6in overall, had 11in barrels and weighed 8.15lb loaded. The detachable box magazines held twenty rounds and the cyclic rate was about 550 rds/min. The Model 50 had a conventional stock, whereas the Model 55 'Paratrooper' (which also lacked a compensator) had a flimsy folding wire butt and a pistol grip.

The U.D. 42, designed by Carl Swebilius of High Standard in 1940, was made by Marlin Firearms Company for the government-owned Defence Supply Corporation. Most of the 15,000 made in 1942–4 went to the O.S.S. or, eventually, to the Soviet Union. The U.D. was a selective-fire blowback, firing from an open bolt, and had a non-reciprocating cocking slide. A combined safety/selector lay on the right side of the trigger housing, a hold-open was fitted, and the back sight was an unusual elevating-bar pattern. The U.D., which measured 31.8in overall, had an 11in barrel and weighed about 10lb loaded. The box magazine held twenty rounds and the cyclic rate was approximately 700 rds/min. Unlike the Reising, the U.D. was sturdy, accurate, very efficient and greatly appreciated by its users. However, as it was comparatively difficult to make, it was passed over in U.S. service in favour of the abortive M2 and then the M3 'Grease Gun'.

Handguns. There is very little evidence to show that the Germans ever made use of the large numbers of handguns that came into their possession after Operation 'Barbarossa'. The 7.62mm Tokarev or 'Tula-Tokarev' ('T.T.') pistol had been approved in 1930, altered in 1933 after service experience had shown the need for modifications, but had been challenged in the 1930s by the venerable obr. 1895 Nagant revolver.

The Tokarev embodied a minor modification of the Colt-Browning tipping barrel lock and had a considerable external affinity with the 1903-pattern F.N.-Brownings that had been used in Russia prior to the 1917 Revolution. However, the Tokarev had its lock work packaged in a detachable sub-assembly and (at least in the perfected form) locking ribs that encircled the barrel. These were much easier to machine than lugs that occupied only a small part of the circumference. The Soviet designers also tried to improve the feed by machining the feed lips inside the magazine-well instead of relying on the shaping of the magazine-top to position the cartridges accurately. This was partly a condemnation of the poor quality of Soviet metalworking skills, but answered a very real problem that affected many of the service pistols that were being used in other countries.

The Tokarev pistols had two major problems: firstly, there was no manual safety other than a half-cock notch on the hammer (a source of danger that few other armies would have tolerated); and the crewmen of armoured vehicles disliked the recoiling barrel, which made it difficult to use firing ports. An expedient was provided simply by recommencing production of the Nagant revolver, and experiments with fixed-barrel pistols began. However, the incomplete trials were abandoned when the Germans invaded the Soviet Union and the T.T. 33 was ordered back into mass production.

The Tokarev had the merit, from the German viewpoint, of firing ammunition that was dimensionally identical with the 7.63mm Mauser type. Though the German cartridges were usually loaded to give less power, it seems that most Soviet pistols would still fire them at the expense of more jams than normal.

The 7.62mm obr. 1895 Nagant revolver was an interesting design that cammed the cylinder forward at the instant of firing to allow the extended cartridge case (which entirely enveloped the bullet) to expand momentarily to seal the joint between the chamber and the bore. The goal was to minimise the leak of gas from the cylinder/barrel joint, though experiments subsequently showed that the gains were minimal. Despite the additional complication of the cylinder-camming system, the Nagant was sturdy and reliable. Its worst features were undoubtedly its small calibre and the lightweight bullet, which greatly restricted its 'man-stopping' performance (even though it allowed the Russians to make barrels for handguns and rifles alike on the same machinery).

The earliest revolvers had been supplied from Belgium, though most of those delivered after 1901 came from Tula. Production continued intermittently through the early post-Revolutionary years until the T.T. pistol had been perfected. Work on the revolvers then ceased, only to re-start for the reasons given previously and continue virtually until the end of the war.

The Russians had been enthusiastic purchasers of the Mauser C/96 pistol prior to the Revolution – so popular, indeed, that the short-barrelled version had become known as the 'Bolo' (a derivative of 'Bolshevik'). It is probable that guns were retrieved after 1942, alongside pre-1914 F.N.-Brownings and 6.35mm T.K. ('Tula-Korovin') blowbacks that had been issued in large numbers to party officials and army officers. Guns of this type had also been sold commercially as 'T.O.Z.'.

3) OTHERS

The *Gewehr 98/40* was a derivative of the Hungarian 35.M (Mannlicher) rifle, made in large quantities for the Wehrmacht during the Second World War. However, it is considered to be essentially a German design and is discussed below (see 'Regulation weapons, rifles').

The Germans also made limited use of submachine-guns purchased in Hungary. Credited to Királý, the Hungarian 39.M (fixed stock) and 39.AM (folding stock) guns were sturdily made, accepted bayonets, and had a unique two-piece bolt retarding system. Made by the Danuvia factory in Budapest, the Királý guns had rotary selectors and folding vertical magazines. Only about eight thousand were made before the advent of the simplified 43.M.

The 39.M measured 1,048mm overall, had a 500mm barrel and weighed 4.6kg with a loaded 40-round box magazine. Unlike most of the standard German guns, but in common with the Austrian army MP. 34, they chambered the 9mm Mauser cartridge rather than the ubiquitous 9mm Parabellum. Owing to their weight, long barrel and exemplary standards of manufacture, they were extremely accurate and pleasant to fire. However, only small numbers found their way into German hands after Hungarian units on the Russian Front collapsed, and most guns were ultimately lost in Russia.

Handguns were also purchased from the same source. The first contract for fifty thousand *Pistolen 37 (ü)*, apparently on behalf of the Luftwaffe, was placed in 1941 and completed in February 1942. An additional order for 60,000 guns followed in 1943, but had only been partially fulfilled when the Germans began to evacuate the Danuvia factory machinery in November 1944. A variant of the Hungarian 37.M service pistol with an additional manual safety catch, the P. 37 (ü) was a simple 7.65mm-calibre blowback, acceptably machined from good-quality material but with little else to commend it.

The slides of first-contract guns were marked 'Pistole M.37'; second-contract examples displayed 'P. Mod. 37'. All guns bore the letter-code 'jhv' on the left side of the slide.

Regulation weapons

As the tide of war turned against Germany, losses of equipment reached such colossal proportions that the arms industry simply could not cope with demands made on it. By mid-1942, the authorities were already seeking not only simplified designs but also specialists in advanced production techniques with no previous relevance to gunmaking; for the first time, traditional construction methods were replaced by metal-stamping, welding and other mass-production techniques in a search for less complexity, less wastage of raw material, and greatly increased output.

The first lessons were applied to comparatively conventional weapons, leading from designs such as the Kar. 98k 'Kriegsmodell' and MG. 42 to the MP. 43. But these were all conventional weapons, designed for mass production but nevertheless durable, sophisticated and still relatively expensive. The second stage was to produce the Volkswaffen or 'People's Guns', in which even design was subordinated to ease of production. The change of emphasis can be seen in the handguns, as what had begun with the P. 38 was clearly to finish with hideous (but potentially no less lethal) sheet-steel blowbacks.

The Germans also discovered that much of their weaponry had been developed under the comparatively mild conditions of the German climate, and that its performance was often far worse in the far north of Russia or the deserts of North Africa. Extreme cold was a particular hardship. Not only were the German troops totally unprepared for the harshness of winter on the Eastern Front, lacking properly insulated boots, greatcoats that could keep out the worst of the biting cold, and suitable tents, but the standard small arms were particularly prone to failure. One of the worst examples was the MG. 34, which was made to such fine tolerances that it seized just as easily in cold as when sand got into the mechanism, but even the Kar. 98k was regularly immobilised when the slender tip of the firing pins crystallised and broke.

One of the first 'cold weather' directives instructed the troops to remove all traces of oil and grease from their weapons, but this was easier said than done when temperatures were dropping as low as fifty degrees below zero. Tanks and vehicle ground to a halt, and optical equipment failed. Optical sights marked 'Kf.', for *Kältefest* or 'coldproof' were only protected to −20° Centigrade, little use in Russia (although the later sights with blue-coloured seals were claimed to be able to withstand temperatures as low as −40° C).

Not until the middle of 1942 were low-temperature lubricants available in quantity. These included lubricating oil usable down to −20° C; gun-cleaning oil (−30° C); special frost-resistant oils and cleaners (−40° C); and 'Vakuum Servol 222', issued only in Norway and on the Eastern Front, with an extreme rating of −50° C. These limiting temperatures could be reduced still further by mixing the oils and lubricants with kerosene.

The problems of extreme cold were mirrored in North Africa, where excessive heat caused propellant to sweat and seals to fail. Many stores were marked 'Trop.' or 'Tp.' to show that they could be used in hot climates. However, many were unsatisfactory in temperatures above 25° C . . . when the ambient temperature was likely to exceed 40° C!

Hitler, who was apt to interfere with procurement by changing manufacturing priorities on a whim, created another problem. A week before the invasion of the Soviet Union, for example, he had decreed that the most pressing need was 'to re-equip the field army . . . with [automatic] carbines, machine-guns, light infantry guns, light and heavy field howitzers, and various kinds of [special] ammunition'. In August 1942 he repeated this view: '. . . In the future, small arms must consist of nothing but machine-guns and automatic rifles; and every weapon must have a telescope sight'. Instead of concentrating on accelerating production of existing weapons, therefore, designers were encouraged to find new solutions to problems that did not necessarily exist.

Machine-guns.   After experience in Poland and France, the H.WaA. requested an increase in the fire-rate as detailed studies had shown – at least in the MG. 34 – that dispersion in short bursts could be reduced. The experimental MG. 34S subsequently achieved cyclic rates as high as 1,650 rds/min, but could not sustain such a hammering for more than a few hundred rounds even though the lock had been modified, an improved recoil booster had been fitted, and the recoil buffer had been greatly strengthened.

The MG. 34S measured 1,120mm overall and had a 560mm barrel. Its failure led to the MG. 34/41, 1,707 guns being despatched to the Eastern Front shortly after the invasion of the Soviet Union. To simplify manufacture and increase the cyclic rate to about 1,250 rds/min, virtu-ally every part of the original gun had been redesigned: the bolt had lugs instead of an interrupted-thread; the feed arrangements were refined; and the trigger was reduced to fully-automatic operation only. However, as the prototype MG. 42 was performing well, the otherwise promising 34/41 was abandoned in January 1943 and the standard MG. 34 remained in production until the end of the war.

Even as the MG. 34 was beginning its field trials, the H.WaA. had realised that the Einheitsmaschinengewehr was too complex and much too expensive to mass-produce. Finally, after a time-and-motion study completed in 1937 under the enthusiastic championship of Dr.-Ing. Peter, even the O.K.H. was forced to agree. The race to find a simpler gun had commenced even before the MG. 34 had been formally adopted.

The biggest problem was simply that, though metal-stamping would be essential to lift production to the levels that were being demanded, the appropriate technology was still in its infancy. However, though work needed to be done before a simplified design would encounter success, a draft specification was sent to three leading manu-facturers in February 1937. Only one company had experience of weapons design, the others being production specialists.

Rheinmetall-Borsig A.G. and Stübgen A.G. of Erfurt submitted gas-operated designs, while Grossfuss Metall- & Lackierwarenfabrik of Döbeln proposed the recoil-operated Grüner system. Grossfuss then built a prototype that convinced the Heereswaffenamt of the merits in its roller-locking system.

Representatives of the competing designs had all been completed by April 1938, when trials revealed the unacceptability of the Grossfuss barrel-change. However, as the Rheinmetall and Stübgen designs had been rejected, an improved Grossfuss gun was requested. This incorporated a one-piece receiver and a simplified barrel-changing system, and performed well enough to inspire work on a series of semi-experimental guns that culminated in the MG. 39. Fifty of these were tested at the Döberitz infantry school, and the MG. 39/41, the final pre-production pattern, successfully passed its final field trials in the autumn of 1941.

Though Grüner had retained the basic MG. 34 concept, the standard metal-link ammunition belt and the multiplicity of mounts, the MG. 42 was far easier to make than its predecessor. In 1944, the cost of an MG. 42 was estimated as 250 Reichsmarks compared with 312 for an MG. 34. Many dimensional tolerances were much wider than had previously been deemed acceptable by the procuring agencies, and the wholesale use of stampings, pressing and welding was viewed with horror by the gunmaking fraternity.

By comparison with the pre-war MG. 34, which displayed excellent surface finish and an unimpeachable fit of parts, the MG. 42 was very crudely made. However, it was extremely sturdy, despite a much higher rate of fire, and had an exceptionally simple barrel-change system.

The MG. 42 was approved for mass-production in the summer of 1942, but only 17,250 had been made by the end of the year and the definitive manual – D 166/1 – was not published until September 1943. By the end of the Second World War, however, more than 400,000 had been made by Grossfuss in Döbeln, Gustloff-Werke in Suhl, Maget in Berlin, Mauser-Werke in Berlin-Borsigwalde, and Steyr-Daimler-Puch A.G. in Steyr/Oberdonau. Most of these had previously been making the MG. 34; indeed, as more than one commentator has noted, considerable generic similarity is evident between the two machine-gun designs if Grüner is considered to have simply translated the older breech-lock into a single plane.

Though there are few important variants of the MG. 42, many changes were made during the war to simplify production. The butt, which had originally been of wood, became a synthetic injection moulding; the bipod was greatly simplified; the original straight charging handle was replaced with a toggle-grip lever to ease the cocking effort;

and the dimensions of the barrel/barrel-bush assembly were so substantially changed that interchangeability could not be guaranteed.

Usually mounted on its simple bipod, the Zweibein 42, the MG. 42 could be transferred to sophisticated, if complicated buffered quadrupod mounts – the MG.-Lafette 42 and 43 – utilising the standard MG. Z. 34 or MG. Z. 40 optical sights. Mount-types multiplied as the war progressed; not only could the MG. 42 be adapted to fit the standard MG. 34 tripods (Dreifuss 34 and 40) but there were also several differing pedestal, vehicle and anti-aircraft mounts in service by 1945.

The unusually high fire-rate, which soon gained the gun the sobriquet *Hitlersäge* ('Hitler's Saw'), proved to be a weakness in service even though it rarely failed to impress the men who faced it. Allied observers described the characteristic noise as 'like ripping linoleum', but the guns consumed huge quantities of ammunition and even the buffered mounts began to vibrate during long periods of firing. It was not uncommon to see the German gunners weighting the mounts with sandbags in an attempt to prevent excessive dispersion of fire.

The rapid operating cycle also placed emphasis on the availability of good-quality ammunition. That this had not always been possible is evident in O.K.H. directives banning the use, first of the Czechoslovakian 7.9mm rounds in the MG. 34 and MG. 42 (1943), owing to persistent chamber jams, and then of any non-German ammunition (1944).[9]

When the Western Allies captured the first MG. 42, ordnance experts were amazed. The U.S. Army, indeed, attempted to have two 'T24' MG. 42-type guns made by Harrington & Richardson for detailed evaluation. Ironically, these guns would fire only a single shot and then jam – quite unlike the reliable feed of their German prototypes. Only when it was realised that no allowance had been made for the longer case of the standard American .30 rifle cartridge was the problem revealed: the T24 simply did not recoil far enough to feed the second round into the action!

Other than this exception to the general efficiency of the MG. 42, which still serves the Federal German army (as the MG. 42/59 and MG3) and has been made in quantity in Turkey, Yugoslavia and elsewhere, few basic problems were encountered. Original pre-1945 guns will still be encountered in South America, in the hands of African guerrillas, and sometimes also in the Far East.

The original guns could occasionally fire before the rollers had properly locked – probably as a result of excessive wear or poor wartime construction – but an auxiliary bolt-catch was added to delay movement of the firing-pin support block and ensure proper roller engagement. However, some of the manufacturers were still making first-pattern guns in May 1945.

Automatic rifles.   Though substantial research had been undertaken during the Weimar Republic, only the Selbstladegewehre Rh. 28 and Rh. 29 are readily identifable. Designed by Karl Heinemann for Rheinmetall, these guns had distinctive lateral toggle-locks on the right rear of the receiver, box magazines that protruded from the left side of the receiver, and Bang-type muzzle cups to trap and divert propelling gases onto the actuating rod. Mauser produced the experimental Selbstladegewehr M. 35 in the mid 1930s and Walther may have experimented with the forerunner of the MKb. 42 (W)[10], but neither design had impressed the Heereswaffenamt prior to 1939.

Analysis of the Polish campaign then suggested several improvements in German small arms. Demands for optically sighted rifles that could be issued to the best marksmen in the infantry squads resulted in the Kar. 98k–Zf. 41, but something was needed to combat the Browning Automatic Rifles issued in the Polish army.

Late in 1940, therefore, well before Operation 'Barbarossa' commenced, the H.WaA. issued outline specifications for a new semi-automatic rifle to Mauser, Walther and, presumably, other interested parties such as Krieghoff. Mauser and Walther soon responded, and sufficient quantities of both rifles were ordered so that field trials could be undertaken. The muzzle-cup gas system and fixed ten-round box magazines that could be loaded from chargers or with loose rounds, features that were shared by both guns, were presumably specified by the H.WaA.

The *Gewehr 41 (M)*, made in Mauser-Werke's factory in Oberndorf (code 'byf'), had a distinctive receiver with a non-reciprocating bolt-type cocking handle on the right, whereas its Walther competitor, the *Gewehr*

41 (W), made in Zella-Mehlis ('ac'), was cocked by retracting the breech cover.

Internally, the actions were similar in concept but markedly different in detail. Both guns trapped propelling gases in the muzzle chamber, where it expanded to push back on an operating rod. The actuating rods of the Mauser and Walther rifles lay beneath and above the barrel respectively. Mauser relied on a two piece 'straight-pull' bolt with a rotary bolt head, not unlike some of the pre-1918 Austrian Mannlicher rifles, whereas Walther fitted a modified Friberg-Kjellman flap-lock. The Gew. 41 (M) and 41 (W) were fully stocked, had tangent-leaf back sights and accepted the standard SG. 84/98.

The development paths of these two rifles remain uncertain. However, according to a report made on 27 January 1942 by the staff of Wa. Stab. to the Chief of Staff of the Heereswaffenamt, 'development contracts' had been placed with Mauser and Walther eighteen months previously (i.e. in the summer of 1940). The report also noted that the Walther rifles had all been delivered, but only 1,673 Mausers had been completed and production had been 'halted temporarily owing to problems with materials'. It was anticipated that the Mausers 'would all be available by May 1942'.

The papers reveal that the Mauser had suffered teething troubles that had supposedly been overcome, and that the 'M' pattern was regarded as equal to the 'W'. Both manufacturers had been given additional orders for five thousand 'series production guns', but the inadequacy of the Zella-Mehlis factory remained a concern. It was suggested, therefore, that Walther should concentrate on the 'MP. 42', as Mauser had been given a preliminary order for 50,000 Gew. 41 (M) and was claiming to be able to deliver sixty thousand guns by 1 April 1943.

A problem is highlighted by the H.WaA. procurement figures summarised by Fritz Hahn in *Waffen- und Geheime Waffen*, which suggest that 6,673 Gewehre 41 (M) had been delivered by the end of the 1941 accounting year (it is not clear if this was identical with the calendar year) . . . but that no Walthers had been made until 6,778 had been accepted in 1942! There are several plausible explanations. One is simply that the Walthers had all been delivered into store in the few weeks prior to the 27 January report, but it is much more likely that the alleged delivery of

'6,673' Gew. 41 (M) in 1941 consisted of five thousand Walthers – the original 'development' order' – and the 1,673 Mausers mentioned in the January 1942 report.[11] A transcription mistake could easily have been made, particularly as the letters 'M' and 'W' are often similar when handwritten.

Combat experience in Russia soon showed that the Gew. 41 (M) was a poor design, and it is suspected that Mauser never entirely corrected its problems. Indeed, production may have been limited to the original 1,673 guns. The Walther was much more efficient, though the muzzle-cap system was undoubtedly a serious weakness in its overall design. The H.WaA. elected to mass-produce the Gew. 41 (W), which was adopted in December 1942 as the 'Gewehr 41' without a distinguishing suffix.[12] The mechanical hold-open of the prototype was eliminated and – possibly after production had commenced – the safety system was radically revised to prevent damaging the internal components if the safety lever were rotated when the gun was cocked. A rail for the Zf. 41 telescope sight was also added on the left side of the back-sight base.

The desire to provide large numbers of semi-automatic rifles as rapidly as possible was eased by recruiting a second contractor, Berlin-Lübecker Maschinenfabrik (code 'duv') and creating another Walther factory. A map reproduced by Richard Law in *Sniper Variations of the German K98k Rifle*, reveals that the Walther factory was in Buchenwald. The first 1,713 rifles were delivered in September 1942; the revised manual D191/1 *Gewehr 41. Beschreibung, Handhabung und Behandlung* was published on 16 February 1943, and, by August 1943, more than ten thousand guns were being made each month.

Production of the Gew. 41 stopped in favour of the Gew. 43 at the end of 1943, though there were sufficient parts on hand to assemble 12,000 guns in January, 10,383 in February and finally 2,085 1941-type rifles in March 1944. Output of Gew. 41 totalled about 123,000, excluding the five thousand Gew. 41 (W), which shows that the rifle was not as statistically insignificant as many post-war writers have claimed.

The campaigns in Russia had exposed the unacceptably muzzle-heavy balance of the Gew. 41, revealed the limitations of the charger-loaded internal box magazine, highlighted the susceptibility of the muzzle-cup system to corrosion, and proved that the gas system was very difficult to clean. The simplest solution was to combine the gas system of the Soviet S.V.T. 40 (Tokarev) rifle and a detachable box magazine with the breech-locking mechanism of the Gew. 41, producing a shorter, lighter and much more combat-worthy design. This, the *Gewehr 43*, was substituted for its predecessor on 30 April 1943.[13]

Unfortunately, the Gew. 43 was ordered into full-scale production before development was complete, and never entirely overcame a reputation for unreliability. A trial undertaken by the U.S. Army in 1946 concluded disparagingly that 'the general performance and endurance of the weapons tested were poor, as excessive malfunctions and breakages were encountered . . . The weapon does not appear to possess any outstandingly meritorious design features.' One interesting conclusion was that the test rifle was 'overpowered, resulting in frequent ejection failures', but there is no evidence to suggest that this applied to others of the same type.

The receiver of the Gew. 43 resembled the Gew. 41 pattern externally, but the half-stock had a full-length handguard and a slender unsupported barrel protruding from a simple nosecap. The gas-tube, piston and actuating-rod assembly lay above the barrel. When the gun was fired, a portion of the propelling gas bled back into a hollow piston chamber to tap the actuating rod back against the breech cover. As the cover retreated, it pulled the firing pin away from the breech and cammed the locking arms back into the breechblock.

The butt had a typically German sling slot, and a rail for the Zf. 4 telescope sight was attached to the left side of the receiver. The earliest guns had rails without the vertical locator for the spring-loaded latch on the optical-sight mount, but later examples have a prominent groove midway along the face of the rail. Like its predecessor, the Gew. 43 chambered the standard 7.9mm S-Patrone. However, it did not accept the SG. 84/98.

The principal manufacturers included Walther (code 'qve') and Berlin-Lübecker Maschinenfabrik ('duv'), though a few guns were assembled in the Gustloff-Werke factory in Weimar ('bcd'). Production was substantial, beginning with fifteen delivered in October 1943 and rising to 38,006 in February 1945. About a third of these February deliveries were *Zielfernrohr-Karabiner 43*, fitted with 4× Zf. 4 sights in special swept-back monoblock mounts made exclusively by Hermann Weihrauch of Zella-Mehlis.

Despite the attention paid to the MP. 43 assault rifle in the immediate post-war period, and the greatly inflated reputation of the limited-production FG. 42 (see Chapter Seven), the Gewehr 43 was considered to be the true replacement for the Kar. 98k. The H.WaA. still took the view that the standard 7.9×57mm cartridge was the only pattern acceptable for universal military service, restricting the intermediate cartridge to theatres where a need for firepower outweighed limitations on maximum engagement range. Consequently, production of Gewehre 43 totalled 399,504, excluding the unknown number delivered in April 1945; 53,500 of these were classifed as Zf.-Kar. 43.

Most of the guns are comparatively crudely finished, with visible tool marks on the metalwork and stocks, sometimes laminated, that had received minimal fine sanding and often lacked even a coat of varnish. Many K. 43 made in 1945 lacked the mechanical hold-open and the half-length cleaning rod, but had an additional bolt-guide rib to improve reliability. An obvious change was made to the breech cover in January 1945, removing the original raised tip, with a characteristic rolled edge, and reducing the length of the cover from 87mm to 80mm.[14]

Though the Gew. 43/Kar. 43 was undoubtedly among the best semi-automatic rifles to reach active service during the Second World War, attempts to reduce machine-time and conserve raw materials hamstrung the production programme. Though the guns were generally well finished internally, external finish was often rough and the tolerances of non-essential components fluctuated enormously. Allied with poor accuracy[15] and material of suspect quality, particularly on guns made towards the end of hostilities, these problems now obscure the guns' genuinely outstanding qualities.

Assault rifles. The Haenel Maschinenkarabiner, the first of the German assault rifles, resulted from trials that had been undertaken with intermediate cartridges since the 1920s (see Chapter Three). It was designed largely by Hugo Schmeisser, who had been responsible for the MP.18 during the First World War, and was readied for trials with the perfected short 7.9mm Polte cartridge in 1940.

However, as Haenel had little experience of simplified manufacturing techniques, transforming the prototype into a mass-production reality was entrusted to Merz-Werke GmbH of Frankfurt am Main, a company with unrivalled experience of metal stamping, precision casting and spot-welding. By this time, the German authorities, for once realizing that speed was vital, had formed the 'Sonderauschuss für Maschinenpistolen und Maschinenkarabiner' ('Sd. Au. MP. u. MKb.'). This special sub-committee was to supervise production of the new machine-carbines alongside the existing submachine-guns; it answered to the Hauptauschuss Waffen (Ha.W.), which in turn reported directly to the Reichsministerium für Rüstungs- & Kriegsproduction.

While Haenel was producing the MKb. 42 (H) prototypes, a design team led by Erich Walther had also begun work. Evidently believing that a better gun could be produced, Walther had completed an experimental gas-operated machine-carbine by the beginning of 1941. It was satisfactorily demonstrated to Wa.-Prüf 2 and a contract for two hundred pre-production guns was approved late in January 1942.

Only two guns had been supplied by July 1942, when extensive trials should have been undertaken at Schiessplatz Kummersdorf. Walther's traditions of quality pistol production were unquestioned, but the company had even less experience of stamped-metal production techniques than Haenel.

Unwilling to wait for the results of protracted trials, the H.WaA. ordered both carbines into production; detailed drawings and sufficient machinery were to be ready by July 1942, Haenel was to begin work in November 1942, and Walther was expected to progress from making five hundred guns in October 1942 to 15,000 per month by March 1943.

The H.WaA. then added bayonet lugs and grenade launchers to the Maschinenkarabiner specification as an afterthought, severely disrupting progress, while unforeseen manufacturing difficulties – and sub-contractors' failure to reach targets – slowed progress to a crawl. None of the guns expected in October 1942 could be delivered, only 25 of the November quota of 500 were forthcoming, and then came a mere 91 of the thousand anticipated in December.

Most of the tooling problems had been resolved by the beginning of 1943, however, and the delivery of 500 guns in January represented a shortfall of only 200. Walther and Haenel then exceeded the thousand-gun February quota by 217.

The MKb. 42 (H) and MKb. 42 (W) were superficially similar, owing to the rigidity of the H.WaA. specification and extensive use of stamping, pressing and welding. The Haenel design looked relatively conventional, with a gas-tube extending forward above the barrel almost to the muzzle, but the MKb. 42 (W) had a more pronounced straight-line design with the back sight on a tall block. The annular gas piston/barrel construction of the Walther carbine permitted a cylindrical fore-end casing from which only the barrel protruded.

Both guns accepted the SG. 84/98, and had curved thirty-round box magazines protruding from the underside of the receiver ahead of the trigger/pistol-grip group. The Haenel carbine, relying on a tilting-block locking mechanism, fired from an open breech; the Walther, firing from a closed breech, incorporated a rotary bolt. The MKb. 42 (H) was 940mm overall, had a 365mm barrel, and weighed 5.02kg empty; comparative figures for the MKb. 42 (W) were 933mm, 409mm and 4.42kg respectively. Cyclic rates were generally 550–600 rds/min.

Though the Walther was lighter, better balanced and more accurate, the Haenel had the merit of simplicity. The H.WaA. recommended standardising the MKb. 42 (H), but only after an adaptation of the hammer-fired Walther trigger system had replaced the original Haenel striker pattern. The finalised MP. 43, like the MKb. 42 (W), fired from a closed breech.

Approximately eight thousand carbines had been delivered by the middle of 1943 – 2,800 Walthers and 5,200 Haenels – and only about 14,000 had been accepted by the end of the year. Problems encountered in series production and with the quality of the ammunition were still proving difficult to overcome.

The MP. 43 was the refined Haenel Maschinenkarabiner, the term 'Maschinenpistole' being adopted to camouflage the assault rifle as a sub-machine-gun and overcome Hitler's prejudices. It greatly resembled the MKb. 42, but lacked the distinctively extended gas-tube; instead, a ball-tipped rod projected from the gas-port assembly.

Among the known variants were the MP. 43/1, with the muzzle threaded for the MKb. Gewehrgranatgerät (later known as the MP.

GwGrGt. 43), whereas the MP. 43, MP. 44 and StG. 44 had a shorter muzzle for the Kar. 98k-type grenade launcher. The MP. 44 appears to have been nothing more than the original MP. 43 renamed, and the StG. 44 was nothing but the MP. 44 renamed!

Most MP. 43/1 and some MP. 44 have been seen with side-rail mounts for the Zf. 4 optical sight or the Zielgerät 1229 'Vampir' (ZG. 1229) infrared night sight. Experimental muzzle brakes and sights have been found, in addition to *Krummlauf* (curved barrel) adaptations that included the 30-degree 'Vorsatz J', 40-degree 'Vorsatz V' and 90-degree 'Vorsatz P'.

Production was entrusted largely to C.G. Haenel Waffen- & Fahrradfabrik of Suhl (code 'fxo') and Erfurter Maschinenfabrik B. Geipel G.m.b.H. 'Erma-Werk' of Erfurt ('ayf'), while Mauser-Werke A.G. of Oberndorf ('byf') and an unidentified company using the code 'sup' made receivers. However, many lesser contractors became involved in the MP. 43 production line, including Merz-Werke Gebr. Merz of Frankfurt am Main ('cos'); Württembergische Metallwarenfabrik of Geislingen-Steige ('awt'); J.G. Anschütz Germaniawaffen-Fabrik of Zella-Mehlis; Progress-Werk; Lux; J.P. Sauer & Sohn of Suhl ('ce'); Erste Nordböhmische Waffenfabrik Adolf Rossler of Niederinseidel ('fnh'); L.W. Zeug- & Metallwarenfabrik; and, allegedly, Trippel-Werke Hanns Trippel of Molsheim/Elsass. However, Trippel's code, 'glu', has probably been mistaken for 'qlv'.

It has often been claimed that Maschinenkarabiner enabled Kampfgruppe Scherer to fight its way out of the Kholm Pocket on the Eastern Front in the early days of 1942. The story originally appeared in 'Das Sturmgewehre' in *Wehrkunde* early in 1953, was repeated in Eckardt & Morawietz's *Die Handwaffen des brandenburgisch-preussisch-deutschen Heeres 1640–1945* (Verlag Helmut Gerhard Schulz, Hamburg, 1957), and then by so many other authors that it became accepted as 'fact'.

However, the defenders of the Kholm Pocket broke out of encircle-ment in February 1942. Only a few Haenel prototypes had reached the H.WaA. by that time, and it is most unlikely that valuable test-pieces would be dropped into an obscure part of Russia. The guns concerned are much more likely to have been Gew. 41 (M) or Gew. 41 (W), as suffi-cient pre-production examples of each pattern were available by the end of 1941.

The first full combat trials of the new Maschinenkarabiner were undertaken in the spring of 1943 by S.S.- Division 'Wiking', more than half the firers reporting that the new gun would be a suitable replacement for the MP. 40 and the Kar. 98k. The combination of firepower and controllability so impressed the élite troops that three army commanders reputedly asked Hitler to begin series production of the MP. 43 immediately. As he had been told that the development programme had been cancelled, the requests doubtless came as a great surprise. After seeking the opinions of the rank-and-file personally, however, Hitler reversed his low opinion of the Maschinenkarabiner concept at the expense of the FG. 42 and Gew. 43. In December 1944, the MP. 43 was officially renamed 'Sturmgewehr 44' (StG. 44) in recognition of its capabilities, though manual D 1854/3, *Sturmgewehr 44, Gebrauchsanleitung* dated from 3 June 1944.[16]

Each gun was accompanied by six magazines, a magazine filler, a sling, three '98.'-type muzzle protectors ('MP.' if the gun had a muzzle nut) and two three-magazine pouches, in addition to a *Lösedorn* and a cleaning brush for the gas cylinder in a leather wallet. A kit of spare parts (an extractor, an extractor pin, an extractor spring and a striker) was to be carried in the right-hand magazine pouch.

The MP. 43/StG. 44 was one of the first military weapons to be mass-produced on the sub-contract system that later became commonplace. Like all pioneering efforts, however, this did not proceed smoothly; parts made by outworkers were not always satisfactory and too much handwork was needed to ensure the guns worked. So many problems were discovered during tooling that initial deliveries were erratic; an acceptable production rate was reached only in the summer of 1944.

The new assault rifles excited great interest, but were never issued in sufficient quantity to influence the fighting. Production continued into 1945 and, as it had always been made largely from crude-looking stampings, the assault rifle did not suffer the visible deterioration that characterised the Kar. 98k or the Gew. 43. Only the last batches were bonderised (a process similar to Parkerising) rather than thinly blued, had laminated rather than solid wood butts, and wooden grips substituted by cheap plastic mouldings.

Rifles.   The start of the Russian campaign coincided with the introduction of a new telescope sight, the Zf. 41, which was announced in July 1941[17] and described in an addition to the Kar. 98k manual – *Richtlinien für technische Lieferbedingungen. Karabiner K98k–Z.F. 41 (Zielfernrohrgewehr)* published on 3 October. A separate manual, D 136, *Karabiner 98k–Zf 41 (Zielfernrohrgewehr) und Zielfernrohr 41 (Zf 41)* followed in February 1942 and was eventually superseded by a corrected and amended version, D 136/1, in October 1943.

The Zf. 41 was one of the catastrophes of German military technology. It had been created in answer to requests made during the Polish campaign for rifles that could be issued to the best marksmen in each infantry unit, allowing them to make better use of their skills than the standard open sights allowed. However, instead of extending the range of engagement, the sights were *actually* requested to give a better chance of hitting targets such as the vision slits on pillboxes or vital parts of vehicles at comparatively close range.

Experimental Zf. 40 sights were tested shortly after the attack on Poland was completed, to be superseded by the Zf. 40+ and the Zf. 41 before series production began. The most important features of the sights were their small size, comparatively light weight and an eye relief that was long enough to allow them to be mounted on a rail attached to the left side of the back sight. The goal was to provide a sight that could be mounted over the bore, yet still allow the rifle to be fired without the firer being forced to raise his cheek from the butt. In addition, a standard five-round charger could be used, unlike guns fitted with Zielvier and Zf. 39.

The Zf. 41 could be removed to allow the Kar. 98k to revert to standard open sights, though the transition could prove to be difficult if the firer were wearing gloves. The relatively small magnification, 1.5×, was chosen partly because the sights were intended for use at ordinary combat ranges and partly to encourage marksmen to fire with both eyes open.

Trials showed that the original side rails, which were milled flat to accept mounts with plain cylindrical tensioning rollers, were not rigid enough to maintain zero. Later examples had a bevelled groove and bevelled rollers on the sight base, to force the mount down and outward (improving rigidity) and to help maintain zero if the sight were detached.

However, very few soldiers liked the Zf. 41; its light-gathering capabilities were poor, owing to too many lenses in the light-path and the small diameter of the objective lens. It had been intended to issue adaptors that could be fitted to any standard Kar. 98k, but experience soon showed that, as the sight bases had not been manufactured with a view to attaching optical sights, tolerances varied too greatly to guarantee that the Zf. 41 aligned satisfactorily with the axis of the bore. Adaptors were soon abandoned, and most of the true Kar. 98k–Zf. 41 combinations were purpose-built by Mauser-Werke, in Berlin-Borsigwalde or Oberndorf (codes 'ar' and 'byf' respectively), and by Berlin-Lübecker Maschinenfabrik ('duv').

Tubular sheet-steel rain guards were issued with the sights from the beginning, and the introduction of a light-filter, *Aufsteckfilter für Zielfernrohr 41*, was announced in April 1943.[18]

Unlike the Gewehr 33/40, which was based on a Czechoslovakian Mauser, the *Gewehr 98/40* was an adaptation of the Hungarian 35.M Mannlicher rifle, adopted in October 1941[19] and purchased from 'Metallwaren-, Waffen- & Maschinenfabrik' – the Hungarian state firearms factory in Budapest, code 'jhv'. Many thousands were delivered to the Wehrmacht from 1941 until November 1944.

The Gew. 98/40 was easily distinguished from the 35.M by its German-style charger-loaded magazine, a 4cm bayonet bar beneath the muzzle instead of a short peg on the nose cap, sights for the 7.9mm S-Patrone, a bolt handle that was turned downward against the stock, and a sling-slot in the butt. The rifles also had split-bridge receivers and British-type stocks with separate fore-ends. The butts were held in the action-body sockets by sturdy bolts that ran up through the pistol grip.

The 98/40 was sturdy and reliable, though the butts occasionally worked loose, and sharp edges on the bolt-retaining catch, which snagged clothing, had to be rounded from September 1942.[20] Impressed, the Hungarians subsequently rechambered the German action for the 8mm 31.M cartridge, changed the nose cap to accept the Hungarian bayonet, and adopted the 98/40 as the 'Huzagol 43.M'.

Another introduction was a grenade launcher for the Kar. 98k, known as the *Gewehrgranatgerät*, 'GGGt.' or 'GwGrGt.', a cup-type launcher that was designed to throw a variety of projectiles to a maximum range of about 500 metres. Introduced in April 1942[21], the GwGrGt. consisted of an extended collar and a short 'barrel' with prominent rifling grooves. The collar located on the base of the front sight, where it could be locked by pivoting a block over the top of the barrel and clamping it in place by turning a large radial lever. The barrel screwed into the front of the collar. Lands on a drive band on the tail of the grenade engaged the rifling grooves in the bore, a special blank cartridge was fired, and the grenade was spinning as it left the muzzle.

Each GwGrGt. was issued with a grenade-launching sight, a pouch, a spanner to remove the rifled barrel, and a pair of cases or bags for the grenades. Three grenades were introduced at the same time: the high-explosive Gewehr-Sprenggranate, the armour-piercing Gewehr-Panzergranate, and the Gewehr-Sprenggranate Üb. for practice.[22] Separate launching blanks were issued for each grenade, including the 'Gewehrkartusche für Gewehr-Sprenggranate' ('G. Kart. für G. Sprgr.'), together with a carton or *Packhülle* and a packing case or *Kasten*. An enlarged armour-piercing grenade, the Grosse Gewehr-Panzergranate ('G. G.Pzgr.') appeared in October 1942, and was improved by the substitution of a stronger rifled shaft early in 1943. Details will be found in Appendix One.

The grenade launchers were put to good use, though accuracy was comparatively poor. In addition, a large number of accidents had arisen when men had tried to handle grenades that had failed to ignite. So bad did the problem become that the O.K.H. issued a directive banning anyone from touching these 'duds', other than personnel trained in the disposal of munitions.[23] This was particularly important in areas where live-firing practice was being undertaken.

A change was soon made to the contours of the collar, the height of the walls around the front sight being reduced to 8.5mm[24], and issues continued. In October 1942, these were defined as one GwGrGt. with thirty Gewehr-Sprenggranaten and thirty Gewehr-Panzergranaten to each company or squadron of Schützen, Gebirgsjäger, Jäger, Panzer-Grenadier, Krad.-Schütz, Pioniere, Reiter and Radfahrer units. Two launchers, with the same total ammunition allocation, were to be given to each battery of light and heavy artillery (including 21cm gun batteries) and the Nebeltruppe, but not to the Heeres-Küsten-Artillerie.[25]

Service experience revealed that many of the captured Mauser-type rifles that had been impressed into German service did not feed cartridges from their magazines as efficiently as the Kar. 98k. In September 1942, the O.K.H. ordered that the magazines of Czechoslovakian, Polish and Yugoslavian rifles, short rifles and carbines should be fitted with German-made magazine followers, apparently by using parts for the Gew. 98 and Kar. 98b that were being held in store.[26] The alterations were to be undertaken by the armourers attached to individual units.

In addition, in May 1943, a special clamping mount was introduced to allow the Kar. 98k to be fixed to a bicycle, very important in the context of the number of troops and police who were expected to travel in this way.

Anti-tank rifles.   By the time Operation 'Barbarossa' began, the small-calibre German anti-tank rifles had been all but discarded; captured Russian weapons, particularly the simple 14.5mm P.T.R.D., were to prove much more useful, but something had to be done with the thousands of PzB. 39 that had been made by Havelwerk, Gustloff-Werke and others. Apart from anti-tank rifles serving in North Africa and the Balkans, where uses could still be found, most survivors were converted to *Granatbüchsen 39* (GrB. 39) by removing the fore-end, shortening the barrel and attaching a grenade discharger cup. The GrB. 39 was much shorter and appreciably lighter than the PzB. 39, but had a limited role. Only a few guns survived until the end of the war. They fired the same ammunition as the Kar. 98k equipped with the GwGrGt.

The continual struggle between the tank and the gun, which had reduced the standard German anti-tank rifles to impotence, fuelled a search for more useful weapons. This was partly satisfied by increases in power, allowing the calibres associated with conventional anti-tank artillery to progress from 3.7cm to 12.8cm by the end of the Second World War[27], and partly by seeking advances in technology.

Small numbers of wz. 35 hyper-velocity rifle-calibre guns had been seized in Poland, but they offered little advance on the German Panzerbüchsen and required tungsten-cored ammunition. Some use was made of the 2cm Solothurn S-18/1000, known in German service as the Panzerbüchse 41 (PzB. 41), which was a powerful recoil-operated semi-

automatic cannon offering acceptable power, good penetrative capability (30mm at 250m) and a useful offensive payload in its large-calibre
shell. However, the guns were long and very heavy (2.1m overall, 44kg),
and were also needlessly complicated – incorporating a Stange collar-
lock, five- or ten-round box magazines, and a cocking system in which
a crank and a toothed chain were needed to overcome the strength of the
recoil springs. The PzB. 41 also proved to be useless against the frontal
armour of the Russian T-34 tank, survivors being sent to North Africa
and Italy later in the war.

As the H.WaA. moved away from rifle calibres to other and better
ideas, the Waffen-SS also began to seek anti-tank weapons. None could
be obtained through regular procurement channels in 1940–1, but,
shortly before the German occupation, work on small-calibre anti-tank
rifles had commenced in Czechoslovakia. After rejecting a handful of
prototypes, including several Janeček squeezebores, the Czechs had
settled on the Československá Zbrojovka Z.K. 395 (12mm and 15mm)
and the Z.K. 405–407 series (7.9mm, some manually operated and
others semi-automatic).

Marketed as the 'Protitankova puška vz. 41', a few of the large-
calibre guns went to Italy while the SS took appreciable numbers of the
smaller versions, which were generally known as 'M. SS-41' in German
paramilitary service.

The SS-41 was beautifully made, but much too complicated to be
suited to arduous service. After the gun had been fired, the pistol grip
was rotated laterally to the right to unlock the breech and pushed
forward. This pulled the breech-sleeve away from the standing breech to
expose the spent cartridge case. At the end of the opening stroke, the
ejector kicked the case clear of the gun, allowing the pistol grip and sleeve
assembly to be pulled back to reload the action from a detachable ten-
round box magazine. Turning the grip back to its original vertical position then secured the system ready for the next shot. The SS-41 was
about 1.2m long and weighed 18kg when empty. Muzzle velocity was
about 1,220 m/sec, which gave a penetrative capability similar to that of
the obsolescent PzB. 38 and PzB. 39.

The Germans, typically, continued to seek much more sophisticated
solutions to the anti-tank question. Squeeze-bore guns were developed

from the ideas of Ernst Gerlich, who had died in 1934, but a reliance on tungsten-cored shot proved their undoing. Though the performance of the 28/21mm taper-bore was spectacular for a gun of its size and weight, shortages of tungsten soon meant an absence of ammunition. Later developments are described in Chapter Seven.

Submachine-guns. A dual-magazine version of the MP. 40, known as the 'MP. 40/II.', was made exclusively in Steyr in 1942–3 specifically for use on the Eastern Front, where the German troops were facing Russian P.P.Sh. submachine-guns with 70-round drum magazines. The MP. 40/II. had two standard magazines side-by-side in a special magazine housing, but the additional weight and complexity prevented universal adoption.

Hybrid 'Maschinenpistolen 41' combined the receiver and barrel of the MP. 40 with the stock and trigger of the MP. 28. A typical gun measured 864mm overall, had a 250mm barrel and weighed 4.37kg when loaded; cyclic rate was about 500 rds/min. However, the origins of the MP. 41 remain mysterious; though fashionably supposed to have been produced for a 'friendly foreign power', Haenel may simply have been expending superfluous MP. 28 components. The MP. 41 bears no special marks, apart from those of Haenel and the principal sub-contractor Merz-Werke.

The advent of the 7.9mm Maschinenpistolen, the first assault rifles, threatened to make the conventional pistol-ammunition weapons obsolete. Eventually, in the autumn of 1944, the O.K.H. directed that surviving MP. 38, MP. 40 and impressed submachine-guns should be withdrawn from front-line service to be given to 'battalion and regimental reserves, special-purpose units and irregular forces'. The Kar. 98k, Kar. 43 and MP. 44/StG. 44 series were to be given priority.

Handguns. The adoption of the P. 38 made the older P. 08 (Parabellum) obsolescent, and Mauser was officially ordered to cease making the latter in 1941, freeing additional manufacturing capacity for the P. 38. However, though none were accepted for the Wehrmacht after October 1942, Parabellums were still being assembled in small numbers as late as 1945 (including 7.65mm examples destined for the German forestry service). Small batches of unwanted P. 08 were even exported to friendly states in 1942/3 – principally Bulgaria and Portugal – and others went to police or paramilitary organisations. Total production in 1934–45 amounted to slightly more than one million Parabellums, including more than 31,000 for commercial sale, and nearly twelve thousand for agencies such as the Reichs-Finanz-Verwaltung and the police. Between March 1939 and October 1942, 499,448 P.08 had been supplied to the Wehrmacht; 359,247 to the army, 131,451 to the Luftwaffe and a mere 8,750 for the navy.

The authorities soon realised that handguns would be required in such great numbers that Walther would never cope alone, even though approximately 590,000 P. 38 were delivered to the Wehrmacht in 1939–45. The army inventory in September 1940 had stood at 552,962 pistols (almost all P. 08), with an additional 186,000 P. 08 serving the Luftwaffe and nearly 36,000 assorted pistols – P. 08 and Mauser blow-backs – in the Kriegsmarine. By August 1944, the total army inventory had risen to 1,600,000 despite stupendous losses – 12,381 pistols in December 1943, rising to 52,090 in July 1944 alone. By the end of the war, the army had purchased more than three million pistols since the beginning of 1939.

It is popularly believed that Mauser-Werke was the second contractor to deliver the P. 38 to the armed forces, but the honour actually fell to Spreewerke G.m.b.H. of Spandau. Spreewerke, better known for field guns and howitzers, was impressed into the production of Walther-type pistols in 1941 and delivered the first fifty in May 1942; 7,050 had been accepted by New Year's Day 1943. The company ultimately achieved the highest production, but only at the expense of quality. Total production amounted to about 275,000 P. 38, mostly displaying 'cyq'. However, a few show what appears to be 'cvq', caused by the 'y' tail breaking away from the die unnoticed.

Some (if not all) of Spreewerke's pistol production was undertaken in a subsidiary plant at Kratzau, now Hradkou in northern Czechoslovakia, where three thousand guns were assembled for the Czechoslovak army in 1945–6. This may also explain why the Spreewerke guns contain so many components made by Czechoslovakian subcontractors.

Mauser-Werke was ordered to stop producing the P. 08 in 1941, though assembly continued well into the following year, and the first 700 Mauser-made Pistolen 38 were delivered in December 1942. Work continued until the French arrived in April 1945, by which time more than 308,000 had been made in several recognisably differing subvarieties. Mauser products displayed the code-group 'byf' until the beginning of 1945, when the appearance of 'svw' may indicate dispersal of P. 38 production elsewhere in southern Württemberg.

Production of the P. 38 was accelerated as much as possible, but the design was complicated and difficult to mass-produce at a level that enabled spiralling losses on the Eastern Front to be replaced. Gradually, thoughts turned to the development of simplified handguns known as 'Volkspistolen'. These are described in greater detail in the next chapter.

Signal pistols. The Walther-type Heeresmodell was complicated, expensive to make and difficult to maintain under service conditions. Consequently, a search, begun by the H.WaA. in the early 1940s, resulted in the approval of the simplified *Leuchtpistole 42* ('LP. 42'). Adapted from a pre-war Moritz & Gerstenberger 'EM-GE' design, the LP. 42 had a single tipping barrel locked by a bolt running laterally through the frame above and behind the trigger. Pressing the bolt to the left released the barrel after the hammer had been retracted. There was no safety catch.

The LP. 42 was made largely from crude pressings and had coarsely-ribbed Bakelite grips. It measured 220mm overall, had a barrel of 155mm and weighed about 1,125gm. Only two contractors have been identified: HASAG–Hugo Schneider A.G., Abteilung Lampenfabrik, Leipzig (code 'wa') and C. & W. Meinel-Scholer of Klingenthal in Sachsen ('euh'). The Meinel-Scholer guns are particularly poorly made, which suggests 1944–5 as the likeliest date of manufacture. A rifled version of the basic pattern, the *Gezogene Leuchtpistole 42*, was also made in small numbers.

The Gezogene Leuchtpistole, also known as the 'Leuchtpistole 42 Z.' or 'Kampfpistole', was derived from the Heeresmodell on the basis of experience of war in the USSR. This had suggested that a small hand-held grenade projector could be used to knock out vehicles, tanks and small strongpoints, and the rifled Kampfpistole appeared soon after the first phases of Operation 'Barbarossa' had been completed. The introductory pamphlet, *Merkblatt für die Erprobung der Leuchtpistole Z, sowie der Sondermunition . . .* was published on 25 March 1942.

Details of the special projectiles will be found in Appendix One. All were fired from die-cast aluminium (more rarely, brass or steel) cartridge cases, and had pre-rifled shell bodies that engaged the rifling cut into the barrels of otherwise-standard signal pistols. The grooves were about 7mm wide and 0.125mm deep, the rifled portion of the barrel measuring 120mm. An elevating quadrant and spirit level were added to the left side of the frame behind the breech and a large luminous 'Z' was applied on the left side of the barrel near the breech.

The purpose-built Walther Leuchtpistolen Z. (distinguished by the code 'ac') exhibited a glossy brownish-black finish, but some matt-black Erma guns ('ayf') were converted from standard flare pistols.

The *Sturmpistole* was a 1943-vintage Heeresmodell conversion with a rifled barrel liner, reducing the bore diameter to about 22mm. A sleeve carrying a special sight was then clamped to the barrel and a folding shoulder stock was attached to the frame. The ammunition issued with the *Sturmpistole* could not be interchanged with either standard flare-pistol or *Leuchtpistole* Z. patterns.

The muzzle-loaded 'Panzer-Wurfkörper 42 für Leuchtpistole' was a hollow-charge bomb relying on the Munroe Effect to destroy Russian T-34 or KV-1 tanks; as much as 10cm of armour plate could be penetrated at close range. The Sturmpistole could also fire a breech-loaded high-explosive shell, but this had an unreliable combustion fuze with a mere one-second delay and was universally mistrusted. Its packaging was always marked ACHTUNG! NUR AUS PANZERN ODER GLEICHVERTIGER DECKUNG VERFEUEREN! ('Danger! Only fire from tanks or similar cover!').

Sturmpistolen bore no special marks. Heartily disliked for their violent recoil, they were about 345mm long with the stock folded (550mm with the stock extended), had 135mm smooth-bore barrels with a rifled liner, and weighed about 3kg.

7

Seeds of Doubt

By the autumn of 1942, the enthusiasm for the Russian campaign, never strong with some sections of the Wehrmacht, was diminishing fast. Reichsmarschall Göring was still declaiming that the Luftwaffe could supply the Sixth Army, penned in Stalingrad, just as it had done earlier at Demyansk and Kholm. But the severity of winter and renewed Russian air presence soon showed his boasts to be empty. Though fifty thousand men, many sick or injured, were airlifted out of Stalingrad in a remarkable feat of organisation, more than a hundred thousand (including Generalfeldmarschall Paulus and more than twenty generals) capitulated on 31 January 1943.

For 75,000 Germans, Stalingrad was a grave. The myth of Teutonic invincibility had been shattered, and after the awesome battle of Kursk in July 1943 the question was no longer a matter of who would win, but simply when the Red Army would reach Berlin.

Kursk was a titanic confrontation of armour and air power, and a turning point in the war on the Eastern Front that may have hinged on German battle-plans that had been passed to the U.S.S.R. by a popular actress working for Goebbels' propaganda ministry. It has been estimated that 2,600 German tanks and assault guns battered away remorselessly at 3,300 Soviet assault guns and tanks, beneath a canopy of four thousand aircraft vying for supremacy. The casualty figures were on a similarly epic scale. Virtually half of the Soviet armoured vehicles were knocked out, but though the balance of casualties favoured the Germans, whose tanks, self-propelled guns and anti-tank artillery were handled with greater discipline, the losses were too much for hard-pressed German industry to restore overnight.

The Soviet initiative marked a perceptible change in the course of the war and, by the summer of 1943, the arms industry was able to out-strip not only the ability of the Red Army to lose matériel, but also Germany's capacity to supply the Wehrmacht. Output of T-34/76, T-34/85 and KV-1 tanks, particularly, reached prodigious heights. Moreover, what the Soviet weapons lacked in quality, which could be considerable, was more than offset by quantity.

By 1943, the Soviet small-arms industry was producing many mil-lions of weapons per annum. Though these included obsolescent Mosin-Nagant rifles, Maxim and Degtyarev machine-guns, sufficient time had been bought to resurrect re-equipment plans mooted prior to Operation 'Barbarossa'. The success of the P.P.Sh. submachine-gun had encouraged the concept of tank-borne infantrymen, though the simpler P.P.S. was increasingly preferred as the war ran its course. The Germans were unable to introduce an auto-loading rifle in sufficient numbers to influ-ence the fighting, and the Gewehr 41, adopted in December 1942, was clearly destined to fail. The advent of the Gewehr 43 and the MP. 43 series had little impact, as production did not begin in earnest until 1944, and problems with the Fallschirmjägergewehr (FG. 42) were not resolved until the last few months of the war.

Throughout the winter of 1943–4, and on into the summer of 1944, the Soviet Army made inroads into what had been Russian terri-tory prior to June 1941, catching the Germans where they were weakest. Forced to defend a lengthy boundary with insufficient men, the Wehrmacht could do little but fall back. Once Soviet units had raised the siege of Leningrad on 27 January 1944, pressure was easily brought on the Finns to sue for peace and diplomatic moves in the south, with promise of territory claimed by Hungary, caused Romania to question its motives for war.

A coup d'état on 23 August 1944 then overthrew Antonescu, the Romanian dictator, and a surrender was immediately concluded with the

Soviet Union. As the Germans had also been forced to cover the withdrawal of Italy from the war and prevent an Anglo-American advance up the Italian promontory into Vichy France, the elasticity of the Wehrmacht was being stretched to its limit.

Captured and non-standard weapons

The Wehrmacht continued to issue submachine-guns that had been seized from enemy and even co-belligerent forces. Possibly the best liked was the Italian Beretta Mo. 938A, known to the Germans as the 'Maschinenpistole 739 (i)'. Designed by Tullio Marengoni and introduced in 1935 as a semi-automatic carbine, the Beretta reappeared as a twin-trigger submachine-gun at the beginning of 1938. The original version had a slotted barrel jacket and a simple compensator, but, by the time guns were acquired by the Germans, the production pattern had acquired a pierced jacket and an efficient four-baffle compensator.

The Mo. 938A was 946mm long, with a 315mm barrel, and weighed a little under 5kg when empty. Cyclic rate was about 600 rds/min, but single shots could be fired by pressing the front trigger. Most guns had a radial safety on the left side of the stock above the triggers and a blocking-bar behind the rear trigger to prevent accidental automatic fire. Widely carried by paratroops and Waffen-SS, often in preference to the MP. 38 and MP. 40, the Beretta was sturdy, reliable and regarded as supremely accurate for a gun of its class.

After the fall of Italy, the Germans continued to acquire an improved version of the Beretta, usually designated 'M38A/42'. This had been altered to accelerate production, and can be recognised by a short barrel, lacking the sophisticated barrel jacket of the M938, and a simplified back sight. The quality is also noticeably poorer than the original guns, with notable machining marks on the receiver. Work continued until the end of 1944.

German forces in Italy also received small quantities of the F.N.A.B. submachine-gun, made by Fabbrica Nazionale d'Armi of Brescia in 1943–4. This was a complicated delayed blowback design, firing from a closed breech, with a folding magazine housing and a radial selector on the left side of the frame above the grip. It was regarded as well made and accurate, but unnecessarily complicated for a submachine-gun. Only about seven thousand were made.

Co-belligerent forces provided small quantities of Finnish Suomi m/31, Hungarian 39.M and Romanian Orita guns, which found their way into the Wehrmacht inventory as the fronts collapsed in 1944–5.

Designed by Aimo Lahti, the Suomi was a selective-fire blowback with a control lever that slid through the front of the trigger guard. Made by Oy Tikkakoski (and under licence by Husqvarna, Madsen and Hispano-Suiza), the m/31 was an influential but surprisingly traditional design. The service weapon of virtually all Scandinavia, in addition to Spain, Bolivia and elsewhere in South America prior to 1939, the Suomi was strong and reliable. Overall length was about 870mm, with a 315mm barrel, though weight was excessive: with a loaded 71-round drum magazine, the m/31 weighed more than 7kg. Box or drum magazines could be used, but the largest drum remained the most popular option.

The Romanian M1940 and M1941 Orita submachine-guns, with fixed wood and folding metal stocks respectively, were designed by Leopold Jaška and made by CMC at Cŭgir. The M1941 bore a superficial resemblance to the MP. 38, but had a crossbolt safety ahead of the trigger, a sliding selector on the right side of the receiver, and a unique design of tangent back-sight. It is believed that about 25,000 Oritas were made, but most were subsequently lost with the Romanian troops fighting alongside the Germans on the Russian Front.

Lanchester, Sten, Thompson M1 and M1A1, and U.S. M3/M3A1 'Grease Guns', captured from the Western Allies, were reissued in the last days of the war. The British guns were particularly useful, as they could fire standard 9mm pistol ammunition.

Regulation weapons

Machine-guns. Efforts were concentrated on accelerating production of the MG. 42, though Mauser and others were still experimenting with alternative designs. None of these had much effect on the service weapons of the Wehrmacht, as emphasis had been switched to airborne weapons that could defeat Allied aircraft, particularly the heavily armed B-17 Flying Fortress, and the growing numbers of Soviet tanks. These goals could not be achieved by small-arms ammunition; consequently, most of the conventional weapons were 30mm or even 5cm-calibre cannon.

Automatic rifles.   The Luftwaffe had once asked the army to participate in the development of a special rifle to arm paratroops. The specification requested the standard 7.9×57 chambering, selective fire, overall length no greater than one metre, weight that about the same as the Kar. 98k, and a large-capacity magazine. The army speedily rejected the proposal as unattainable, so the O.K.L. simply contacted Rheinmetall, Krieghoff, Mauser, Gustloff-Werke, Walther and other well-established arms makers independently.

Only Rheinmetall and Krieghoff responded, but the rising-block Krieghoff prototype was rejected in favour of the Stange-designed Rheinmetall gun. After development of the latter had been completed in the Rheinmetall-Borsig factory in Sömmerda, production of the *Fallschirmjägergewehr 42* began, ironically, in the Krieghoff factory in Suhl (code 'fzs').

The original FG. 42 had a 'straight-line' configuration, folding sights high above the bore, a pressed-steel butt, a sharply angled pistol grip to improve control, a short wooden fore-end/handguard, and a permanently attached bipod pivoted at the breech. A twenty-round box magazine fed laterally from the left side of the breech, and a special reversible spike bayonet was carried beneath the barrel.

The rifle was gas operated, relying on a long-stroke piston/bolt carrier to rotate the twin locking lugs on the bolt head. Among the oddest features was the method of selecting single shots or fully automatic fire by two differing sear/bolt carrier engagement notches. The bolt closed and locked in semi-automatic mode, the firing pin (mounted on the bolt carrier) reaching the cartridge only after the trigger was pressed; in automatic fire, the bolt and the bolt carrier were both released together from the rearmost position.

This gave an equally odd reloading procedure. Once the magazine had been emptied and removed, the bolt remained open only if the selector was set for fully automatic fire; pulling the trigger once the new magazine had been inserted caused the bolt to close, loading a new round, and the bolt carrier followed immediately to fire the gun. If single shots were being fired, however, the bolt shut as the spent magazine was withdrawn and the action needed to be retracted manually before shooting could recommence.

Progress with the FG. 42 was much slower than had been hoped. A report made in mid-July 1944 to the *Sonderauschuss für Maschinenpistolen & Maschinenkarabiner* (Sd. Au. MP u. MKb, 'Special Commission for Infantry Weapons') noted that Krieghoff had only delivered 250 guns. Field trials were still underway. Shortly afterwards, the gun was radically redesigned to save manganese steel. Carbon steel was substituted, but so many parts needed strengthening that the opportunity to redesign the FG. 42 to incorporate lessons learned from the field trials had been unexpectedly presented.

Changes included improving the muzzle brake; moving the bipod pivot to the muzzle, which enhanced stability; providing a variable-orifice gas regulator to cope with variations in ammunition pressure (or cumulative propellant fouling); packaging the trigger into a detachable unit; re-positioning the safety catch; fitting a wooden butt and a more conventional plastic pistol-grip; and adding a magazine cover and a spent case deflector. As the bolt stroke had been lengthened to reduce the violence of the breech movement, the FG. 42 II. was appreciably longer and larger than its predecessor. Only the bayonet remained unchanged. Like the earlier gun, the Model II was made by Krieghoff, but only a few thousand had been made before the end of the war. H.WaA. inventories indicate that 524 guns were accepted in 1944 and 3,873 early in 1945, but it is not clear whether others had been sent directly to the Luftwaffe. By 1944, theoretically at least, all small-arms procurement should have been channelled through the army authorities.

The FG. 42 has since attained a reputation entirely out of proportion to its numbers. The achievement seemed impressive enough to seduce many post-1945 commentators, but the gun had serious faults – difficult to control in automatic fire, a badly-placed magazine – as a result of a desire to provide an assault weapon chambered for the 7.9mm rifle cartridge.

It was also a glorious waste of resources, typifying the lack of control over the armed forces and the arms industry. The Soviet A.V.S. (Simonov) rifle had showed the perils of including a selective-fire capability in a gun of infantry-rifle weight, and the .30-calibre Johnson light machine-gun, which sought some of the same goals as the FG. 42, was appreciably heavier than the German gun. It is also worth recording that the tactical role of the FG. 42 was undefined; the Browning Automatic Rifle (B.A.R.) of 1918, successful if somewhat heavy in its intended role, had metamorphosed in the U.S. Army into a comparatively unsuccessful light machine-gun.

The severe losses suffered by the Fallschirmjäger during the attack on Crete in 1940 had severely damaged their image of invulnerability, and though proponents of airborne assault enjoyed periodic successes, these were never on a grand enough scale to impress Hitler. The development facilities and production-time wasted on the FG. 42 should rightly have been used to accelerate production of the MP. 43/St.G. 44 series.

Rifles.   In 1943, mindful of the declining economic situation, Mauser-Werke proposed introducing a simplified ('Vereinfachener') version of the Kar. 98k to eliminate unnecessary machining operations, conserve raw material, and accelerate production. The Oberkommando des Heeres accepted that the bolt-disassembly disc was to be replaced by a small cupped hole drilled through the extended sides of the buttplate; that the bayonet bar was to be replaced by a small sheet-metal plate attached to the tip of the fore-end with a wood screw (a change that was accepted particularly grudgingly); and that the cleaning rod was finally to be abandoned. These revisions ultimately created the Kar. 98k Kriegsmodell ('war model').

However, some of the more radical proposals were rejected. Mauser had wanted to leave the stock, the receiver and the bolt in their roughly machined state, except where bearing surfaces were involved, simplify the cocking piece/safety catch assembly, and fit butt plates that had not been hardened. Most military observers were concerned that changes of this type would suggest too openly that the progress of the war was no longer favouring the Germans. The same had happened when the British introduced the No. 4 rifle to replace the old Lee-Enfield No. 1 Mk III*, even though the changes were not based on any need to conserve materials or machine time but instead on a desire to modernise a pre-1914 design. The German military authorities resisted the most radical suggestions virtually until the end of the war; the ultra-crude *Volksgewehre* and *Volkskarabiner* had origins that were more political than military.

Most, but by no means all Kriegsmodelle displayed barrel bands that were stamped from sheet steel and welded along the bottom edge, and had thinly varnished laminated stocks, the result of trials that had stretched through the 1930s. Though plastic-coated metal stocks had been a failure, plywood laminates proved to be more resistant to warping than the conventional one-piece patterns; as a bonus, the wood did not require lengthy maturing and there was much less waste. It has been estimated that only two in every hundred laminated stocks failed inspection, compared with ten solid ones.

Variants of the Kar. 98k included the *Gebirgsjäger-Karabiner 98k*, a semi-experimental pattern with a large cast-steel plate on the left side of the butt. There were also several *Fallschirmjäger-Karabiner 98k* (paratroop rifles), at least one survivor having a hinged butt and another relying on a detachable barrel with an interrupted-screw joint ahead of the receiver.

Interest in sniping rifles still remained very high. Issue of the Zielfernrohrkarabiner 98k–Zf. 41 was greatly extended in February 1943, but the combination of gun and sight had been universally condemned by 1944. The objective lens of the sight was regarded as too small, light-gathering abilities were poor, the sight was prone to damage, and the magnification of just 1.5× was too small. The problems had arisen largely because the original demand for a sight of this type, for use on pillboxes and vehicles at normal ranges of engagement, had become lost in a desire to compete with the good long-range performance of the Russian Mosin-Nagant M91/30 sniping rifle.

The Germans tried a variety of solutions, including the introduction of a special long-rail side mount said to have been developed by J.P. Sauer & Sohn (code 'ce') in the autumn of 1943. The rail was attached to a specially thickened receiver wall that had been milled flat to increase the contact area between the rail and the gun. Guns of this type were made in quantity in the Gustloff-Werke factory in Weimar, and possibly on a more limited basis by Sauer. But the long-rail mount was no more successful than its predecessors, as the inferior accuracy of the rifle remained the limiting factor.

Single-claw mounts were also used, though possibly only by the police and SS units. These relied on one claw hooking into a base above the chamber and another entering a base on the receiver bridge, the unit being locked in place either by a sliding latch on the rear base or sprung catches on the rear claw. The design was neither particularly rigid nor 'zero-secure', and the manufacturers were allowed too much latitude to achieve any uniformity. A few two-claw commercial-type mounts have also been reported, probably used towards the end of the war when anything that could shoot was pressed into service.

The introduction of the Zielfernrohr K. 43 (Zf. K. 43) was intended to answer the problems. Eventually renamed 'Zf. 4' in December 1944[1], the sight was essentially a copy of the Russian P.U. in a one-piece mount that was clamped to the side rail with a radial lever. The sights had distinctive flattened sides. Hitler demanded that 25,000 sights should be made with the highest priority, fitted to Kar. 43 (Walthers) and sent to the Eastern Front. Even though the initial orders had not been fulfilled by July 1944, the request was then amplified to 25,000 sights monthly.

Most of the army experts regarded this as an indefensible waste of optical-industry capacity, as the accuracy of the Kar. 98k was still causing concern and the guns could not be trusted to achieve one-shot kills at anything over 200 metres. The Kar. 43 had proved to be even worse, and the assembly of 'sniping' auto-loaders was regarded as a complete waste of time. Even Fritz Walther had reported that the K. 43 could never be improved to shoot better than the bolt-action Mausers, but this did not stop the delivery of 53,435 optically sighted Karabiner 43 in 1944–5.

A few special monoblock side-rail mounts, made by Weihrauch ('eeo'), allowed Zf. 4 sights to be issed with the Kar. 98k. However, the probability of hits on a *man*-size target (not the desired head-size target!) was gloomily assessed in March 1945 as 80 per cent at 800 metres, 60 per cent at 1,000 metres, and only 40 per cent at 1,200 metres.

Another problem was caused by a shortage of special sights for the GwGrGt grenade launcher. In August 1944, therefore, the O.K.H. published details of a way in which sighting could be undertaken by using the existing back sight and various parts of the gun, such as the centre of the nosecap or the barrel band.[2] This ensured that fired grenades fell somewhere in the vicinity of the target in terms of range, though it was difficult to place them accurately owing to the impossibility of getting a proper sight picture through the rifle body!

Handguns. Experiments with the first simplified 'Volkspistolen' began in earnest, but had no tangible effects. The development of these guns is discussed in greater detail in Chapter Eight; the Wehrmacht continued to rely heavily on the P. 38 and a host of impressments.

Signal pistols. As the war progressed, so the quality of material declined and the standards of external finish deteriorated. Walther made some Heeresmodell signal pistols with steel barrels and frames in 1943, to conserve the valuable alloy for more important tasks, and a zinc-frame variant was developed in 1944. Apart from a noticeable increase in weight (to about 1,250gm), the guns were identical with the preceding alloy pattern apart from displaying 'ZINK 4' on their frames.

No Walther-made zinc-frame pistol has been identified, excepting some prototypes. However, guns of this type were made in quantity in 1944–5 by Erfurter Maschinenfabrik B. Geipel G.m.b.H., 'Erma-Werke' (code 'ayf') and Berlin-Lübecker Maschinenfabrik ('duv'), both of which had been making standard alloy-frame guns since 1940–1. An automotive battery maker, Motor-Condensator-Kompagnie Scholz K.G. of München ('dtd') also made a few zinc frame signal pistols in this period.

8

A Bitter End

On D-Day, 6 June 1944, the 'Second Front' was opened. Massive Allied forces, landing unexpectedly in Normandy instead of the Pas de Calais, soon consolidated their bridgeheads and broke out. By 29 June, Cherbourg had been liberated; on 9 July, the British entered Caen; Rennes fell to the U.S. 3rd Army on 4 August (the day Florence had fallen to the 8th Army in Italy); and the Seine had been reached by 20 August. By 11 September, most of France, Belgium and the Netherlands had been liberated, and the first U.S. Army patrols had crossed into German territory.

Despite the debacle at Arnhem, a vigorous German counter-attack aimed at regaining Nijmegen, and the so-called 'Battle of the Bulge' against U.S. forces in the Ardennes (16 December 1944–28 January 1945), the Allied advance on Germany rolled onward.

After a wholesale reorganisation of its resources on the Eastern Front, the Red Army had prepared Operation 'Bagration', an attack by the three White Russian Fronts and the First Baltic Front on German Army Group Centre. So many of the German units were under-strength that the Red Army could field four soldiers for each German, and six tanks for every Panzer.

'Bagration' was set for 22 June 1944, the third anniversary of the German invasion of the Soviet Union in 1941. Though the German commander of Group Centre foresaw the attack, his request to effect a strategic withdrawal fell on deaf ears; instead of the twenty-kilometre retreat recommended by Guderian, Hitler and Model would grant just three kilometres.

The result was a disaster for Germany. The massive Allied invasion through Normandy had forced the Wehrmacht to fight on two fronts instead of one, stretching resources to their limit, while the defection of Romania and then Bulgaria to the Allied cause brought the collapse of the Balkan theatre. Soon, the Red Army massed on the pre-war border with Poland. With merely 75 divisions, the Wehrmacht was to attempt to hold a front line stretching 1,100km against troops outnumbering them at least ten to one. Such had been the Soviet industrial recovery that there were now seven tanks for every Panzer; twenty Soviet field-guns for each German one; and perhaps twenty Soviet aircraft for each fighter the Luftwaffe could put into the air. Qualitatively, the Germans still held an important edge, but technical superiority had been frittered away uselessly; quantitatively, the Red Army now had a vast superiority in men, matériel and, perhaps, the will to win.

By early 1945, the Red Army stood on the borders of Germany in the east. Anglo-American forces, having broken through the Siegfried Line and pressed on across the Saarland, were approaching the river Rhein. On 16 February, Guderian mounted a last desperate counter-offensive to persuade the Russians to abandon a dash for Berlin and, instead, concentrate resources for a mass attack later in the spring. More than half a million German casualties had occurred during the retreat across Poland from the Vistula to the Oder.

As Soviet forces cleared the eastern part of the Reich and penetrated eastern Czechoslovakia, the Germans launched their final riposte – *Frühlingerwachsen*, 'awakening of spring'. Beginning on 6 March, the offensive achieved modest successes until the Red Army correctly selected one of the pro-German Hungarian armies blocking the route to Austria as the weakest part of the chain. Though the remnants of the German Panzer-Armee were successfully extricated, the collapse of the Hungarians allowed Tolbukhin, the Soviet Front commander, to march into Austria. Wien (Vienna) surrendered on 13 April 1945.

The day before Frühlingerwachsen had been launched, Köln (Cologne) had capitulated in the west; the day afterwards, 7 March, the

U.S. 1st Army crossed the river Rhein at Remagen; and, by the end of March, American, British and Canadian troops were racing across western Germany. These thrusts forced the Germans to draw units away from the Eastern Front and indirectly assisted the Russian passage to Berlin. With a distinct geographical advantage, Stalin had determined to be there first.

Early in April, having cleared the Oder-Neisse line, the Red Army formed three new Fronts under the command of Rokossovsky, Zhukov and Koniev. Zhukov had used his standing with Stalin to stake a claim for the final thrust, though the U.S.S.R. was also keen to prevent the Allies gaining too much of a foothold in territory that the Yalta Conference had accepted as the Russian Zone of post-war influence. The U.S. Army was already making great inroads towards the river Elbe and up into the Thüringerwald.

The final offensive was launched on 16 April 1945. The Germans managed to halt Soviet units in several places, and Zhukov's First Byelorussian Front, under Sokolovsky, initially failed to breach the German defences. By 19 April, however, Koniev had crossed the river Spree close to Spremberg; and Sokolovsky had taken Muncheberg, less than thirty kilometres east of Berlin.

Hitler's 56th birthday, on 20 April 1945, was marked by sporadic counter-attacks. These sorties, often undertaken by very few men without any effective armour or artillery support, were doomed to fail. On 21 April, the Russian 2nd Guards Tank Army breached the outer ring of Berlin's defences at Werneuchen, the 1st Guards Tank Army and 8th Guards Army reached the south-eastern suburbs, and the 3rd Guards Tank Army was occupying Königswusterhausen – just a few kilometres south of Berlin.

The German high command vainly awaited the initiative that was to be taken by General Steiner, whose army existed largely on paper. The trap was closing. Ammunition was almost all spent, morale was distintegrating, SS death squads were arbitrarily executing 'slackers' and 'cowards', and the fate of Germany's capital lay with the old men, invalids and child-soldiers who faced the Soviet juggernaut. Berlin was, however, being taken street by street, block by block, against defenders just as tenacious as the Russians had been at Stalingrad. Finally, on 30

April 1945, the red and gold hammer-and-sickle flag flew above the shattered Reichstag.

Within 24 hours, Hitler had committed suicide, Berlin had capitulated, and the surrender of all the remaining German forces was delayed
for little more than a week. The cost to Germany had been two million
soldiers killed or missing (few of the prisoners were ever to return) and
2.2 million civilian dead, most of whom had perished in the great
retreats of 1944–5 and Russian revenge for German rampages through
the Ukraine and the Baltic States in 1941–2.

To put these figures into context, British and Commonwealth casualties (dead, wounded and missing) to 10 April 1945 had amounted to
1.3 million servicemen, merchant seamen and civilians; and the U.S.
armed forces had lost about 400,000 dead, mostly in the Pacific Theatre.
However, the Soviet Union had lost 13.7 million men in combat, and
eleven million civilians to war, privation and disease. The total death-roll
of perhaps 55–60 million men, women and children is perhaps best
understood in the context of the death of the entire population of Britain
or France, or of one in every four American citizens.

The arms industry

The effects of the loss of occupied territory on arms production soon
became obvious. With the loss of Oberschlesien and the sequestered
facilities in Poland, hard-pressed German industry could deliver no
greater than a quarter of the monthly ammunition requirements, even
though the output of the weapons themselves was maintained surprisingly well. The biggest problem was a shortage of fuel for the aircraft and
the tanks, and the inability of the German railway system – rapidly being
wrecked by Allied bombing – to transport arms and munitions to where
they were most needed. The quality of small arms went into irreversible
decline in the first weeks of 1945, as did the fighting qualities of the conscripts. Virtually anything that could fire was pressed into service with
the Volkssturm (Home Guard) and the Hitler Youth.

Optimistic evacuation plans were laid, though little could be done
before the Third Reich collapsed. Nothing is known about the overall
scheme, though components from Radom were transported to Steyr

shortly before the Russians arrived and it is possible that much of Spreewerke P. 38 production was switched from Spandau to northern Bohemia.

Instructions sent in April 1945 from the Ministry of Armaments to the Mauser-Werke factory in Oberndorf noted that, if evacuation proved to be necessary, priority should be given to infantry weapons, the 2cm Flak. 38 and the MG. 151. The most important individual priority was the MK. 213 barrel-making plant, followed by the Kar. 98k barrel-making machinery, one entire production line for the Kar. 98k, and the original manufacturing drawings for the unexploited Mauser-Volksgewehr.[1]

The arms industry could not hope to equip an estimated 3.5 million home-defence troops with traditionally-made weapons, and it is assumed that the production of Volkswaffen was sanctioned on a local basis. Most of these were horrible – crudely made of bad materials, and often sources of potential danger to the firer. The most interesting was the *Volks-Gerät 1-5* (VG 1-5), sometimes known as the 'VG-5'[2], a delayed blowback autoloader designed by Barnitzke of Gustloff-Werke under orders from the Gauleiter of Thüringen, but comparatively few were made.

Volkskarabiner 98, based on the standard Kar. 98k, were made in the Walther and Steyr factories, while many workshops had been impressed to make submachine-guns modelled on the British Sten Gun. The story of these guns has never been satisfactorily told and, indeed, may never be known.

One of the most important problems that had faced German designers was caused by the Soviet tanks, which had rapidly advanced from the crude designs of the 1930s to the 'IS' (Iosif Stalin) of 1944, armed with a potent 122mm gun. The rapid failure of conventional Pz.B. 38 and Pz.B. 39, and the withdrawal of the s. Pz.B. 41 and its tungsten-cored shot, deprived German infantrymen of lightweight anti-tank weapons. Need became desperation when the T-34/76, T-34/85 and KV-1 tanks appeared in vast numbers, with armour that was thick enough to defeat all but the most powerful German anti-tank guns.

Anti-tank measures were soon helped considerably by the rediscovery of the Munroe Effect, originally used in railway construction, which allowed a cone-shape liner and a comparatively small charge of high explosive to pierce incredible thicknesses of steel plate. Most other forms of specialised anti-armour projectiles were immediately rendered obsolescent.

However, though hollow-charge ammunition could be provided for guns above 7.5cm calibre without exceeding bore diameter – and simply fired from the breech – small-calibre guns were far less suitable. As early as 1941, attempts were made to improve the performance of the obsolescent 3.7cm Pak. 36 and 5cm Pak. 38 by issuing finned *Steilgranaten*, with tail-rods protruding down the bore, but low velocity limited the engagement range to 200–300m.

Issued with guns as diverse as 3.7cm anti-aircraft guns and 15cm heavy infantry guns (s.IG. 33), a Steilgranate could penetrate as much as 18cm of armour plate and threatened even the best Soviet tanks, but the 5cm Pak. 38 weighed 1,000kg in action and was scarcely ideal for 'shoot and run' engagements necessitated by short-range projectiles. Consequently, Steilgranaten were little more than last-ditch weapons to be used when the gun was seriously threatened. By 1943, lighter and more mobile solutions were vital.

Though recoilless guns promised a useful combination of light weight and power, they had also proved extremely wasteful of propellant, and excessive back-blast from the venturi-type breech instantly revealed the gun's position to the enemy after each shot. These would not be the answer to the anti-tank problem.

A better 'one-man' solution came in the form of a copy of the U.S. 2.36 M1 Bazooka, the 8.8cm Raketenpanzerbüchse 54 (R. Pz.B. 54), which was not officially adopted until August 1944.[3] Though the R. Pz.B. 54 still suffered excessive back-blast, it weighed less than 11kg and was easily moved to a new site after each shot. Issued widely to Panzerzerstörer-Bataillone and Panzer-Grenadiere by the end of the Second World War, the 'German Bazooka' was made in two versions: R. Pz.B. 54 of August 1944, with a bar igniter; and the later R. Pz.B. 54/I. of 20 December 1944 with a ring-contact system.

The perfected single-shot throwaway Panzerfaust ('armoured fist'), designed by Dr Langweiler of Hugo Schneider A.G. ('HASAG'), Leipzig, appeared in the summer of 1943. Comprising a large hollow-charge stick bomb loaded into a tube containing the propellant, Panzerfaust came with a crude sight and trigger system. At short range, it was exceptionally effective and could penetrate 14–20cm of armour plate. Disadvantages included a back-blast that gave a two-metre sheet of flame.

Several versions were made, beginning with the Panzerfaust 30 (two versions, with small- and large-head bombs), then progressing to Panzerfaust 60 and Panzerfaust 100. The figures indicated the recommended maximum engagement range, though the Panzerfaust 60 was sighted to 80m and the Panzerfaust 100 was sighted to 150m. Loaded weight varied between 3.1 and 6.8kg, depending on size, while overall length was 1.03m (Models 30 and 60) or 1.15m (Model 100). Manufacturers included the HASAG factories in Leipzig (code 'wa') and Schlieben ('wk'), Oerlikon Bührle & Co., and, apparently, Rheinische Gummi- & Celluloid-Fabrik of Mannheim ('dsu'). They were issued to the army and the Waffen-SS, and then to the Volkssturm.

The effective range of the Raketenpanzerbüchse and Panzerfaust was comparatively short, resulting in a demand for a mobile but lightweight weapon capable of consistently hitting one-metre square targets 750m away. As this seemed to be beyond the capability of anything other than conventional anti-tank artillery, a new solution was sought in the 'high/low pressure system', credited to Rheinmetall-Borsig though the basic idea had been tried in the Zalinski Dynamite Gun late in the nineteenth century.

Zalinski had used the propellant to compress air through an intermediary piston, allowing the smooth launch of a delicate projectile laden with comparatively unstable explosive. The Zalinski shell had a leisurely flight and restricted range, but undoubtedly worked well within its limitations. In the context of 1944-vintage anti-tank warfare, the advantages of the system were perceived to be greater than the drawbacks.

Rheinmetall's Panzer-Abwehr-Werfer 600 (Paw. 600), later rechristened 'Panzer-Abwehr-Kanone [Pak.] 8H63', was very light for its bore-size – even the perfected weapon weighed a mere 600kg in action. It fired the unique W.Gr. Patr. Hl. 4462, comprising a modified 8cm mortar-bomb attached to a heavy iron plate over which the mouth of a standard 10.5cm le. FH. 18 cartridge-case had been crimped. The Paw. 600 was loaded and fired conventionally, but events thereafter were anything but conventional; gas bled through the venturi holes into the space between the mortar-bomb sealing rings and the base-plate, but at greatly reduced pressure compared with the confinement chamber (the shell case). A shear-pin connecting the tail of the bomb with the base-plate ruptured once the pressure behind the bomb had increased to the desired level, and the projectile flew forward out of the muzzle.

The smoothbore Paw. 600 could defeat 14cm of armour plate even at its maximum effective engagement range of 750m, while consuming only about 360gm of standard propellant. However, the perfection of the system coincided with declining German fortunes; only about 250 guns were made in the last four months of the Second World War.

To supplement conventional infantry weapons, German scientists also dreamed up several extraordinary ideas. Among them were the *Wirbelgeschütz* ('vortex gun') and the sound cannon, both originating at an aerodynamic institute in the Tirol. The vortex gun made use of the well-known ability of slow-burning explosive to create vortices that would wrench aircraft apart, or so its designer hoped, but the problem of achieving sufficient height was never solved. The sound cannon featured a three-metre diameter parabolic mirror, amplifiers and a series of detonating chambers to produce a continuous high-pitched note that could kill small animals at short range. But neither of these freakish ideas was battle-worthy in any sense of the term.

Nor was the Hänsler Electric Gun, which relied on a variation of the linear motor principle to launch a continuous stream of projectiles at London . . . but was found to need a colossal power station to do so. Another fruitless exercise was the Cönders *Tausendfüßler* ('millipede'), a long-barrelled multi-chamber gun designed to bombard London from a site at Mimoyèques, near Calais. Lateral chambers connected to the bore contained additional propellant charges fired a microsecond or two after the projectile passed, the goal being hyper-velocity, but the developers were never able to time the ignition of the boosters accurately. The Royal Air Force destroyed the Mimoyèques site before any Cönders guns could be installed.

The *höhere Feuerfolge* (HF) system had more relevance to small-arms technology. It sought to achieve ultra-high rates of fire by using a single large propellant charge in a special cartridge to push separate projectiles

– from eight to twenty-seven, according to a Kummersdorf report in August 1943 – around a helical channel and then up and out through the barrel. The goal was a theoretical fire-rate in excess of 20,000 rounds per minute.

Designed and patented by Bela Zettl, an employee of the Hungarian state optical manufactory, the basic idea proved to work regardless of the grave doubts expressed by the German military small-arms experts. However, continual jamming was never satisfactorily conquered and what began as a promising anti-aircraft weapon finally disappeared into anonymity.

The HF15, which was to have been fed from a six-chamber cylinder, used a nine-round cartridge. Overall gun-length was 1.58m and it weighed about 20kg. A proposed five-barrel installation was calculated to have a theoretical fire-rate of 107,000 rds/min! Experimental guns were actually made and fired. However, even disregarding declining muzzle velocity, evident in the last three bullets of each series, ballistics were very unpredictable and the use of nose-fuzed high-explosive projectiles proved catastrophic.

Accuracy at 100m was quite acceptable – the bursts usually fell in a 10cm-diameter circle – but the severe problems were never entirely resolved and, it is believed, the whole project had already been abandoned when fighting ceased. A 7.9mm-calibre single-barrel 'one salvo' (nine-projectile) Zettl infantry rifle, claimed to have been developed by Gustloff-Werke in Suhl, had also proved abortive.

Captured and non-standard weapons

As the situation worsened for the Germans, and the Soviet noose grew tighter, increasing numbers of non-standard weapons were pressed into service. Attempts were made to convert a variety of captured small arms to chamber the 7.9mm Patrone s.S., but the success of these endeavours is very difficult to determine. In August 1944, the Generalstab des Heeres ordered a variety of machine-gun conversions to be given distinctive marks.[4]

These included the Soviet le. MG 120 (r) and 's. MG. Maxim (r)', and three Italian guns – le. MG 099 (i), s. MG. 255 (i) and s. MG. 259

(i) – that were to be given the marks 'S S' to remind firers that they chambered German ammunition. One of the Soviet submachine-guns, the MP 717 (r), altered to chamber the 9mm Pist. Patr. 08, displayed a large 'D' beneath the serial number on the receiver. These supplementary letters, to be at least 10mm high, were applied in a variety of positions specified in the directive, but usually so that they could be seen by looking down on top of the action.

The Italian machine-guns are believed to have been the 6.5mm Mo. 30 Breda, which had also been made in 7.35mm for the Italian army and 7.92mm for export; the 8mm FIAT-Revelli Mo. 35; and the 8mm Mo. 37 Breda ground gun. As only the gas-operated 8mm Mo. 37 made an effective weapon (the others were delayed blowbacks), the transformation process smacks of desperation.

The 1930-type Breda was a particularly unusual gun, crammed with strange features. The pivoting magazine lay on the right side of the breech, spent cases being ejected across the firer, and the butt had a folding shoulder plate. The feed lips were machined in the breech – instead of relying on comparatively flimsy box magazines – and the guns had a reputation for reliable performance as long as the magazine case was undamaged. More than 28,000 of them were on hand in August 1939, and work continued throughout the war. It is suspected that many were seized after the Italians withdrew from the war, but only 150 are known to have been supplied to the German forces (in May 1944).

Mystery surrounds the 15,420 'Italienisches Gewehre' ('Italian rifles') acquired by the O.K.H. in 1945. These may be 7.9mm conversions of 7.35mm Mo. 38 Mannlicher-Carcano short rifles, undertaken in Cremona during the German withdrawal northward and subsequently evacuated with the troops. Distinguished by a large 'S' above the chamber, these guns were only marginally strong enough to withstand the additional chamber pressure.

Regulation weapons

Machine-guns.   As the war ran its course, supplies of conventional ground machine-guns ran too short to arm the Volkssturm and other last-ditch units formed to defend the Fatherland. One expedient was to convert many surviving aircraft machine-guns to ground roles, the most favoured being rifle-calibre observers' guns. The addition of simple bipods and rudimentary stocks soon provided many serviceable designs, lacking only the replaceable barrels of the best land-service guns. Though these conversions were generally incapable of prolonged sustained fire, they did provide effective light-support weapons for troops who would otherwise have had none.

As rifle-calibre guns had become increasingly ineffective against aircraft from 1941 onward, presaging a move to the 15mm MG. 151 and then to 20mm cannon, it is suspected that the earliest conversions were made about 1943 for Luftwaffe ground-defence forces. By the end of the war, however, many other combinations had been tried.

Though the MG. 42 was still being made in 1945 and a strengthened buffered MG.-Lafette 43 was being tested, the German authorities were also experimenting with the so-called MG. 42V (or 'MG. 45'). Apparently being developed by Mauser at Oberndorf, this resembled the standard gun except for its delayed-blowback breech – the forerunner, in fact, of the post-war Heckler & Koch patterns. The first MG. 42V, with a distinctive half-length barrel shroud, dated from June 1944. Five similar weapons followed immediately, and improved patterns appeared towards the end of the year. Total production is unlikely to have exceeded ten.

The MG. 45 weighed a little less than 9kg, fired the standard metal-link belt and offered a remarkable cyclic rate of 1,800rpm that would have made it impossible to control satisfactorily on a bipod. One gun allegedly fired 120,000 specially manufactured steel-case cartridges with practically no trouble, a testimony to the qualities of the basic design and the care with which the ammunition had been prepared.

Assault rifles.   Despite the success of the MP. 43, or perhaps because of it, many other companies commenced work on assault rifles as early as 1942. Among them was Mauser, whose Gerät 06 featured a gas-operated roller-locked breech system generally credited to Wilhelm Stähle. The project was subsequently developed by a research team lead by Ernst Altenburger and Lugwig Vorgrimler, whose names are most often associated with it.

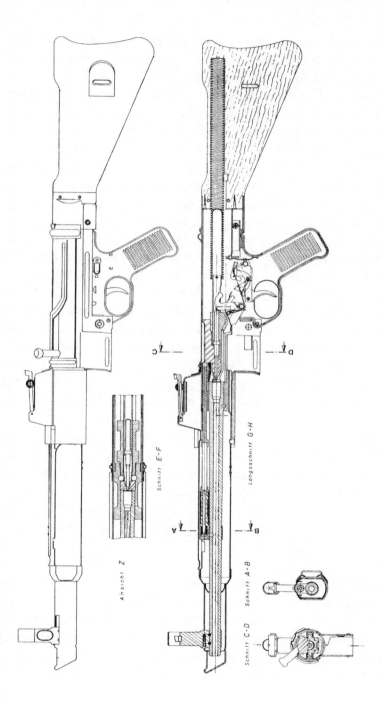

Schnitt E–F

Ansicht Z

Langsschnitt G–H

Schnitt A–B

Schnitt C–D

9. Drawings of the StG. 45 (M) or Gerät 06 (H), a gas-operated assault rifle developed as a potential replacement for the MP. 43 series. The roller-locked breech was an adaptation of the MG. 42, and led directly to the post-war CETME/Heckler & Koch designs.

Identifying the Mauser prototypes is hindered by confusion in surviving documents. There were two basic designs: a gas-operated locked-breech gun intended for the H.WaA.; and a delayed blowback developed privately. The locked-breech guns were apparently allotted development codes V. 5823 (first prototype) and V. 5911 (for an improved gun with a 'new shape' receiver), while the blowback was M. 7066. These suggest dates of early 1943 and the middle of 1944 respectively. Should this be true, then the designation 'StG. 45 (M)' applies to Gerät 06 rather than Gerät 06 (H).

Gerät 06, apparently V. 5823, vaguely resembled the old Walther-made MKb. 42 (W), with a straight-line layout and the back sight carried on a high block. However, the detachable box magazine was positioned much closer to the trigger/pistol-grip group and a cranked cocking aperture lay on the left side of the breech. The gun had a light sheet-metal barrel casing, a distinctive muzzle-brake/compensator and an MP. 43-type butt. The Gerät 06 No. 2 (V. 5911?) was essentially similar, but once had a simpler butt and lacked the muzzle brake. The surviving gun has a plain flat-sided sheet-metal barrel jacket, although its butt has (some time in the past) become detached and lost.

The third gun, Gerät 06 (H), probably M. 7066, had a modified breech in which the rollers simply delayed the opening stroke. This permitted the gas system to be deleted altogether. Owing to the similarity between Geräte 06 and 06 (H), it is assumed that development was concurrent. The H.WaA. is known to have been suspicious of the delayed blowback design, though Mauser apparently favoured it on the grounds of simplicity. The guns all chamber the 7.9mm Pist. Patr. 43 or 'Kurz-Patrone'.

Guns other than Mausers were tested by the H.WaA., but few are identifiable. In December 1944, for example, the Gerät 06 was to be tested against Rheinmetall-Borsig and Grossfuss designs (expected to be delivered in January 1945) and possibly also a Haenel. Nothing is known about the Rheinmetall gun, though the Grossfuss pattern had a gas-retarded wedge-lock. The so-called Haenel StG. 45 (H) was a greatly simplified MP. 43, somewhat resembling the MKb. 42 (H), but remained incomplete by the end of the war. An additional Gustloff-Werke prototype, credited to Barnitzke, relied on gas impinging on a muzzle cup to delay the MP. 43 breech-stroke, despite the removal of the locking lugs, while Spreewerke and Steyr-Daimler-Puch are also said to have participated in the design competition.

Most of the small arms that reached service were relatively conventional. Small-calibre rocket or ramjet projectiles, briefly mentioned in the ammunition Appendix, were never likely to succeed; indeed, neither were the full-size shells. Among the more optimistic ideas was the curved barrel, or Krummlauf device.

This was conceived to protect tank and armoured vehicle crews whose firing ports had blind spots. Originally to be used in conjunction with ball mounts, Krummläufe were developed for the Kar. 98k in several differing guises. Considerable experimentation was necessary to find not only the ideal form for the barrel-attachment system, but also the radius of the barrel-curve and adjustment needed in the bore dimensions. Many of the earliest prototypes ruptured either on the first shot or after sufficient shots had been fired to weaken the outer side of the curve.

After the introduction of the MP. 43, the Krummlauf was adapted to provide an urban infantry weapon that could shoot around corners without the firer exposing his head or body to enemy retaliation. A reflector sight was incorporated in the Krummlauf body-hood, the extent of deflection being 30-, 40- or even 90 degrees. Needless to say, even though the concept was eventually made to work efficiently, few Krummläufe were ever issued for service. Whether they had any true utility can only be questioned.

Excepting the Tokarev, the Germans impressed few semi-automatic rifles prior to the Allied invasions of North Africa, Italy and Europe, when small numbers of M1 Garands and M1 Carbines (or 'Selbstladekarabiner 655 [a]') were captured. A few semi-experimental rifles were seized after the invasion of Czechoslovakia, but none of these had attained anything other than limited export sales. The most commonly reported were the Holek-designed Č.Z.-made Z.H. 29, which had been made in appreciable quantity, and a handful of Č.Z. vz. 'S' (c. 1929) and vz. 35 guns. As even the strangest weapons were pressed into service in the last desperate days of the war, it is not surprising that Czechoslovakian semi-automatics – particularly those chambering standard 7.9mm cartridges – were taken from German troops in 1944–5. This simply makes their importance seem greater than it actually was.

The most interesting Volksgewehre was the Versuchs-Gerät 1-5 (sometimes called 'Volksgewehr 1-5', VG. 1-5 or VG-5), produced by Gustloff-Werke in 1945 to the design of Barnitszke. Though the rifle was very crudely made, with a sheet-steel barrel casing, a folded-strip back sight and badly-finished woodwork riveted to the frame, it embodied a sophisticated delayed-blowback action relying on gas bled from the barrel into the annular gap between the barrel and its outer casing. This opposed the breech stroke until chamber pressure declined to a safe level.

Volksgewehre were rarely sanctioned officially; their development was generally kept secret from Hitler, who disapproved greatly of such crudity. Indeed, the VG. 1-5 was apparently developed solely on the initiative of the Gauleiter of the Thüringen district – which was particularly vulnerable to the Russians. Most surviving examples lack Waffenamt marks, but have identifiers such as 'Th.1839' stamped into the butt.

A requirement for an assault rifle chambering the full-power 7.9mm rifle round caused Mauser to begin work on several projects – apparently Geräte 02, 03 and 07 – while a Gustloff prototype known as the MKb. 42 (G) 'für Gewehrpatrone' later developed into the Gew. 43 (G). The Gustloff gun, based on the old MG. 13 light machine-gun, featured a tipping bolt and a 25-round box magazine. A very distinctive prototype made by Knorr-Bremse also survived the war, together with at least one unidentifable weapon. Whether these are contemporary with the FG. 42, MKb. 42, or even the Gew. 43, is not yet known.

Rifles.   The Kar. 98k had been made in colossal numbers by legions of contractors. In addition to two Mauser-owned factories in Oberndorf am Neckar ('S/42', '42', 'byf' and 'svw') and Berlin-Borsigwalde ('S/243', '243' and 'ar'), guns had been made by Sauer & Sohn of Suhl ('S/147', '147' and 'ce'), Berlin-Lübecker Maschinenfabrik of Lübeck ('S/237' or '237'), Waffenwerk Brünn AG of Brno ('dot') and Povaska Bystrica ('dou'), Feinmechanische Werke GmbH of Erfurt ('S/27', '27' and 'ax'), Gustloff-Werke of Weimar ('bcd') and Steyr-Daimler-Puch AG of Steyr/Oberdonau ('660', 'bnz'). Many others made components, particularly the companies that had operated as part of the 'Sachsengruppe' prior to the Second World War. These had supplied components marked with a single letter ('a'–'z') to the Gustloff-Werke factory in Weimar, where the guns were assembled.

The total output of Kar. 98k remains unknown. The most comprehensive assessment is probably slightly greater than 14 million, made by Robert Jensen and Ralph Riccio, in Richard Law, *Sniper Variations of the German K98k Rifle* (1996).

Interestingly, working with much less data, I concluded in *The German Rifle* (1979) that the total would be about 15 million, and there may yet be information to find. The total for the Mauser factory in Oberndorf given in the Jensen/Riccio figurework, for example, is substantially higher than that given in the postwar Allied C.I.O.S. report.

H.WaA. procurement figures record acceptance of 7,413,767 Kar. 98k and 126,981 'Zf.-Kar. 98k' from 2 September 1939 to 1 April 1945, in addition to 699,758 essentially similar Gew. 24 (t) and Gew. 29 (p).[5] These totals probably include rifles issued in the navy, but not those that were destined for the Luftwaffe, which were procured and inventoried separately (at least until 1943).

The Zielfernrohrkarabiner, K98k–Zf. 41 had been downgraded to simply 'Karabiner' in the summer of 1944, reflecting the universal lack of faith in the sight, but few changes were made to the design or construction of the Kar. 98k in the last years of the war. Though winter triggers for the Kar. 98k and MP. 40 were introduced officially in October 1944[6], similar fittings had been issued in Russia in 1941–2, on a local basis, and had even been the subject of an instruction leaflet issued in October 1943.[7]

Typical of the unrealistic view taken of the military situation by Hitler and his immediate circle was a request for forty thousand sniping rifles to be delivered to the Wehrmacht in 1945. Fulfilment was delayed by shortages of Zf. 4 (even though production was supposed to be proceeding at 25,000 per month), and because production of the special spring-steel retaining rings was entrusted to just one manufacturer, Weihrauch of Zella-Mehlis.

A last-minute attempt was also made to issue snipers with explosive 'B'-Patronen to counter the use by the Russians of similar ammunition. Rounds of this type were theoretically banned by the Geneva Convention, but the approval of deliberate anti-personnel use at the highest levels reflected just how low the conduct of the war had sunk.

The final deterioration of the German bolt-action rifles was the ultra-crude *Volksgewehr* or "People's Rifle". The earliest apparently dates from the autumn of 1944, though specifications had been circulated some months previously. The goal was a simplified rifle that could be made with a minimum of machine-time or raw material.

A simplified Kar. 98k was developed by Mauser-Werke, the Volkskarabiner 98 (VK. 98) were made by Steyr-Daimler-Puch (code 'bnz'), Walther ('qve') and others, and Volksgewehre were contributed by many anonymous machine shops. Most of these guns chambered the standard 7.9mm S-Patrone, though the Mauser-Volkskarabiner I and II accepted the 7.9mm Kurz ammunition.

Excepting the 'last-ditch' Volksgewehre made in Thüringen in April 1945, the guns all had conventional Mauser-type bolt actions. VK. 98 had half stocks, fixed-notch backsights and roughly finished 'stepped' or cylindrical barrels. However, though their finish was notably rough, they were not as poorly made as the Volksgewehre ('VG.').

Chambering either 7.9mm S-Patrone or Pist. Patr. 43, the Volksgewehre have been credited to Erfurter Maschinenfabrik B. Geipel G.m.b.H. 'Erma-Werke' ('ayf'), among others. Most featured stamped and welded receivers, and had simple bolts with no more than two locking lugs. They had plain cylindrical bolt handles made from bar-stock, roughly planed woodwork (often with separate butts and fore-ends), and accepted neither bayonets nor grenade launchers. Though standard Gew. 43 box magazines were usually fitted, some of the last guns were single-shot only.

No official orders governing the introduction of these Volkswaffen have ever been found, though the H.WaA. was ordered to develop an effectual weapon and army procurement figures indicate the acceptance in 1945 of 53,033 guns (type unknown). It is suspected that these were VK. 98, and that most of the cruder guns were procured on a local basis; some may have been made by the manufacturers purely for last-ditch local defence, without even telling local Party officials.

Submachine-guns.   The MP. 40 was made until the very end of the war, though manufacturing quality declined appreciably in the last months of 1944 and the guns made in 1945 were characterised by a particularly high rate of failure at final inspection. A winter-trigger unit, the Winterabzug MP., was officially introduced in October 1944 simultaneously with the Winterabzug 98 for the Kar. 98k (q.v.), though similar designs were being used unofficially on the Eastern Front as early as the autumn of 1942.

As the war progressed, the emphasis had shifted from quality to quantity. Based on surviving Heereswaffenamt proof-house returns, about 1.11 million submachine-guns were accepted from the beginning of 1940 to the end of the war. However, this figure included a quantity of Beretta and other guns, and it is generally agreed that production of MP. 40 (peaking in July 1943 at about 20,600 monthly) did not exceed 950,000. Changes made in construction included the addition of flutes in the magazine body to improve feed[8] and revisions in the design of the receiver. Most of the guns made in the Steyr factory from the autumn of 1943 onwards, for example, had the frame and receiver-cap made integrally instead of separately. Some of the guns made in 1944–5 were fitted with MG. 42 springs that had been cut in half – much easier to make than the complicated Vollmer-type telescoping-spring assembly – but the stiffness of the machine-gun springs increased the cyclic rate to a virtually uncontrollable 1,100–1,200 rds/min.

Erma-Werke had produced a prototype all-metal submachine-gun in 1943 (the so-called 'EMP. 44'), but it had been rejected by the H.WaA. and only a handful of guns were completed. However, the EMP. 44 was an interesting design, with a double magazine unit and a pivoting 'flip-over' back sight in a prominent housing above the magazine feedway. It is now difficult to decide whether the gun would have been refined had it reached production status, or if it was a special-purpose design with a hollow tubular pistol grip that acted as part of a mount.

Though the MP. 40 was reasonably simple, captured British Sten Guns had shown the Germans that submachine-guns could be produced much more crudely, yet still work acceptably. The first German attempt to copy the Sten was the so-called 'Gerät Potsdam', a precise copy of the Sten Mk II – even to the minor proof- and inspectors' marks – developed by the Mauser-Werke factory in Oberndorf as project V. 7081, apparently under contract to the Reichssicherheitshauptamt ('RSHA'). The drawings had been completed by October 1944, production commencing in November and finishing in January 1945. 28,000 guns were to be issued to pro-German forces behind the Allied lines, but Mauser made only 10,000 of them. Assuming the contracts were completed, Haenel and Sauer may have been the other contractors.

Though Gerät Potsdam guns were subsequently issued to the Volkssturm and other emergency units defending the Reich to the bitter end, they never fulfilled the role for which they had been conceived.

Concurrently with work on Gerät Potsdam, Mauser modified the Sten design so that it could be made by metalworking companies with the most meagre equipment. Known as Project V. 7083, the resulting MP. 3008 or 'Gerät Neumünster' was put into immediate production in the autumn of 1944. However, none of the 50,000 expected in December was delivered and management of the project was given to Sonderkommission Waffen 12 in January 1945.

Work was entrusted to companies with no previous experience of gunmaking. Despite optimistic predictions that monthly production, initially set at 1,000 guns per plant, would rapidly reach 200,000, it is believed that less than 10,000 guns were accepted before the end of the war. Several differing patterns have been identified, which indicates the degree of latitude in the basic design.

The MP. 3008 was a near facsimile of the Sten Mk II, but had a vertical MP. 40-type magazine and a trigger retained with staked pins. A selector ran laterally through the trigger housing above and ahead of the trigger guard, permitting single shots to be fired when it was pressed to the right and fully automatic operation when pressed to the left. The stock was originally a skeletal pattern, but some guns were made (apparently by 'tjk') with a reinforced tubular strut.

A typical MP. 3008 was 800mm long, had a 200mm barrel and weighed 2.95kg when empty. The guns were usually very poorly made, with phosphated components and brick red or black stove-enamelling on the barrel, receiver and frame. Among the manufacturers said to have been involved in the programme were Mauser-Werke of Oberndorf (codes 'byf' and 'svw'); Haenel of Suhl ('fxo'); Mitteldeutsche-Schweiz-Industrie of Weissenfels; Frebel of Oldenburg; W.J. Hölzen of Löhne; Carl Eickhorn of Solingen ('cof'); Gustav Appel of Berlin; Walter Steiner Eisenkonstruktion of Suhl ('nea'); Blohm & Voss of Hamburg; and

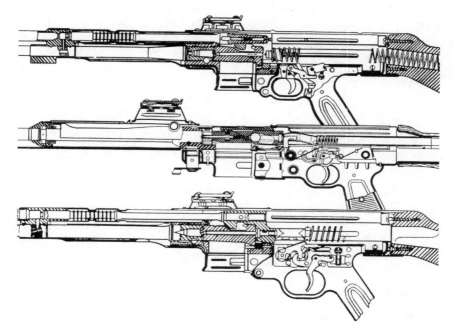

10. Comparative sectional drawings of the Maschinenkarabiner: *top to bottom*, the MKb. 42 (H), MKb. 42 (W) and MP 43.

Gottfried Linder A.G. of Bremen. Unidentified codes 'rde', 'tjk' and 'tvw' have also been found.

The status of some of these in relation to the MP. 3008 is questionable. No guns have even been reported with Mauser or Haenel markings, the former being involved merely as the originator of the project, and the identification of those attributed to Blohm & Voss relies solely on the appearance of a 'B&V' trademark on the frame of a very non-standard gun. Steiner's MP. 3008 may be distinguished from the others by the knurled cocking handle and a flat cross-brace inside the skeletal butt-frame.

Requests that the MP. 3008 should be tested as a grenade launcher, apparently made by the R.S.H.A. were initially treated with derision. However, trials undertaken in January 1945 with specially-loaded 9mm Pl. Patr. 08 showed that, despite its crudity, the MP. 3008 was strong enough to project grenades an appreciable distance. The major problem was that the pre-rifled ammunition tended to twist the gun in the firer's hands, making firing unnecessarily tiring.

Handguns.   Guns seized from vanquished armies, made in sequestered facilities or purchased abroad were supplemented with Italian Mo. 34 (9mm Short) and Mo. 35 (7.65mm Auto) Beretta blowbacks – some taken after the collapse of the Italian army in 1943, though about 19,800 additional Mo. 34 were made specifically for the Italian socialist army and Italian-based German units in 1944–5.

Webley, Colt and Smith & Wesson revolvers were captured from the Anglo-American forces; U.S. .45 M1911A1 Colt-Browning pistols, taken from the U.S. Army, were greatly appreciated on account of their prodigious stopping power; and obr. 1895g gas-seal Nagant revolvers, plus smaller quantities of obr. 1930g Tokarev pistols, were still being used in Russia.

Another solution was sought in the form of a *Volkspistole*, or "people's pistol", that was simple enough to be produced in enormous quantities in factories that had had no previous experience of precision metalworking. Mauser's so-called 'Gerät 40' pre-dated a visit by senior Wa.-Prüf. officials to the Oberndorf factory in June 1943, but only drawings and a wooden model had been made.

Though the project had originated late in 1942, when it had been allotted the identifier 'M. 7057', the first prototype was not ready until February 1944 and a second followed in June. The guns were made largely of sheet-steel, and were locked by tipping the barrel so that a transverse channel above the chamber engaged a shoulder that had been crimped inside the slide. M. 7057 had a double-action trigger with an exposed hammer spur and a radial safety high on the left side of the slide above the ribbed pressed-metal grips. Two single-strand wire recoil springs in the butt, one each side of the magazine, were the ultimate expression of the patent granted to Mauser engineers Altenburger & Seidel in 1938 (DRP 17,799). However, M. 7057 failed to elicit official backing and was abandoned in January 1945; nothing had been done since October 1944.

The true Mauser Volkspistole apparently bore the internal development code 'V. 7082'. It was originally a double-action striker-fired blowback, made from heavy-gauge steel pressings, and had been completed by October 1944. It was tested by Wa.-Prüf. 2 in November, against a double-action Walther blowback, but a hold-open and a lanyard ring were requested and the guns were returned to their promoters. Trials undertaken at Döberitz in December 1944 then led to the rejection of the double-action trigger system and a request that a breech-opening delay should be incorporated. A single-action blowback was the immediate result, though the Oberndorf development department was conducting simultaneous trials with fluted chambers and 'gas pockets' to delay the initial rearward movement of the breech.

Previously often attributed to Gustloff-Werke, one surviving modified V. 7082 features a unique gas-bleed delay in which part of the gas propelling the bullet seeps through ports in the barrel to impinge on the inner surfaces of the slide. This helps to keep the breech shut until residual chamber pressure decays to a safe level. On 20 January 1945, one gun of this type and another with an experimental lead buffer were tested in Oberndorf against a conventional double-action blowback numbered 'V.102'.

Walther's first projects included a 9mm pistol with a rotating-barrel lock adapted from the Austrian Steyr-Pistole M. 12, plus a blowback sharing an essentially similar frame. Though made largely of stampings, the surprisingly good finish, the attention to detail in the small parts and the quality of the blueing suggest pre-1944 origins. It is assumed that the rotating-barrel gun competed against the M. 7057 Mauser design. A variant of the P. 38 with a lengthened frame and a full-length stamped-sheet slide may date from this period. The surviving specimen actually bears 'No. 2' beneath a small Walther banner, but the identity of 'No. 1' (unless it is the rotating barrel gun) remains to be determined. Mauser also made a few examples of the HSc with stamped slides, but these are unlikely to have made the savings in machine time and material that the O.K.H. was demanding.

Walther then proceeded to much cruder sheet-steel guns, including a greatly simplified version of the the P. 38 – sometimes identified as the original pistol prototype – and a single-action blowback. The locked-breech gun, incorporating a radical revision of the Barthelmes lock found in the P. 38, was made largely of sturdy pressings and is suspected to date from the later period of the Volkspistole (probably the autumn or winter of 1944).

The oldest type of Walther blowback offered comparatively good quality, a double-action trigger system, wood grips, blued finish and acceptable attention to detail. It is assumed to be the pattern tested against Mauser's original double-action V. 7082 in November 1944; as the Walther offers much better quality than the Mauser, it would have been more expensive and time-consuming to produce – precisely the opinion offered in surviving documents. This gun was probably followed by a simplified double-action pattern in December 1944 and, finally, by the well-known single-action type that must date from early 1945.

Gustloff-Werke's participation in the simplified pistol and Volkspistole projects is confirmed by surviving Mauser documents, though no guns have yet been identified. There were also three simple revolvers submitted by Mauser, Deutsche-Werke and Böhmische Waffenfabrik, but no details have been located.

Appendix 1: Small-arms Ammunition

The details that follow are concerned only with ammunition that was considered to be standardised in the Wehrmacht. However, the impressment of so many captured weapons added an additional dimension to the quartermasters' jobs. Though most of the Czechoslovakian, Polish and Yugoslavian weapons chambered cartridges that were supposedly identical with the German 7.9mm Gewehr-Patrone, fractional differences in tolerances created feed problems in automatic weapons; eventually, in 1944, the use of non-standard ammunition in the MG. 34 and MG. 42 was expressly prohibited.

Captures of 7.62×54mm rimmed Soviet ammunition were so great, indeed, that the Germans did not attempt to convert Soviet weapons for their own cartridges until the end of the war. Belgian 7.65×53mm semi-rim rounds were among those that were typically issued for training purposes, an O.K.H. directive dating from 1943 indicating that the 'Patr. 260 (b)', loaded with an ogival bullet, could be used at distances up to 600 metres in the Mauser rifles, Gew. 262 (b) and 263 (b), and in the FN-Browning Mle 1930 automatic rifle, le. MG. 127 (b).[1]

6.35mm Auto

This, the standard .25 ACP round introduced with the Baby Browning pistol in 1906, was rare in German service. However, it chambered in the Astra 200 as well as the many pocket pistols purchased by individual soldiers as a last-resort defence. Ammunition was purchased from commercial stocks.

7.65mm Auto

A larger predecessor of the 6.35mm Auto, about seven years older, this Browning-developed cartridge chambered in most of the double-action blow-backs – such as the Walther PP, Mauser HSc and Sauer M38 – plus many of the captured weapons originating in Czechoslovakia, Belgium and the Netherlands. The loading generally comprised a jacketed lead-core bullet in a straight-sided brass rimless case, but was ineffective at anything other than close range.

7.65mm Mauser

Originally introduced in the 1890s as the '7.65mm Borchardt', this bottleneck pistol cartridge is similar to (but larger than) the 7.65mm Parabellum. It chambered only in the Mauser C/96 and Spanish-made copies. Power was much the same as the 9mm Pist. Patr. 08, but the lightweight bullet had a greater tendency to penetrate and often passed through an animate target.

7.65mm Parabellum

Sharing the case-head dimensions of the 9mm Pist. Patr. 08, this reduced-calibre bottleneck-case variant was official issue in Switzerland. However, it was also chambered in some privately purchased Parabellums and some of those issued to the German forestry service in an attempt to exhaust existing commercial stockpiles. Velocity was somewhat higher than the 9mm Pist. Patr. 08, but the lighter bullet reduced hitting power considerably.

7.9mm *Gewehr-Patrone*

The standard 7.9mm rifle cartridge, generally known as the '7.9×57mm', was originally made with a brass bottleneck case. However, successful attempts were made in the mid-1930s to develop steel cases, freeing supplies of brass for more vital tasks, though the first patterns usually had to be brass- or copper-washed to guarantee smooth feed. An acceptable greyish-green lacquer coating was subsequently perfected, but even this failed to prevent auto-feed troubles and an additional wax coating had to be approved early in 1944. Though the wax was durable, and virtually insensitive to temperature and humidity, it became sticky when contaminated with oil or grease; consequently, feed problems were never entirely cured prior to 1945.

Virtually all 7.9mm projectiles made since the appearance of the *Spitzgeschoss* ('pointed bullet') in 1903 have been streamlined, often with a boat-tail. The bullet envelopes were initially made of steel, coated with gilding metal, but zinc envelopes and mild-steel cores were successfully developed in the interests of economy.

7.9mm Patr. s. S. The pre-1918 *schwere Spitzgeschoss* ('heavy pointed bullet') had a lead core within a gilding-metal clad steel envelope and weighed 12.83gm. The cartridge case – measuring 57.0±0.03mm – had a distinctive green primer annulus, though the bullet was invariably unmarked. Propelled by 2.88gm of Nitrozellulosegewehrpulver ('Nz. Gew. P.'), s. S. bullets attained a muzzle velocity of about 765 m/sec. The loaded cartridges measured 80–81mm overall and weighed about 26.1gm.

7.9mm *Nahpatrone.* Though widely believed to have been developed for silenced weapons, this low-power short-range round was originally introduced for practice on ranges where the full-power round was too dangerous. The Nahpatrone generally had a green primer annulus and an additional green-lacquered case or case-mouth seal. Though the bullet was much the same size and shape as the standard s. S. pattern, the Nahpatrone contained only 0.60gm of Nitropentagewehrpulver (Np. Gew. P., a mixture of nitrocellulose and P.E.T.N.), weighed only about 23.5gm complete, and attained a velocity of only 275 m/sec.

7.9mm Patr. S. m. E. The *Spitzgeschoss mit Eisenkern* ('iron-core pointed bullet') had a mild-steel core, developed for economic reasons, and sometimes also a zinc bullet envelope. The bullet was originally about 35.5mm long, though this was soon increased to 37.3mm; it generally weighed about 11.5–11.6gm, 5.8–5.9gm being contributed by cores that were made from special steel wire on lathes or swaging machinery. The bullet envelope was conventionally plated or galvanized zinc. The zinc treatment authorised in November 1942 was regarded as inferior to any other method, but acceptable in an emergency. It was originally exclusive to Langbein-Pfannhäuser-Werke of Leipzig, using material from the D.W.M. factory in Lübeck-Schlutup. The primer annulus of S. m. E. rounds was generally blue. The loaded cartridge weighed about 24.6gm and the projectile, driven by a 2.85gm charge of Nz. Gew. P., attained a muzzle velocity of about 700 m/sec. A special high-quality loading was developed for snipers' use; 'Patr. S. m. E. für Scharfschützen geeignet' generally appears on the packing labels.

7.9mm Patr. S. m. E. Lang. Approved in 1944, this variant of the standard S. m. E. cartridge contained a 39.5mm 12gm bullet intended to compensate for the replacement of the original heavyweight lead core by lighter mild steel. The two types of cartridge shared the same external dimensions, as the longer bullet was simply seated more deeply in the case. The only identifying mark was a practically colourless lacquered coating on the primer.

7.9mm Patr. S. m. K. The *Spitzgeschoss mit Kern* ('cored pointed bullet') was the standard armour-piercing design, the 11.53gm projectile containing a

5.77gm steel core inside a plated steel envelope. The primer had a red annulus, but the cartridge case was otherwise unmarked. The loaded round weighed about 25gm, developed a muzzle velocity of about 800 m/sec, and 12mm of mild-steel plate could be penetrated at 100m if the bullet struck at 90° to the plate surface. A high-power 'verbesserte' version was made for aircraft machine-guns. Loaded with 3.37gm of Np. Gew. P. and distinguished by an additional green ring on the bullet, it weighed 25.5gm complete and could attain 860 m/sec. Penetration of 14.5mm of mild-steel plate was possible at 100m.

7.9mm Patr. S. m. K. Leuchtspur. The standard tracer round, weighing about 23.5gm complete, this had a red primer annulus and an additional black bullet tip. The standard bullet weighed about 10.17gm, including the trace compound and a 2.53gm steel core. The core gave the tracer a residual armour-piercing capability, generally regarded as 8mm of mild-steel plate at 100m. Propelled by 2.88gm of Nz. Gew. P., the projectile attained about 830 m/sec in the Kar. 98k.

Several types of trace were used, the most common in the opening phases of the war being all-yellow. All-green versions are also known, together with a bi-colour trace that changed from green-to-red or red-to-green about 500m from the muzzle. The labels of these cartridges displayed 'grünrot' and 'rotgrün' respectively. The trace burned out at 800–1,000m.

'Patr. S. m. K. Leuchtspur 100/600' was made for aerial use, the figures referring to the ignition and extinction distances. The cartridge generally exhibited a red primer annulus, while the bullet had a black tip.

The essentially similar 'Patr. S. m. K. Glimmspur' (visible from 150m to 800–1,000m) and 'Patr. S. m. K. Glimmspur 100/600' were low-intensity tracers that would not temporarily blind firers at night. They were distinguished by a 5mm black bullet-tip, half the normal measurement. The rarely encountered 'Dunkelspur' was an ultra-dim trace apparently intended for burst-firing at night; it was so dim, indeed, that the trace of a single round was practically invisible.

Most tracers were also made in high-velocity 'v' loads for aircraft machine-guns, distinguished either by a green bullet-tip on early examples or an additional 2mm-broad green ring. Charges of 3.53gm Np. Gew. P. raised the weight of a complete round to about 24gm and the muzzle velocity to 895–900 m/sec. Armour-piercing performance was slightly enhanced.

Tracer cartridges incorporating a self-destruct element ('mit Zerleger') were also made, but are now rarely seen. In these, a pellet compounded of lead azide, P.E.T.N. and tetracene destroyed the bullet after it had travelled about

2km. However, not only was the self-destruction unreliable, but fragments were scattered so widely that issue of ammunition of this type was greatly restricted.

7.9mm Patr. S. m. K. H. Officially adopted in August 1939, this cartridge was loaded with a special 12.57gm armour-piercing bullet containing an 8.25gm tungsten core. The loaded round was difficult to distinguish from the standard S. m. K., apart from its markings. Cartridges made in 1938–9 had plain tombak-plated bullet envelopes and red primer annuli, while those made later in 1939 featured cupro-nickel cladding and a red primer. Unfortunately, the case-head marks were hidden when the rounds were packed in chargers. Painting bands on the chargers themselves was unsatisfactory; from January 1940 until production was abandoned in March 1942, therefore, the bullet was blacked. A complete cartridge weighs about 26.6gm, a charge of 3.61gm Np. Gew. P. giving a muzzle velocity of about 910 m/sec. However, the increase in power was accompanied by an increase in recoil and firing S. m. K. H. ammunition in automatic weapons had to be restricted to short bursts. Penetration of mild-steel plate at 100m was 19mm when struck at 90°, or 12.5mm at an angle of 30°. Production was discontinued in 1941 to conserve valuable tungsten for more vital tasks.

7.9mm Patr. le. S., or l. S. The *leichte Spitzgeschoss* had a green band across the case-head. Intended for relatively safe practice, particularly in the air, it had a lightweight (5.58gm) bullet with a 2.7gm aluminium core; consequently, complete rounds weighed merely 19.4gm. A practice tracer was identified by an additional black bullet tip and (occasionally) a green band across the case head. The tracer bullet weighed 6.03gm, 1.62gm being contributed by the aluminium core and 0.6gm by the white phosphorus filling. Muzzle velocity was about 930 m/sec, and the yellow or yellowish-white trace was visible to about 800m.

7.9mm Pl. Patr. The *Platzpatrone* 33, the standard bulleted blank, was easily distinguished by its 31mm-long red or reddish-purple wooden bullet. The primer annulus was generally plain. These blanks were originally loaded in brass cases that had already been fired once. A knurled ring (1. Sorte) was milled into the case when reloaded as a blank; after use, the expended blank was then returned, reloaded and a second ring (2. Sorte) was added. Cases were discarded after the second blank charge had been fired. Once steel cases became available, however, the ring-marking distinction was dropped. Despite being loaded with a frangible wood bullet, Pl. Patr. 33 could still be dangerous at 25 metres.

Grenade-launching blanks. Specialised blanks were made for GwGrGt. issued with the Kar. 98k, varying considerably in propellant loading. According to an O.K.H. announcement made in the summer of 1944, they included a 1gm load with a yellow annulus; a 1.1gm load with a black annulus; a 1.5gm load with a short yellow wooden bullet; a 1.7gm load with a red annulus; and a 1.9gm load with a black primer annulus.[2] In September 1944, however, a new blank with a 1gm load superseded the original 1gm pattern ('lg. Gew. Kart.') used with the Gewehrsprenggranat. This was distinguished by a blue wooden bullet with a 9mm deep hole bored in the tip.[3]

7.9mm B. Patr. This explosive incendiary round or *Beobachtungs-Patrone* – weighing about 24.1gm complete – contained a special 10.82gm bullet, 39.7mm overall, with a base fuze, a detonator and a striker. A small charge of 0.4gm phosphorus in the bullet sufficed as an indicator, giving a cloud of blue-white smoke visible 2km away in perfect conditions, while the detonator contained about 0.45gm of compounded lead styphnate, barium peroxide and calcium silicide. A charge of 2.9gm Nz. Gew. P. gave a muzzle velocity of about 815 m/sec in the Kar. 98k. The earliest cartridges were distinguished either by a chromium-tipped bullet or, later, by a black bullet with a natural metal tip.

The Beobachtungs-Patrone was conceived as a 'spotter' round, performing so well that it was subsequently adopted by several post-war Allied armies. However, respectable incendiary performance led to a change in its primary role as the war progressed. A high-power 'verbesserte' pattern, made for use in aircraft machine-guns, had an additional 2mm-broad green ring on the bullet. Slightly heavier than the standard pattern – 24.6 instead of 24.1gm – it attained a velocity of 895 m/sec with a charge of 3.43gm Np. Gew. P.

7.9mm Patr. P. m. K. The high-explosive-incendiary bulletted cartridge ('Phosphorgeschoss mit Kern') was distinguished by a black primer annulus. The 10.17gm bullet – 37.3mm overall – had a narrow green ring if the case contained Np. Gew. P., but was otherwise unmarked. The bullet contained a 2.46gm steel core and 0.4gm of phosphorus. The standard Nz. Gew. P. charge permitted a velocity of about 835 m/sec; white smoke was emitted to about 450–500m, and 8mm of mild-steel plate could be pierced at 100m provided it was struck at 90° to its surface. The high-power 'v' pattern attained 915 m/sec, enhancing armour-piercing performance and increasing loaded-round weight from 23.3 to 23.8gm.

The original P. m. K. bullets proved to be very sensitive, particularly when temperatures rose above 45° C on tropical service. Though great care was taken to seal the basal joint between the core and the bullet envelope, often with silver or gold lacquer, premature explosions still occurred. In 1943, therefore, a new-pattern ('neuer Art', n. A.) S. m. K. bullet was authorised. Better base-closure and the elimination of the sidewall vent resulted in a bullet stable at temperatures as high as 95° C, though losing the ability of the earlier bullets to ignite thin-skinned fuel tanks simply by passing through them.

Werkzeug-Patronen. 'Tool-cartridges' allowed armourers to test the action of weapons without actually firing them. They were strongly made (virtually all in Polte-Werke's Magdeburg factory) and could be considered as gauges. The earliest pattern had a coil-spring in the case between the bullet and the base, but proved to be insufficiently durable; later examples, therefore, had a magnesium-alloy or sturdy plastic strut between the purpose-built 'bullet' and the base of the cartridge case.

Exerzierpatronen. Many dummy rounds were one-piece extrusions in the shape of the bulleted case, often fluted longitudinally, but others had standard bullets pinned into fluted brass or steel cases. The last and best pattern, confined to 1941–4, amalgamated a sturdily shanked metal base with a solid plastic body. Made by Polte, Pirkl and Servotechna, among others, synthetic-body dummies remained comparatively uncommon in service.

Captured ammunition. The Wehrmacht seized vast stocks of German-type 7.9mm ('7.92mm') ammunition in Czechoslovakia, Greece, Poland and Yugoslavia. However, owing to minuscule differences in dimensions and production tolerances, problems sometimes arose when captured ammunition was used in German small arms. The most vulnerable were the automatic weapons, especially machine-guns, and the H.WaA. or the O.K.H. were occasionally forced to issue clarification. These documents could be extremely complicated.

In December 1939, faced with a tremendous influx of Czechoslovakian weapons and ammunition, the O.K.H. observed that all the standard German 7.9mm rounds could be used in the Gew. 24 (t); the le. MG. 26 (t) could accept all but the S. m. K. H. and the Pl. Patr. 33; the s. MG. 37 (t) could fire all but the Pl. Patr. 33; but that the s. MG. 07/24 (t), the antiquated Schwarzlose, was to be restricted in German service to the s. S., S. m. K. L'Spur and B.-Patr. ammunition.

All Czechoslovakian cartridges – ball, heavy ball, tracer, armour-piercing and observation – could be used in any of the rifles and machine-guns, but the employment of blanks needed care. All of these had wooden bullets and brass cases with black primer annuli, but black-bulleted rounds were restricted to the s. MG. 07/24 (t) (Schwarzlose); yellow-bulletted rounds to the le. MG. 26 (t) and s. MG. 37 (t); and red-bulletted rounds to the Gew. 24 (t).[4]

Equally typical of the complication was an order issued in May 1944 restricting the use of one Czechoslovakian ('M. 35 (t) o. L.') and two Yugoslav blank cartridges ('M. 88a (j) o.L.' and 'M. 98 (j) o. L.') to manually-operated weapons.[5]

Czech rounds included the vz. 23 ball cartridge, similar to the German S.-Patr. but with a blue (later black) primer annulus; the vz. 27 ball cartridge intended for short-range practice and target-shooting, with a 'T' in the head-stamp and a blue-black primer annulus; a vz. 28 tracer, with a flat-base bullet and a red annulus; three patterns of vz. 30 blank, with red, black or yellow wooden bullets; the vz. 34 heavy ball, comparable to the German s. S. pattern but with a green annulus; a vz. 34 armour-piercing pattern, with a steel-cored bullet and a white annulus; an observation round with a yellow annulus; and a vz. 35 blank, with a natural-colour wood bullet.

Greek ammunition included old German ball rounds ('Patr. S. [g]') dating prior to 1918, and new 'Patr. s. S. (g)' made by the Greek Powder Company. The older cartridges had black primer annuli, and headstamps that were typically 'S67 | 7 | 17 | C'. The newer rounds also had black annuli and tombak-plated bullets, but their headstamps contained an 'ΕΠΚ' monogram (with 'Π' springing from the central bar of 'Ε'), the letters 'Ε' and 'Σ' (for Hellas, 'Greece') and dates such as '1936' or '39'. In August 1943, all Greek 7.9mm rounds were restricted to rifles and carbines for practice at ranges up to 600 metres. The sight settings on the rifles were to be set 200m above the actual range.[6]

Polish cartridges were similar to the Czechoslovakian issue, including 'S' (standard) and 's. S.' (heavy) ball rounds, with black and green primer annuli respectively; an armour-piercing round with a red annulus; an armour-piercing tracer, with a blue annulus and a blue or occasionally black-tipped bullet; a yellow-annulus incendiary round for rifles (yellow-tipped bullet) or machine-guns (black bullet); and a selection of blanks, among them a red wood-bulleted pattern for rifles and a blue one for machine-guns.

Yugoslavian cartridges were seized in large quantities, but the chronology and designations are not yet clear. There were, however, at least two forms of blank: one with a natural-colour pointed wood bullet (known to the Germans as the 'Pl. Patr. M. 88a (j) o. L.') and another with a light brown ogival papier-mâché bullet with a blackened tip ('Pl. Patr. M. 98 (j) o. L.').

7.9mm Kurz-Patrone

Introduced for the Maschinenkarabiner after a development history that had stretched back into the 1930s, this intermediate cartridge had the official German designation 'Pist. Patr. 43' but was known colloquially as the '7.9mm Kurz' or 7.9×33mm. It may be distinguished from standard rifle ammunition by its shorter case, despite identical case-head design. The standard m. E. ball cartridge weighed 16.7gm complete and measured 47.9mm overall. Its 7.95–8.25gm bullet (overall length 25.4–26mm) had a mild-steel core weighing about 3.9gm inside a gilding-metal plated steel envelope. The charge of 1.57gm of Nz. Gew. P. gave a muzzle velocity of about 700 m/sec in the short-barrelled Maschinenkarabiner, though armour-penetrating performance at 100m was not particularly impressive: merely 6.5mm mild-steel plate if the target were struck at 90° to its surface, or 4.5mm at 45°.

In addition to standard m. E. and S. E. ball cartridges, experimental semi-armour piercing (S. m. K.), tracer (S. m. K. L'spur) and short-range practice rounds loaded with round lead balls (*Zielpatronen*) have been found; there are also yellow wood-bulleted blanks for grenade launching, and even 'Werkzeug' tool-rounds. Only eight manufacturers have been linked with Pist. Patr. 43: Draht- und Metallwarenfabrik of Salzwedel (code: 'fva'); Hugo Schneider Lampenfabrik in Leipzig ('wa') and Skarzysko-Kamienna ('kam'); Metallwarenfabrik Treuenbritzen, Sebaldushof ('hla'); Polte-Werke's factories in Magdeburg ('aux') and Arnstadt ('auy'); the former Sellier & Bellot plant in Vlasim ('ak'), Teuto Metallwerke of Osnabrück ('oxo'); the former Zbrojovka Brno plant in Povaška Bystrica ('dou'); and an unidentified factory using the code 'de'.

Kurzpatronen carriers generally contained either thirty 14-round or twenty-two 20-round cardboard cartons. Five carriers fitted into the standard wooden Patronenkasten 88 (PK. 88, 'ammunition box'), giving a total capacity of 2,100 or 2,200 rounds respectively. The packed box weighed about 50kg.

7.9mm Patrone 318

Conceived as an anti-tank rifle cartridge, this was basically a rifle bullet – 33mm overall and weighing about 14.6gm – inserted into a modified 13mm T-Gewehr cartridge case. The projectile is usually listed as 'S. m. K. H. Rs. L'spur': *Spitzgeschoss mit gehärtetem Kern, Reizstoff und Leuchtspur* ('pointed bullet with hardened core, lachrymator and trace'). The bullet had a 10mm black tip, and the primer had a red annulus. A charge of about 14.7gm of Nitrozellulose Röhrenpulver (Nz. R. P.) could develop a muzzle velocity approaching 1,080m/sec.

The Patr. 318 chambered in the principal anti-tank rifles, PzB. 38 and PzB. 39, and also in an experimental machine-gun. Though 31mm of armour-plate could be defeated at 100 metres, the small bullet could not offer the capacity of 20mm or 30mm cannon-shells and soon faded into obscurity. Five cartridges were contained in each box, whose distinctive red/blue diagonally split label gave details of the precise charge. It seems that propellant loadings were adjusted from batch to batch to maintain constant performance.

The cartridge cases were initially brass, then lacquered or bonderised-and-lacquered steel. Production seems to have been confined almost exclusively to Polte-Werke, Magdeburg (code: 'aux'), and Theodor Bergmann K.G., Velten ('cdo'). In addition to the standard ball loading, wood-bulleted blanks and a selection of dummies have been reported.

9mm Kurz/9mm Short/.380 ACP

The largest of the original Browning pistol-cartridge series, this dates from 1912. Generally regarded as the smallest pistol cartridge acceptable for military use, it offers better stopping power than the 7.65mm pattern simply because of its greater cross-sectional area. Though chambered in some Walther, Mauser, Sauer and F.N. blowbacks, and most of the pistols that had been seized in Czechoslovakia, it was never popular with the Wehrmacht. The ammunition was obtained from commercial sources, and was headstamped accordingly.

9mm Parabellum

The standard German pistol and submachine-gun cartridge, the Pist. Patr. 08 was introduced with the Parabellum pistol in 1908 though experiments to enlarge the 7.65mm round had been underway since 1902. A jacketed lead-core bullet had originally been set in a straight-sided brass case, but various substitute bullets (together with steel cases) were introduced prior to 1945. 9mm Pist. Patr. 08 were packed sixteen to a carton, 52 of which fitted into each carrier. Five carriers then went into the Patronenkasten 88 – 4,160 rounds, about 60kg.

9mm Pist. Patr. 08. The standard ball cartridge contained an ogival jacketed lead-core bullet weighing 7.5–8gm. The case was brass or steel, the latter being washed with brass, copper or lacquer. The primer usually had a black annulus.

9mm Pist. Patr. 08 m. E. Introduced in 1940, this cartridge contained a lightweight bullet (6.3–6.5gm) with a mild-steel core and a lead cup in the base of the steel bullet envelope. The bullet is almost always lacquered black.

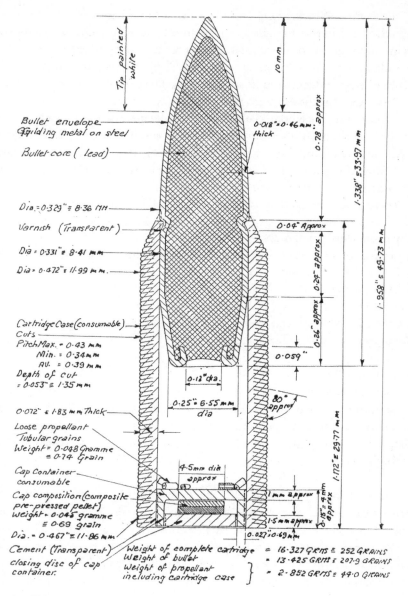

Tip painted white

Bullet envelope — Gilding metal on steel

Bullet core (lead)

0.018" = 0.46 mm thick

0.78" approx

10 mm

1.338" = 33.97 mm

Dia = 0.329" = 8.36 mm

Varnish (Transparent)

Dia = 0.331" = 8.41 mm

Dia = 0.472" = 11.99 mm.

0.04" Approx

0.24" approx

1.958" = 49.73 mm

Cartridge Case (consumable)
Cuts
Pitch Max. = 0.43 mm
Min. = 0.34 mm
Av. = 0.39 mm
Depth of cut
= 0.053" = 1.35 mm

0.26" approx

0.25" = 6.55 mm dia

0.13" dia

0.059"

80° approx

0.072" = 1.83 mm Thick

Loose propellant
Tubular grains
Weight = 0.048 Gramme
= 0.74 Grain

Cap Container
consumable

Cap composition (composite
pre-pressed pellet)
weight = 0.045 gramme
= 0.69 grain

Dia. = 0.467" = 11.86 mm

Cement (Transparent)
closing disc of cap
container.

4.5 mm dia approx

1.172" = 29.77 mm

1 mm approx

1.5 mm approx

0.18" = 4 mm approx

0.027" = 0.69 mm

Weight of complete cartridge = 16.327 GRMS = 252 GRAINS
Weight of bullet = 13.425 GRMS = 207.9 GRAINS
Weight of propellant
including cartridge case = 2.852 GRMS = 44.0 GRAINS

11. This drawing shows that the Germans had made appreciable progress with a self-contained 'caseless' cartridge, an attractive proposition that Heckler & Koch eventually perfected in the 1980s – only for the funds necessary for re-equipment to be withheld by the German government.

9mm Pist. Patr. 08 S. E. Introduced in 1942, these had bullets made of sintered iron. They were lighter even than the m. E. pattern, weighing only 5.9gm, and attained a substantially higher muzzle velocity than the standard '08' bullet; unfortunately, the combination of light bullet and steel case gave persistent feed troubles in automatic weapons. These were never entirely solved.

9mm Ex. Patr. 08. The *Exerzierpatronen* were dummies intended for drill purposes. Mostly the work of Polte-Werke of Magdeburg, the Third Reich patterns generally comprise a one-piece nickelled case/bullet unit, longitudinally fluted and often transversely holed. Ex. Patr. 08 K (Kunststoff, 'plastic material'), with plastic bodies and reinforced metal bases, were made by Polte-Werke, Pirkl and Servotechna in 1940–3.

9mm Nahpatrone 08. Originally developed for short-range practice, with a heavyweight bullet and a reduced charge to guarantee subsonic velocity, Nahpatronen eventually achieved more notoriety as silencer ammunition – for which their reduced power was ideal. Their headstamps were generally nothing but 'X'.

9mm Steyr

Chambered in the Austrian pistols and submachine-guns assimilated into the German military and police forces in 1938.

9mm Mauser Export

Originating in an attempt by Waffenfabrik Mauser to compete with the 9mm Parabellum, this was chambered in variants of the C/96 and also some of the delayed blowbacks developed shortly before the First World War began. Some of the submachine-guns acquired in Austria and Hungary fired this particular cartridge.

Unusual cartridges

The Germans were masters at wasting valuable development time on exotic ammunition. The development of small 8mm, 9mm and 11mm-calibre *rocket cartridges,* for example, was never likely to affect the production of conventional small-arms patterns. The rockets carried virtually no payload, and their accuracy was seriously compromised by the continual change in the centre of gravity as the propellant was consumed. The only advantage was that the rockets could be fired from a very simple gun.

In an attempt to squeeze the maximum performance out of 7.9mm weapons, a few experiments were undertaken with collapsing-skirt projectiles on the Gerlich principle. Tapering the bore towards the muzzle permitted the pressure on the projectile base to increase as it moved forward. Gerlich's goal had been power, and the 7.9/5.3mm collapsing-skirt bullet achieved stupendous velocities approaching 1,400m/sec. However, it did so at such great expense that the project was soon adjudged a failure – the tapered bore was difficult to machine and tungsten was too valuable to waste in bullet cores. The taper-bore system achieved short-lived success only in the 28/21mm taper-bore s. Pz. B. 41.

The 7.9mm *Bernstein* bullet was a serious attempt to simplify production when raw material was running low towards the end of the war. Made from mild steel bar-stock, the bullet's claim to fame lay in the driving bands midway along the body. Made of compressed paper, lead or a suitable alloy, these prevented the projectile contacting the bore-wall along its entire length; the mild steel would otherwise have caused excessive bore wear. The principle was similar to that employed in artillery shells, but the war ended while trials of the unique bullet were still underway.

If the Bernstein design was a realistic solution to potentially serious problems, the *Matter Bullet* came from the realms of fiction. Its envelope contained three pellets of a powerful detonator, lead azide, held under increasing pressure. The pellet nearest the muzzle was the most sensitive; that at the tail, the least sensitive. The promoters asserted that as pressure was released when the Matter bullet struck a hard target, the lead azide would explode with shattering force. By 1945, the Germans appear to have doubted that manufacturing complexity justified the potential gains, even though the Matter Bullet was insensitive under all normal conditions and required no separate fuze.

The most intriguing development was the *caseless cartridge* – allegedly made at the request of the Reichssicherheitshauptamt, which wished to avoid leaving spent cartridge cases at the scene of an assassination. A conventional white-tipped 8.4mm-diameter s. S.-type bullet, weighing about 13gm, was partially enveloped by a glazed orange-red combustible case containing conventional Nitrozellulosegewehrpulver. A special primer was set in the base, sandwiched between two wafers of the combustible body material. The cartridge was apparently to be fired in a single-shot gun with a longitudinally split breech system.

Captured Russian 7.65mm *poison bullets,* deliberately (but erroneously) headstamped 'GECO', were found to contain aconitin. As the Russian ammunition was potentially deadly, minuscule quantities of 9mm Kampfstoff-Patronen 08 (K. Patr. 08) were subsequently prepared under the supervision of section 'Chem. g 27' of the Reichssicherheitshauptamt. Made in the spring of 1944, they had a unique bullet with a nose cavity, a core-channel, a capsule of potassium cyanate, and an 'after core'. When the projectile struck a comparatively unyielding target, the after core flew forward. This crushed the capsule and forced the poison out through the nose.

Pyrotechnics for all signal pistols

Leuchtpatronen. These were projectable day/night signals, visible for several kilometres under ideal conditions. The earliest, which may have been designated 'Leuchtpatrone 35' had a pale grey body with a white closing wad; the case-head and rim were plain. It was replaced by the Leuchtpatrone 41, visible up to 4km in daytime, which could be projected to a height of about 160m or, when elevated at about 35°, to a range of about 240m. The Leuchtpatrone 41 was replaced by the externally similar (but more powerful) Leuchtpatrone 42 with effect from 27 February 1942.

Individual flares varied between 70,000 and 160,000 candlepower, burning for about seven seconds in the air and then up to five more on the ground. The cartridge was about 83mm long and weighed 100gm. Half the rim of the Leuchtpatrone 41 was serrated and the closing wad was white. The case-body, made of thick paper, was pale grey with a single white ring.

Fallschirmleuchtpatrone 41. This was a starshell, displaying 'FALLSCHIRMLEUCHTPATRONE' on the aluminium case (which had a plain head and a semiserrated rim). A parachute symbol appeared on the white closing wad. A white flare was fired to 80–90m, burning for up to fifteen seconds. As the white parachute descended, the flare illuminated a 200m-diameter circle. The projectile measured about 135mm overall; the old pattern weighed 100gm, the newer weighing 138gm.

Signalpatronen. Signal cartridges came in a wide variety of colour combinations.

Einzelstern Rot, a day/night signal, fired a single red star to about 100m. The signal, which burned for about seven seconds, could be seen 2.5km away. The cartridge was 83mm long and weighed a little over 80gm. Its paper case and closing wad were red, while the case rim was entirely serrated.

Doppelstern Rot was a two-star version, distinguished by an additional black stripe on the red closing wad.

Einzelstern Grün and *Doppelstern Grün* were similar to Einzelstern Rot and Doppelstern Rot, but with plain case rims and markings in green rather than red. Early examples had longitudinal flutes pressed into the case-head walls above the rim, but this distinction was soon abandoned. At only 70gm, Einzelstern Grün was also noticeably lighter and the daylight range of the signal was rated only at 2km.

Einzel- und Doppelstern Gelb, yellow signals introduced prior to 1939, could be distinguished not by the case rims, which were plain, but by the six radial lines pressed into the base. The cardboard case walls and the closing wads were yellow. Doppelstern Gelb had an additional black band on the wad.

Sternbündelpatrone Weiss mit weissem Vorsignal was a tactical day/night signal 135mm long and weighing about 165gm. It fired a single white flare to an altitude of 90m and then followed it almost immediately with six separate white stars visible in daylight to about 2.5km. Marks included the complete designation on its body, together with six white dots around the body and primer. The case-rim was partially serrated, while the mouth was crimped over a white closing wad in such a way that six indentations could be seen or felt.

Sternbündelpatrone Rot mit rotem Vorsignal was identical, except that it followed a red flare with red stars. Red marks replaced white on the body and case-head, the case-rim was entirely serrated, and the closing wad was red.

Sternbündelpatrone Grün mit rotlichem Vorsignal, a minor variant of the preceding two cartridges, followed a red flare with six green stars. Green marks replaced red on the case, closing wad and case-head, the rim of the last being entirely smooth.

Sternbündelpatrone Rot-Grün mit gelbem Vorsignal, a combination starshell weighing 150gm laden, fired a yellow flare followed by three red and three green stars. The body displayed three green and three red dots, which were repeated on the case-head around the primer. The case mouth was closed with a grey wad impressed to give a raised diagonal bar within a circle. The case-rim was smooth.

Sternbündelpatrone Gelb-Rot-Grün, in addition to its full name, also displayed two yellow, two red and two green dots on its body. The marks were repeated on the case-head, running radially from the primer pocket in three colour-groups. The closing was impressed to give the letter 'Y' within a circle.

Signalpatrone Dreistern Grün, marked with three green dots on the body and three more around the primer, had a plain case-rim and three raised circles on the green closing wad. It fired three large green stars to an altitude of about 90m, the duration of each being about seven seconds.

Signalpatrone (See) was used by Kriegsmarine personnel for ship/shore or ship/aircraft communication. It had a 103mm-long brass case loaded with up

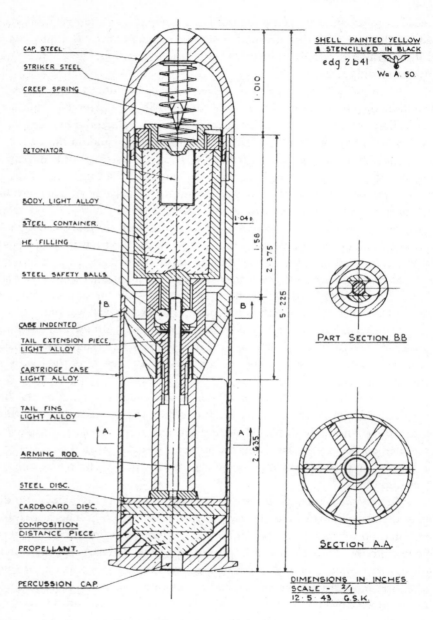

12. A section drawing of the Wurfgranate 326, showing the complexity to be expected in even small-calibre ammunition.

to four white, red or green stars. The case was invariably closed with a lacquered lead-foil seal. Markings on the case showed the colour and number of the stars – e.g., a red '2'.

Pfeifpatrone. Intended solely as a gas-alarm, this 110gm cartridge was distinguished by a blue ring on the case body, a broad blue primer annulus and a smooth case rim; the mark 'pfeifpatrone' was also present. The projectile could reach a ceiling of about 100m when fired at an elevation of 65°, emitting a five-second whistling note audible up to 500m away in still conditions.

Alarmschusspatrone. This 83mm-long cartridge, weighing about 70gm, projected a 15m flare from the signal-pistol barrel for about ten seconds. It could be identified by its black body and half-serrated case rim.

Smoke and obscuration cartridges.

Rauchpatrone. Intended for 'artilleristische Messwecke', this measured 135mm overall and weighed about 100gm. It had a pale grey cardboard body, a grey closing wad and a half-serrated case rim. Fired to a ceiling of 70m, it emitted grey smoke for a minute.

Messpatrone obscuration cartridges fired a smoke charge to a height of 180–200m, the flight time being 2–5 seconds and the smoke visible for up to 8km in daylight. The 83mm-long cartridge, which weighed 105gm, had a particularly powerful charge and was not intended to be fired from the hand. It had a black cardboard body, a raised black 'M' on the white closing wad, and a half-serrated case rim.

Fallschirmpatrone für Windmessung, used to determine wind velocity by measuring the rate and angle of drift, plus drop velocity, had an effective ceiling of about 70m. The cartridge – 135mm long and weighing about 133gm – bore the full designation on its body, the closing wad and the case head being white; the case rim was plain.

Rauchbündelpatrone Violett was used to warn of approaching armoured vehicles in daytime only. It weighed 112gm, and was distinguished by four violet rings around its 135mm-long plain-rimmed aluminium case. Four violet squares were marked around the primer, while the closing wad was also violet. The four smoke pots began to burn after about 3.5 seconds, then for 12–18 seconds on the ground. They could be seen 1.5km away in good conditions.

Fallschirmrauchpatrone, made in two differing patterns, attained a ceiling of about 80m. It could burn for up to nine seconds, the obscuration being effective at up to 1.5km. The aluminium-case cartridge was 125mm long and weighed a mere 80gm. A large coloured parachute symbol (and usually the designation) appeared on the case-wall, together with a similar mark impressed into the case-head. Violet or blue closing wads showed the colour of the smoke. *Rauchzeichenpatronen,* coloured marker flares, were distinguished by large suitably coloured dots on the case-wall and head. The closing wad was also coloured.

Pyrotechnics for Leuchtpistolen Z and 42

1. High-explosive projectiles.
Sprenggranatpatrone für Leuchtpistole Z. had a rimmed diecast aluminium cartridge case containing the primer and propellant. A metal washer above the charge, pierced with ten holes, allowed the expanding gases to act on the projectile, which had a cast-aluminium body left in its natural state. Explosive content was originally 120gm penthrite wax, a nose cavity attempting to capitalise on the Munroe (or Shaped Charge) Effect and improve armour-piercing qualities. The head screwed into the body and the impact fuze, with a setback-type arming mechanism containing six balls, was screwed into the head. Complete rounds were 124mm long, the cartridge-case body having a diameter of about 28.5mm. The diameter of the short pre-rifled section of the projectile was 27.2mm and that of the fuze about 9mm. Cartridge-case heads bore 'SPR. Z.'.

Sprenggranatpatrone für Kampfpistole, similar to the preceding shell, had a more powerful propellant charge in its aluminium cartridge case and could offer a longer range. Introduced in 1943, it had 'SPRGR. PATR. K. P.' stencilled on the case head.

2. Smoke and obscuration cartridges.
Nachrichtenpatrone Z. was similar to the Sprenggranatpatronen, but its cast aluminium body contained a smoke generator, a coloured silk streamer and an ejector charge. The black Bakelite nose contained a message form and a small pencil. Propellant flash ignited the delay pellet in the grenade base-plate, which in turn fired the ejector charge to expel the message container, the smoke generator and the streamer while the projectile was airborne. The case-head was stencilled 'NACHR. Z.'.

Deutpatrone Z. was an aluminium-bodied orange-smoke grenade, externally similar to the high-explosive patterns. Four strands of quickmatch and a black-powder pellet in the centre of the projectile base ignited the smoke generator in flight, compressed paper in the smoke jets being blown clear when the generator ignited. The case-head displayed 'DEUT. Z.'.

Fallschirmleuchtpatrone für Kampfpistole (parachute-flare cartridge) had a cast aluminium body with a white-tipped black Bakelite head. The flare and a parachute lay above the screwed-in base plug, which retained a black-powder pellet. The ejector charge ignited to expel the flare and parachute assembly after a predetermined delay. Case-head markings included 'F. LEUT. Z.'.

Nebelpatrone für Kampfpistole was a smoke cartridge, externally similar to the high-explosive designs but containing a special generator, an impact fuze and a charge of black powder beneath the flash-cap and striker. Impact ignited the flash-cap, which in turn fired the gunpowder charge to blow off the nose cap and eject the smoke generator.

3. Grenade adaptations

Nebeleihandgranate 42/11 was simply a standard oviform hand-grenade adapted to the Kampfpistole by adding a pre-rifled extension and a die-cast aluminium cartridge case.

Wurfkörper 361 für Leuchtpistole was made from the components of the standard Eihandgranate 39. It contained 112gm of T.N.T., a detonator system and a combustion fuze (Brennzünder) with a delay of 4–5 seconds. Mounted on a plastic tube containing the propelling charge and the primer, the muzzle-loaded grenade was armed by removing its lateral safety pin (often omitted from examples made in 1944–5). Wurfkörper had olive-green bodies, were 6.89 inches long, and had an effective range of 60–80m. They were packed in fifteens in a zinc-lined steel packet (Blechbehalter).

Wurfgranatepatrone 326 für Leuchtpistole, with a diecast body painted yellow, had a separate aluminium- or brass-case cartridge containing the primer and propellant. Charged with T.N.T., and not unlike a small mortar shell, the projectile had four stabilising fins. After flying about 12m, airflow pressure armed the Wurfgranate by extracting the automatic safety.

Leuchtpistole grenade. This was an emergency design, dating from the end of 1944 or early 1945, made by attaching the standard Handgranate 24 to spare propelling tubes.

Panzer-Wurfkorper 42 für Leuchtpistole (Pz. Wk. 42 LP.) was basically a grenade with a hollow 'shaped head' charge of T.N.T., the cavity being protected by a thin sheet-steel cap. The propellant tube fitted loosely into the barrel until a pre-rifled band was inserted in the muzzle. Gases generated by firing then drove a shear-bolt forward to cut the pin linking the projectile and propelling tube. The graze fuze was activated during firing by set-back.

Sprenggranate für Leuchtpistole Z. was contained in a varnished steel cartridge case carrying the primer and propellant. A combustion fuze lay in the projectile base, but packing cases bore the legend 'ACHTUNG! NUR AUS PANZERN ODER GLEICHWERTIGER DECKUNG VERFEUEREN! BRENNZEIT 1 SEK.' ('Danger! Only fire from tanks or similar cover! Burning time: 1 second'). As accidents were common, the high-explosive shell was heartily disliked. Issued only in 1944–5, it was regarded as a great secret by the Heereswaffenamt.

Ammunition for Gewehrgranatgerät

Gewehr-Sprenggranate (G. Sprggr.). The standard high-explosive grenade was made in several forms. The most effective had an impact fuze (Aufschlagszünder 5071), a pyrotechnic time fuze (Brennzünder) and delay elements (Verzögerungszeitzündung). The shell-body was painted yellow, the ribbed base-cap could be removed, and a hole was bored through the screw in the centre of the base. Grenades of this type could be used as hand grenades, and also for high angle fire. A similar pattern, without the time-delay elements, made a satisfactory hand grenade but was not to be used for high-angle fire. It lacked the hole in the base screw, and the ribbed base cap was often part of the body; a third version, with only the impact fuze, had the ribbed base cap and the body made integrally. It was unsuitable for high-angle fire, and could not be used as a hand grenade. The launching cartridge, 'Gewehr-Katrusche 1g.', had a yellow primer annulus.

A long-range high-explosive grenade was also made, in the same three patterns. Distinguished by 'WEITSCHUSS' stencilled in black on the yellow body, it was driven by the 'Gewehr-Treibpatrone 1,5g.', with a short yellow wooden bullet. The grenades that were fitted only with impact fuzes had AZ. 5097 instead of AZ. 5071, allowing them to be used for high-angle fire even though accuracy was poor.

Gewehr-Panzergranate (G. Pzgr.). Out of production by the summer of 1944, though still in stock, this armour-piercing projectile had a ballistic cap over a hollow nose. The body was painted black, and the 'Gewehr-Kartusche für G. Pzgr. (1,1g.)' had a black primer annulus. Grenades of this type could not be used as hand grenades, and were unsuitable for anything other than direct fire.

Grosse Gewehr-Panzergranate (G. G. Pzgr.). An enlarged version of the original armour-piercing projectile, introduced in October 1942[7], this weighed about 387gm and required a special blank cartridge with 1.9gm propellant and a black wooden bullet. It had a base fuze, a special primer (Zündhütchen 47), and 'kleine Zündladung 34'. The grenade body was painted black, and the labels and packaging were given distinctive black stripes. An improved form of the G. G. Pzgr. appeared in March 1943[8], with a drive shaft made of Bakelite instead of alloy.

Gewehr-Blendgranate (G. B. Gr.'). Intended for 'flash' or illuminating purposes, this had a field-grey body stencilled 'B' in black. The launching blanks were either the standard 1.5gm Gewehr-Treibpatrone, with a short yellow wooden bullet, or the 1.7gm load developed for the propaganda grenade. An improved form, the Gewehrblendgranate 42 ('Gw. B. Gr. 42.') was introduced in September 1944.[9]

Gewehr-Nebelgranate (G. Nbgr.). The smoke grenade also had a field-grey body, with 'Nb' in black, but also had a distinctive sheet-metal case. It was fired with the 1.5gm Treibpatrone.

Gewehr-Fallschirmleuchtgranate (G. Fall. Lt. Gr.). The parachute grenade, fired with the Treibpatrone 1,5g., had a white-painted nose. The full designation was stencilled in black on the shell body.

Gewehr-Propagandagranate (G. Prop. Gr.). Driven by either the standard Treibpatrone 1,5g. or the 'G.-Kart. F. G. Prop. Gr. 1,7g.', with a red primer annulus, this had a distinctive detachable cap and the full designation stencilled in black on the shell body.

Ammunition packaging and labelling

German small-arms ammunition was packed conventionally. Though the colour of the primer annuli and case-mouth seals varied from calibre to calibre, an identification system was common to all German small-arms packaging.

A white label signified ball ammunition; yellow or buff was tracer; green was incendiary; pink, pale reddish-orange or brick-red identified bulleted blanks; and red-white (divided diagonally) showed that the armour-piercing bullets had tungsten cores.

An additional vertical medial blue stripe identified steel-case ammunition; a green diagonal stripe, running upwards to the right from the bottom left corner, marked practice rounds; and a black horizontal bar along the top edge of the label denoted explosive/incendiary rounds.

Overprinting was generally in black, excepting certain projectile designations (e.g., 'S. m. K.') and some of the major instructions. These were red. Large-scale overprints, also invariably in red ink, showed other characteristics: 'i. L.' or 'in Ladestreifen' for rifle ammunition packed in chargers, only to be used in machine-guns in emergency; 'für M.G.' ('for machine-guns') or 'nur für M.G.' ('only for machine-guns') on machine-gun ammunition, only to be used in rifles in emergency; 'für Gew.' or 'nur für Gew.' for ammunition to be used only in rifles; and 'Inhalt o. L.' – in black – for charger-packed ammunition that had been dismembered into cartons. 'Unbekannt', 'Lief. unbek.' or 'Lieferung unbekannt' indicated ammunition of unknown origin, or collected from mixed batches.

More than one identifier sometimes appeared on a single label. Supplementary rectangular labels provided information such as 'Nicht zur Oberschiessen und Schiessen durch Lucken geeignet' ('unsuitable for overhead fire or for firing through gaps', black on white) or 'Nicht geeignet für Gesteuerte Bordwaffen' ('unsuitable for synchronized guns', red on white). Triangular examples sometimes included 'Nur zu Übungs zwecken' ('only for practice use'), in black on pale green or bluish-green stock.

Cartridges intended specifically for tropical use had an additional case-mouth seal, usually matching the primer annulus, to prevent excessive heat and/or moisture penetrating them. Their box labels usually include 'f. Trop.'.

Appendix 2

German letter codes

The list that follows identifies some of the best known manufacturers' letter codes used during the Second World War, together with the class of product with which they were associated. The list is not exhaustive, but merely a demonstration of the complexity of the coding system. Additional information can be obtained from the reprint of the official codelists, *Liste der Fertigungskennzeichen fur Waffen, Munition and Gerät* . . . (Berlin, 1944), though this gives no additional details. A more comprehensive source of information, though concentrating only on the codes associated with the arms industry, is *German Military Codes 1939–45* by John Walter (Tharston Press and International Military Antiques, Inc., 2004), which, unlike the official *Liste*, has an explanatory introduction and is indexed by code, name and place. *Zahlencode System des Deutschen Heeres von 1925 bis 1940* by Johannes Preuss (Journal-Verlag Schwend, 2002) is the only detailed guide to the numerical codes that preceded the alphabetical systems.

'a': Nähmatag–Nähmaschinenteile AG, Dresden. Gun parts.
'ab': Mundlos AG, Magdeburg-Nord. Bayonets.
'ac': Carl Walther AG, Zella-Mehlis, Thüringen. Small arms.
'ad': Patronen-, Zündhütchen- & Metallwarenfabrik, Schönebeck an der Elbe, Sachsen. Small-arms ammunition.
'aek': F. Dušek, Opočno bei Nachod, Czechoslovakia. Gun parts.
'agv': Berg & Co., Solingen-Ohligs. Bayonets.
'aj': Sörensen & Köster, Neumünster in Holstein (Brachenfeld). Signal-pistol ammunition.

215

'ajf': Junker & Ruh AG, Karlsruhe in Baden. Small arms.

'ak': Munitionsfabriken vormals Sellier & Bellot, Prague, Czechoslovakia (Vlasim works). Small-arms ammunition.

'al': Deutsches Leucht- & Signalmittelwerk, Dr. Feistel KG, Werk Schönhagen bei Trebbin Kreis Teltow (headquarters: Berlin-Charlottenburg, Kaiserdamm 44). Signal-pistol ammunition.

'am': Gustloff-Werke, Otto Eberhardt Patronenfabrik, Hirtenberg, Niederdonau. Small-arms ammunition.

'amn': Mauser-Werke KG, Werk Neuwied. Gun parts.

'amo': Mauser-Werke KG, Werk Waldeck Bezirk Kassel. Gun parts.

'ap': Deutsches Leucht- & Signalmittelwerk, Dr. Feistel KG, Werk Wuppertal-Ronsdorf. Signal-pistol ammunition.

'aqr': R. & O. Lux AG, Marienthal-Bad Lieberstein/Thüringen. Gun parts.

'ar': Mauser-Werke AG, Werk Borsigwalde, Berlin-Borsigwalde, Eichborndamm. Small arms.

'asb': Deutsche Waffen- & Munitionsfabriken AG (DWM), Berlin-Borsigwalde. Small-arms ammunition.

'asr': HAK-Hanseatisches Kettenwerk GmbH, Hamburg. Small-arms ammunition.

'asw': E. & F. Hörster, Solingen. Bayonets.

'auc': Mauser-Werke KG, Köln-Ehrenfeld. Gun parts.

'auj': Monheimer Ketten- & Metallwaren- Industrie Pötz & Sand, Monheim-Düsseldorf. Small-arms- and signal-pistol ammunition.

'aux': Polte-Werke, Werk Magdeburg. Small-arms ammunition.

'auy': Polte-Werke, Werk Grüneberg (Nordbahn). Small-arms ammunition.

'auz': Polte-Werke, Werk Arnstadt, Thüringen. Small-arms ammunition.

'avt': Silva Metallwerke GmbH, Magdeburg. Small-arms ammunition.

'avu': Silva Metallwerke GmbH, Werk Genthin. Small-arms ammunition.

'awj': The Yale & Towne Manufacturing Company, Velbert, Rheinland. Gun parts.

'awt': Württembergische Metallwarenfabrik AG, Geislingen-Steige. Gun parts.

'ax': Feinmechanische Werke GmbH, Erfurt, Thüringen. Small arms.

'axq': Erfurter Laden-Industrie, Erfurt-Nord. Small-arms ammunition.

'ay': Alois Pirkl, Reichenberg/Sudetengau. Small-arms ammunition.

'aye': Olympia Büromaschinenwerke AG, Erfurt. Gun parts.

'ayf': Erma—Erfurter Maschinenfabrik B. Geipel GmbH, Erfurt. Gun parts.

'ba': Sundwiger Messingwerk vorm. Gebr. von der Becke KG, Sundwig Kreis Iserlohn. Small-arms ammunition.

'bcb': Otto Graf, Leipzig. Leatherware.

'bcd': Gustloff-Werke, Werk Weimar. Small arms.

'bdq': Ehrhardt & Kirsten, Tauscha bei Leipzig. Leatherware.

'bdr': Richard Ehrhardt, Pössneck in Thüringen. Leatherware.

'be': Berndorfer Metallwarenfabrik Arthur Krupp AG, Berndorf, Niederdonau. Small-arms ammunition.

'beh': Ernst Leitz GmbH, Wetzlar. Optical equipment.

'bek': Hensoldt Werk für Optik & Mechanik, Inh. Dr Hans Hensoldt, Herborn (Dillkreis). Optical equipment.

'bky': Böhmische Waffenfabrik AG in Prag, Werk Ung. Brod (Mähren). Gun parts.

'bla': E.G. Leuner GmbH, Bautzen. Leatherware.

'blc': Carl Zeiss, Militärabteilung Jena. Optical equipment.

'bmd': Max G. Müller, Nürnberg O., Forsthofstrasse 37. Leatherware.

'bmj': M. Hensoldt & Söhne AG, Wetzlar. Optical equipment.

'bml': Hans Römer, Neu-Ulm/Donau. Leatherware.

'bmn': Böttcher & Renner, Nürnberg O., Rennweg 26–28. Leatherware.

'bmo': Hans Deuter, Augsburg. Leatherware.

'bmz': Minerva Nähmaschinenfabrik AG, Boskowitz, Czechoslovakia. Gun parts.

'bne': Metallwerke Odertal GmbH, Odertal Post Lautaberg/Harz. Small-arms ammunition.

'bnf': Metallwerk Wolfenbüttel GmbH, Wolfenbüttel, Halchterstrasse 21. Small-arms ammunition.

'bnz': Steyr-Daimler-Puch AG, Werk Steyr. Small arms.

'bpd': C.P. Goerz GmbH, Wien. Optical equipment.

'bpr': Johannes Grossfuss, Döbeln in Sachsen. Gun parts.

'bqt': Eugen Müller, Wien XXI. Signal-pistol ammunition.

'bvf': C. Reichert, Wien 107/XVII, Hernalser Hauptstrasse 219. Optical equipment.

'bvv': Rothmüller-Mewa, Wien 20. Signal-pistol ammunition.

'byf': Mauser-Werke KG, Oberndorf am Neckar, Württemberg. Small arms.

'bym': Genossenschafts Maschinenhaus der Büchsenmacher, Ferlach/Kärnten. Bayonets.

'byw': Johannes Schäfer, Stettiner Schraubenwerk, Stettin. Small-arms ammunition.

'bzt': Fritz Wolf, Rob. Sohn, Zella-Mehlis. Gun stocks.

'bzz': IG-Farbenindustrie, Camerawerk München. Optical equipment.

'cad': Karl Kahles, Wien 89, Einwanggasse 48. Optical equipment.

'cag': D. Swarovski, Wattens/Tirol. Optical equipment.

'can': August Wallmeyer, Eisenach in Thüringen. Bayonet scabbards.

'cbl': Vereingte Deutsche Metallwerke AG, Zweigniederlassung Süddeutsche Metallindustrie, Nürnberg W. Signal-pistol ammunition.

'ccx': Optische & Feinmechanische Werke, Hugo Meyer & Co., Görlitz. Optical equipment.

'cdc': Kern, Kläger & Co., Berlin N58, Pappelallee 78–79. Leatherware.

'cdg': Auwaerter & Bubeck KG, Stuttgart, Hasenbergstrasse 31. Leatherware.

'cdo': Theodor Bergmann & Co. KG, Werk Velten (headquarters: Berlin W62). Small-arms ammunition.

'cdp': Theodor Bergmann & Co. KG, Werk Bernau (headquarters: Berlin W62). Small-arms ammunition.

'ce': J.P. Sauer & Sohn, Suhl, Thüringen. Small arms.

'cey': Karl Budischovsky & Söhne, Oesterreichische Lederindustrie AG, Wien, Hintere Zollamtstrasse 17. Leatherware.

'cf': Westfälisch-Anhaltische Sprengstoff AG (WASAG), Werk Oranienburg. Small-arms ammunition.

'cg': Finower Industrie GmbH, Finow/Mark. Small-arms ammunition.

'cgn': Rohrbacher Lederfabrik Jos. Poeschl's Söhne, Rohrbach/Oberdonau. Leatherware.

'cgu': Stolla's Söhne, W.K., K. & A. Stolla, Wien 65, Floriangasse 50. Leatherware.

'ch': Fabrique Nationale d'Armes de Guerre SA, Herstal-lèz-Liége, Belgium ('DWM, Werk Lüttich'). Small arms and ammunition.

'clb': Dr. F.A. Wöhler, Kassel, Wolfsangerstrasse 12. Optical equipment.

'clc': Richard Abr. Herder, Solingen. Bayonets.

'clg': Ernst Melzig, Liegnitz. Leatherware.

'cnd': National Krupp Registrier Kassen GmbH, Fabrik Berlin-Neukölln. Gun parts.

'cny': C. Pose, Berlin O34, Boxhagener Strasse 16. Leatherware.

'cof': Carl Eickhorn, Solingen. Bayonets.

'con': Franz Stock, Berlin-Neukölln. Gun parts.

'cos': Merz-Werke Gebr. Merz, Frankfurt am Main, Rheinland. Gun parts.

'cqh': Clemen & Jung, Solingen. Bayonets.

'cqr': Lederwerk Sedina, Joachim Schell Sportartikelfabrik, Finkenwalde Bezirk Stettin. Leatherware.

'crn': Hanseatische Werkstätten für Feinmechanik & Optik, Friedrichs & Co., Hamburg-Schnelsen, Oldesloer Strasse 59. Optical equipment.

'crs': Paul Weyersberg & Co., Solingen. Bayonets.

'csr': Gebr. Heller GmbH, Marienthal bei Schweina. Gun parts.

'cua': Röhm Gesellschaft, Zella-Mehlis, Thüringen. Gun parts.

'cul': Ernst Pack & Söhne, Solingen. Bayonets.

'cvb': Otto Sindel, Berlin O27, Holzmarktstrasse 67. Leatherware.

'cvc': L. Zeschke Nachfolger, Gebr. Zeuschner, Müllrose bei Frankfurt an der Oder. Leatherware.

'cvg': Vereinigte Deutsche Metallwerke AG, Werk Heddernheim, Frankfurt am Main. Small-arms ammunition.

'cvl': WKC Waffenfabrik GmbH, Solingen-Wald. Bayonets.

'cww': Carl Weiss, Braunschweig. Leatherware.

'cxb': Moll Lederwarenfabrik, Goch, Rheinland. Leatherware.

'cxm': Gustav Genschow & Co. AG, Berlin SO36, Bouchéstrasse 12. Small-arms ammunition; leatherware.

'cxn': Emil Busch AG, Rathenow. Optical sights.

'cyq': Spreewerke GmbH, Berlin-Spandau. Small arms.

'dbg': Dynamit AG, vormals Alfred Nobel & Co., Werk Düneberg. Small-arms ammunition.

'dde': Robert Larsen, Berlin SW68. Leatherware.

'ddl': Remscheider Hobelmesserfabrik Josua Corts Sohn, Remscheid. Bayonets.

'ddx': Voigtländer & Sohn AG, Braunschweig. Optical equipment.

'dfb': Gustloff-Werke, Waffenwerk Suhl. Small arms.

'dfc': L. Ritgen, Karlsruhe. Leatherware.

'dhp': H. Burgsmüller & Söhne GmbH, Kreiensen in Harz. Gun parts.

'dkk': Friedrich Offermann & Söhne, Bensberg. Leatherware.

'dla': Karl Barth, Waldbröhl/Rheinland. Leatherware.

'dlu': Ewald Lüneschloss, Solingen. Leatherware.

'dnf': Rheinisch-Westfälische Sprengstoff AG, Werk Stadeln bei Nürnberg. Small-arms ammunition.

'dnh': Rheinisch-Westfälische Sprengstoff AG, Werk Durlach bei Karlsruhe. Small-arms ammunition.

'dom': Westfälische Metall-Industrie AG, Lippstadt. Small-arms ammunition.

'dot': Waffenwerke Brünn AG, Werk Brünn. Small arms and ammunition.

'dou': Waffenwerke Brünn AG, Werk Povaška Bystrica. Small arms and ammunition.

'dov': Waffenwerke Brünn AG, Werk Wsetin. Small-arms.

'dow': Waffenwerke Brünn AG, Werk Prerau (renamed 'Opticotechna GmbH, Werk Prerau/Protektorat' in 1943). Optical equipment.

'dox': Waffenwerk Brünn AG, Werk Podbrezova. Gun parts.

'dpv': Zeiss-Ikon AG, Dresden. Optical equipment.

'dpw': Zeiss-Ikon AG, Goerzwerk, Berlin-Zehlendorf. Optical equipment.

'dpx': Zeiss-Ikon AG, Contessawerk, Stuttgart. Optical equipment.

'dql': Remo-Gewehr-Fabrik Gebrüder Rempt, Suhl, Thüringen. Gun parts.

'dsh': Ing. F. Janaček, Prag-Nusle II, Czechoslovakia (foundry at Teinitz a/S). Gun parts.

'dta': A. Waldhausen, Inh. M. Bruchmann, Köln. Leatherware.

'dtd': Motor-Condensator-Compagnie Scholz KG, Geschäftsstelle, München 51, Schliessfach 45. Signal pistols.

'dtv': C. Otto Gehrckens, Pinneberg. Leatherware.

'duv': Berlin-Lübecker Maschinenfabriken Bernhard Berghaus, Lübeck. Small arms.

'dvr': Johann Fröhlich, Wien 101/XV, Hütteldorfer Strasse 44–46. Leatherware.

'dye': Erste Alpenländische Pyrotechnikfabrik Ed. Pitschmann & Co., Innsbruck. Signal-pistol ammunition.

'dyo': J.M. Eckart, Ulm-Donau. Leatherware.

'dzl': Optische Anstalt Oigee GmbH, Berlin-Schöneberg. Optical equipment.

'eba': Scharfenberg & Teubert GmbH, Breitungen-Werra. Small-arms ammunition.

'eca': Oskar Fischer GmbH, Markdorf in Baden. Signal-pistol ammunition.

'ecb': Gebr. Bock, Berlin-Buchholz. Signal-pistol ammunition.

'ecc': Oskar Lünig, Möhringen (Fildern). Signal-pistol ammunition.

'ecd': Carl Lippold, Wuppertal-Elberfeld. Signal-pistol ammunition.

'edg': J.A. Henckels Zwillingswerk, Solingen-Gräfrath. Gun parts.

'edq': Deutsche Waffen- & Munitionsfabriken AG, Werk Lübeck-Schlutup, Wesloerstrasse. Small-arms ammunition.

'eea': Hermann Weihrauch, Zella-Mehlis, Thüringen. Gun parts and optical-sight mounts.

'eej': Märkisches Walzwerk GmbH, Strausberg Bezirk Potsdam. Small-arms ammunition.

'eem': Selve-Kronbiegel Dornheim AG, Sömmerda in Sachsen. Small-arms ammunition.

'eeo': Deutsche Waffen- & Munitionsfabriken AG ('DWM'), Werk Posen. Gun parts.

'eeu': Lieferungsgemeinschaft westthüringische Werkzeug- & Metallwaren-fabriken GmbH, Schmalkalden in Thüringen. Signal pistols and gun parts.

'eey': Metallwarenfabrik Treuenbritzen GmbH, Werk Roederhof. Small-arms ammunition.

'elm': J.H. Benecke, Hannoversche Wachstuch- & Ledertuch-Fabrik, Vinnhorst bei Hannover. Leatherware.

'emj': Adalbert Fischer, Berlin C2, Georgenkirchstrasse 24. Leatherware.

'emp': Dynamit AG, vormals Alfred Nobel & Co., Werk Empelde bei Hannover. Small-arms ammunition.

'emr': Adalbert Fischer, Guttstadt in Ostpreussen. Leatherware.

'eom': H. Huck, Nürnberg W. Small-arms ammunition.

'eqf': Karl Böcker, Waldbröhl/Rheinland. Leatherware.

'eqr': G. Passier & Sohn, Hannover i/W. Leatherware.

'eso': G. Rodenstock, München. Optical equipment.

'eue': Otto Reichel, Inh. Rudolf Fischer, Lengefeld/Erzgebirge. Leatherware.

'evg': Max Oswald, Karlsruhe. Leatherware.

'ewx': Franz & Karl Voegels, Köln. Leatherware.

'fa': Mansfeld AG für Bergbau & Hüttenbetrieb, Hettstedt/Südharz. Small-arms ammunition.

'faa': Deutsche Waffen- & Munitionsfabriken AG, Karlsruhe in Baden. Small-arms ammunition.

'fb': Mansfeld AG, Rothenburg/Saale. Small-arms ammunition.

'fd': Stolberger Metallwerke KG von Asten, Lynen & Schleicher, Stolberg/Rheinland. Small-arms ammunition.

'fde': Dynamit AG, vormals Alfred Nobel & Co., Förde. Small-arms ammu-nition.

'fer': Metallwerke Wandhofen GmbH, Schwerte/Ruhr. Small-arms ammuni-tion.

'ffc': Friedr. Abr. Herder Sohn, Solingen, Grünewalder Strasse. Bayonets and gun parts.

'ffk': Wittkop & Co., Bielefeld. Leatherware.

'fkx': Gustav Sudbrack, Bielefeld, Königstrasse 59. Leatherware.

'fla': Ernst Ferd. Waentig KG, Erste Deutsche Ledertuch-Fabrik, Grossenhain in Sachsen. Leatherware.

'fnh': Böhmische Waffenfabrik AG in Prag, Werk Strakonitz. Small arms.

'fnj': Alexander Coppel GmbH ('Alcoso'), Solingen, Auf dem Kamp 58. Bayonets and gun parts.

'fnk': Adolf Hopf AG, Tambach-Dietharz in Thüringen. Signal-pistol ammunition.

'fsx': Albin Scholle, Zeitz, Weissenfelser Strasse 35/36. Leatherware.

'ftc': Frost & Jähnel, Breslau 1, Schlossohle 7–9. Leatherware.

'ftt': Vereinigte Lederwaren-Fabriken Eugen Huber, München 8, Rosenheimerstrasse 17–19. Leatherware.

'fuq': Cottbusser Lederwarenwerk Curt Vogel KG, Cottbuss, Wernerstrasse 62. Leatherware.

'fva': Draht- & Metallwarenfabrik GmbH, Salzwedel. Small-arms ammunition.

'fvx': Cr. Beck & Söhne, Kassel, Wilhelmshöher Allee 40. Optical equipment.

'fxo': C.G. Haenel, Suhl. Small arms.

'fys': Rahm & Kampmann, Wuppertal-Elberfeld. Leatherware.

'fze': F.W. Höller, Solingen. Bayonets.

'fzg': Feinmechanik GmbH, Kassel. Optical equipment.

'fzs': Heinrich Krieghoff, Suhl. Small arms.

'ga': Hirsch Kupfer- & Messingwerke AG, Finow/Mark. Small-arms ammunition.

'gal': Wagner & Co. GmbH, Mühlhausen in Thüringen. Small arms.

'gcy': L.O. Dietrich, Vesta-Nähmaschinenwerke, Altenburg in Thüringen. Gun parts.

'gfg': Carl Hepting & Co., Stuttgart-Feuerbach. Leatherware.

'ghf': Fritz Kiess & Co GmbH, Suhl. Gun parts.

'ghk': Moritz & Gerstenberger, Zella-Mehlis. Signal pistols.

'gmn': Philipp Riebel & Söhne, Ingolstadt, Hindenburgstrasse 31. Leatherware.

'gmo': Rahm & Kampmann, Kaiserslautern. Leatherware.

'gna': Gustav Buchmüller, Stuttgart S., Karlstrasse 15–17. Leatherware.

'gpf': Carl Tesch, Berlin N4, Chausseestrasse 106. Leatherware.

'gpt': Gustav Bittner, Weipert/Sudetengau. Gun parts.

'grz': Gebr. Krüger, Breslau 5, Freiburger Strasse 36. Leatherware.

'gtb': J.F. Eisfeld, Werk Güntersberge. Signal pistols.

'gug': Ungarnische Optische Werke AG, Budapest. Optical equipment.

'guj': Werner D. Kuehn, Berlin-Steglitz, Berlinickestrasse 11. Optical equipment.

'gut': Walter Schürmann & Co., Bielefeld. Leatherware.

'gxc': Adam Reinhold, Oberursel (Taunus). Leatherware.

'gxq': Henseler & Co., Inh. Fritz Henseler, Ulm-Donau, Zinglerstrasse 49. Leatherware.

'gxy': Gebr. Klinge, Dresden-Löbtau, Anton-Weck-Strasse 2–6. Leatherware.

'gyo': Hans Dinkelmeyer, Nürnberg W., Iamnitzerstrasse 14. Leatherware.

'gyq': Anton Wingen jr, Solingen, Gasstrasse 54. Gun parts.

'gyr': Hugo Linder Deltawerk, Solingen. Gun parts.

'ha': Wielandwerke AG, Metallhalbfabrikate, Ulm am Donau. Small-arms ammunition.

'ham': Dynamit AG, vormals Alfred Nobel & Co., Werk Hamm. Small arms and ammunition.

'has': Pulverfabrik Hasloch, Hasloch am Main. Small-arms ammunition.

'hat': Gebr. Gräfrath, Solingen-Widdert. Gun parts.

'hck': Georg A. Lerch GmbH, Berlin C2, Leipzigerstrasse 75/76. Leatherware.

'hee': Ikaria-Werke GmbH, Velten/Mark. Gun parts.

'hfr': Sachs & Deisselberg, Hamburg 11, Rödingsmarkt. Leatherware.

'hft': H. Becker & Co. GmbH, Berlin C2, Marsiliusstrasse 4–6. Leatherware.

'hgs': Gustav W.C. Burmester, Trittau Bezirk Hamburg. Signal-pistol ammunition.

'hhw': Metallwerke Silberhütte GmbH, St. Andreasberg in Harz. Small-arms ammunition.

'hjg': Kimnach & Brunn, Kaiserslautern. Leatherware.

'hjh': Carl Ackva, Bad Kreuznach, Rüdesheimerstrasse 27. Leatherware.

'hla': Metallwarenfabrik Treuenbritzen GmbH, Werk Sebaldushof. Small-arms ammunition.

'hlb': Metallwarenfabrik Treuenbritzen GmbH, Werk Selterhof. Small-arms ammunition.

'hlc': Zieh- & Stanzwerk GmbH, Schleusingen/Thüringen. Small-arms ammunition.

'hlv': Maury & Co., Offenbach am Main, Luisenstrasse 16. Leatherware.

'hou': Press-, Stanz- & Ziehwerk GmbH, Velbert. Small-arms ammunition.

'hre': C.W. Motz & Co., Brandenburg an der Havel. Small-arms ammunition.

'hrn': Presswerk GmbH, Metgethen in Ostpreussen. Small-arms ammunition.

'hsy': Franz Cobau, Berlin-Reinickendorf-Ost, Rezidenzstrasse 133a. Leatherware.

'htg': Polte Werke, Werk Duderstadt. Small-arms ammunition.

'i': Elite Diamantwerke AG, Siegmar-Schönau bei Chemnitz. Bayonets, gun parts.

'jba': A. Wunderlich Nachf., Berlin-Neukölln, Finowstrasse 27. Leatherware.

'jhg': Gustav Genschow & Co. AG, Abteilung Lederwaren-Fabriken, Alstadt-Hachenburg, Westerwald. Leatherware.

'jhv': Metallwaren-, Waffen- & Maschinenfabrik AG, Budapest IX, Sorchksariuc 158, Hungary. Small arms.

'jhz': Jean Weipert, Offenbach am Main, Bernardstrasse 14–16. Leatherware.

'jkh': Carl Busse, Mainz, Kurfürstenstrasse 11. Leatherware.

'jln': Deutsche Lederwerkstätten GmbH, Pirmasens, Margarethenstrasse 3. Leatherware.

'jme': Armeemarinehaus, Inh. Deutscher Offizier-Verein, Berlin-Charlottenburg, Hardenbergstrasse 24. Leatherware.

'jon': Voigtländer-Gevaert, Berlin-Spindlersfeld. Optical equipment.

'jsd': Gustav Reinhardt, Berlin SW68, Brandenburgstrasse 72/73. Leatherware.

'jua': Danuvia Waffen- & Munitionsfabriken AG, Budapest, Angol utca 1–12, Hungary. Guns parts; small-arms ammunition.

'jvb': Wessel & Müller, Luckenwalde. Metal cases for optical sights, gun parts.

'jvd': Erste Nordböhmische Metallwarenfabrik, Adolf Rössler, Niedereinsiedel (Sudetenland). Gun parts.

'jve': Ernst Ludwig, Weixdorf in Sachsen. Optical equipment.

'jvf': Wilhelm Brand, Heidelberg, Eppelheimerstrasse 40. Leatherware.

'jwa': Moritz Stecher, Freiberg in Sachsen. Leatherware.

'jwh': Manufacture Nationale [Staatliche Waffenfabrik], Châtellerault, France. Gun parts; bayonets.

'jxh': F.W. Kinkel, Mainz, Wallstrasse 17. Leatherware.

'k': Luck & Wagner, Suhl, Thüringen. Small arms.

'kam': Hugo Schneider AG, Werk Skarzysko-Kamienna, Poland (from
c. 1943 'Hasag Eisen- und Metallwerke GmbH'). Small-arms
ammunition.

'kfa': Staatliches Arsenal, Sarajewo, Yugoslavia. Small arms.

'kfk': DISA–Dansk Industri Syndikat AS 'Madsen', Kopenhagen. Small
arms.

'kkd': Wilh. Stern KG, Posen, Breitestrasse 1. Leatherware.

'kkj': Leitmeritzer Rucksäcke- & Lederwarenfabrik GmbH, Leitmeritz an der
Elbe. Leatherware.

'klb': J.F. Eisfeld GmbH, Werk Kieselbach. Signal-pistol cartridges.

'kls': Steyr-Daimler-Puch AG, Werk Warschau, Dworska 29, Poland. Gun
parts.

'kot': Adalbert Fischer, Berlin C2, Georgenkirchstrasse 24. Leatherware.

'kov': Établissement Barbier, Benard & Turenne, Paris, Rue Curial 82.
Optical instruments.

'kpm': Franz Cobau, Berlin-Reinickendorf-Ost. Leatherware.

'krd': Lignose AG, Werk Kriewald (renamed ['lt. 8. Nachtrag']
'Sprengstoffwerke Oberschlesien GmbH' in c. 1943). Small-arms
ammunition.

'krl': Dynamit AG, vormals Alfred Nobel & Co., Werk Krümmel. Small-
arms ammunition.

'krm': C. Pose, Berlin O34, Boxhagener Strasse 16. Leatherware.

'kro': Heinrich Döbert, Unterschwarzach/Baden. Leatherware.

'krp': Adolf Weinig, Offenbach am Main, Kaiserstrasse 27. Leatherware.

'krq': Emil Busch AG, Rathenow. Optical equipment.

'kru': Lignose Sprengstoffwerke GmbH, Werk Kruppamühle. Small-arms
ammunition.

'ksd': Walter Winkler, Berlin-Spandau, Schönwalderstrasse 101.
Leatherware.

'kun': J.F. Eisfeld GmbH, Werk Kunigunde. Signal pistols and signal-pistol
ammunition.

'kuu': Carl Henkel, Bielefeld, Herforder Strasse 48. Leatherware.

'kwd': Jagdpatronen-, Zündhütchen- & Metallwarenfabrik AG, Budapest.
Small-arms ammunition.

'la': Dürener Metallwerke AG, Werk Metallhalbfabrikate Düren,
Düren/Rheinland. Small-arms ammunition.

'lae': Heinrich Zeiss/Union Zeiss KG, Werk Gostingen/Wartheland. Optical equipment.

'ldb': Sprengstoff und pyrotechnische Fabriken vorm. Lechfeld & Depyfag GmbH, Werk Berlin-Malchow (renamed 'Deutsche Pyrotechnische-Fabrik' in 1943). Small-arms ammunition.

'ldc': Sprengstoff und pyrotechnische Fabriken vorm. Lechfeld & Depyfag GmbH, Werk Cleebronn ('Deutsche Pyrotechnische-Fabrik' from 1943 onward). Small-arms ammunition.

'ldn': Sprengstoff und pyrotechnische Fabriken vorm. Lechfeld & Depyfag GmbH, Werk Neumarkt/Oberpfalz (renamed 'Deutsche Pyrotechnische-Fabrik' in 1943). Signal-pistol ammunition.

'lgp': Veltener Maschinenbau GmbH, Velten/Mark. Gun parts.

'lhr': Greifelt & Co., Suhl, Schliessfach 18. Gun parts.

'lkm': Munitionsfabriken vorm. Sellier & Bellot, Werk Prag-Veitsberg. Small-arms ammunition.

'lkq': Elwezet-Lederwarenfabrik Werner Zahn, vorm. Fürst & Hoeft, Berlin SW68, Oranienstrasse 70. Leatherware.

'lmq': Carl Zeiss, Jena. Optical equipment.

'lpk': Servotechna AG, Prag IX, Podiebrader Landstrasse 221, Czechoslovakia. Small-arms ammunition.

'ltk': Robert Klass, Solingen-Ohligs, Pfeilstrasse 37. Bayonets; gun parts.

'lww': Huet et Cie, SA des Anciens Établissement et Jumelles Flammarion, Paris. Optical equipment.

'lwx': OPL–Optique et Précision de Levallois, Levallois-Perret/Seine, 102 Rue Chaptal. Optical equipment.

'lwy': SOM–Société d'Optique et Mécanique de Haute Précision, Paris X, 125 Boulevard Davout. Optical equipment.

'lxr': Dianawerk Mayer & Grammelspacher, Rastatt/Baden. Gun parts.

'lza': Mauser-Werke AG, Werk Karlsruhe/Baden. Gun parts.

'ma': F.A. Lange AG, Neusilberfabrikate, Aue/Sachsen. Small-arms ammunition.

'mog': Deutsche Sprengchemie, Werk Moschwig. Small-arms ammunition.

'mpu': Wlaschimer Maschinenfabrik GmbH, Prag XI, Jesseniusstrasse 57, Czechoslovakia. Werk in Wlaschim. Small-arms ammunition.

'na': Westfälische Kupfer- und Messingwerke AG vorm. Caspar Noell, Lüdenscheid in Westfalen. Small-arms ammunition.

'nbe': Hasag Eisen & Metallwerke GmbH, Werk Apparatebau, Tschenstochau. Small-arms ammunition.

'nea': Walter Steiner, Suhl. Gun parts.

'nec': Waffenwerke Brünn AG, Prag, Werk V, Gurein. Gun parts.

'nfx': RWS Munitionsfabrik GmbH, Warschau-Praga, Poland. Small-arms ammunition.

'nhj': J. Brauer, Frankfurt am Main, Bergerstrasse 13. Leatherware.

'nhn': H. Eger & Linde, Seligenthal in Thüringen. Leatherware.

'nhr': Rheinmetall-Borsig AG, Werk Sömmerda. Gun parts.

'nos': Richard Becker, Lesser & Jobst, Vereinigte Möbelstoff-Polstermaterialen & Sattlerwaren grosshandlungen KG, Berlin SW68, Prinzenstrasse 49. Leatherware.

'nqa': Fritz Fürstel, Offenbach/Main, Ludwigstrasse 24. Leatherware.

'nsq': Ernst Opitz, Berlin O112, Frankfurter Allee 316. Leatherware.

'nyw': Gustloff-Werke, Meiningen. Gun parts.

'nzz': Max Oswald, Karlsruhe, Schützenstrasse 42. Leatherware.

'oa': Eduard Hueck, Lüdenscheid in Westfalen. Small-arms ammunition.

'oaz': Max Oswald, Karlsruhe, Schützenstrasse 42. Leatherware.

'oma': Ernst Mahla, Prag-Michl. Small-arms ammunition.

'otg': Heinrich Hinkel, Mühlheim am Main. Leatherware.

'ovt': Josto-Lederwarenfabrik Franz Friedl, Prag XI. Leatherware.

'oxo': Teuto Metallwerke GmbH, Osnabrück, Klosterstrasse 29. Small-arms ammunition.

'oyj': Ateliers de Construction de Tarbes. Small-arms ammunition.

'P': Polte Armaturen- & Maschinenfabrik AG, Magdeburg, Sachsen (later renamed 'Polte-Werke'). Small-arms ammunition.

'pjj': Staatliche Munitionsfabrik, Kopenhagen, Denmark. Small-arms ammunition.

'qa': Wilhelm Prym, Stolberg/Rheinland. Small-arms ammunition.

'qrb': Pirotecnico di Bologna, Italy. Small-arms ammunition.

'qve': Carl Walther, Zella-Mehlis, Thüringen. Small arms.

'r': Westfälisch-Anhaltische Sprengstoff AG (WASAG), Werk Reinsdorf. Small-arms ammunition.

'ra': Deutsche Messingwerke, Carl Eveking AG, Berlin-Niederschönweide. Small-arms ammunition.
'rdf': Westfälisch-Anhaltische Sprengstoff AG (WASAG), Werk Reinsdorf. Small-arms ammunition.
'rhs': Rheinmetall-Borsig AG, Sömmerda. Small-arms ammunition.
'rln': Carl Zeiss, Jena (?). Optical equipment.

'sta': Rheinisch-Westfälische Sprengstoff AG, Stadeln bei Nürnberg. Small-arms ammunition.
'svw': Mauser-Werke AG, Oberndorf am Neckar. Small arms.

'ta': Dürener Metallwerke AG, Hauptverwaltung Berlin-Borsigwalde. Small-arms ammunition.

'ua': Osnabrücker Kupfer- & Drahtwerke AG, Osnabrück. Small-arms ammunition.

'va': Kabel- & Metallwerke Neumeyer AG, Nürnberg. Small-arms ammunition.

'wa': Hugo Schneider AG, Abteilung Lampenfabrik, Leipzig O5 (later 'HASAG-Eisen- & Metallwerke GmbH'). Small-arms ammunition.
'wb': Hugo Schneider AG, Berlin-Köpenick. Small-arms ammunition.
'wg': Hugo Schneider AG, Altenburg in Thüringen. Small-arms ammunition.

'xa': Busch-Jaeger, Lüdenscheider Metallwerke AG, Lüdenscheid in Westfalen. Small-arms ammunition.

'y': Jagdpatronen-, Zündhütchen- & Metallwarenfabrik AG, Budapest, Werk Nagýtetený. Small-arms ammunition.
'ya': Sächsische Metallwarenfabrik August Wellner Söhne AG, Aue/Sachsen. Small-arms ammunition; fuze and primer components.

'z': Waffenwerke Brünn AG, Povaška Bystrica. Small arms; small-arms ammunition.
'zb': Kupferwerk Ilsenburg AG, Ilsenburg/Harz. Small-arms ammunition.

GLOSSARY

Original German names have been used for towns – e.g., München for 'Munich', Nürnberg for 'Nuremburg' – but not for provinces such as Bavaria and Prussia, unless they occur unavoidably in company names. No attempt has been made to indicate the differing genders in the following glossary; the dual-language *Wörterbuch der Waffentechnik* by Glück & Görtz (Journal-Verlag Schwend GmbH, Schwäbisch Hall, 1972) provides more comprehensive coverage.

Abteilung: battalion (artillery), detachment.
Abzug: trigger.
Abzugsbügel: trigger-guard.
Abzugsfeder: trigger spring.
Abzugshebel: trigger lever.
Abzugsstange: sear or trigger-bar.
Aktiengesellschaft: joint-stock company.
alter Art (a.A.): old pattern.
Amboss, Amboß: anvil (in a primer).
amtlich: official.
ansteckbar: detachable.

Ansteckmagazin: detachable magazine.
aptiert: adapted.
Armee: army.
Artillerie: artillery.
aufklappen: tipping.
Aufrüstung: rearmament.
Aufschlag: impact.
Aufschlagpunkt: point of impact.
Aufschlagzünder: impact fuze.
aufsteckbar: detachable.
ausbrennen: to erode.
Auslösung: release.
Ausführung: pattern, model, type.

ausrüsten: to arm, equip, outfit.

Ausschuss: scrap, waste.

Ausstosser or Auswerfer: ejector.

Auszieher: extractor.

automatisch: automatic.

Backe: cheekpiece.

Bajonett: bayonet ('Seitengewehr' was generally used in German service for all but socket bayonets).

Balkenkorn: square-post sight.

Bataillon: battalion.

Batterie: battery (of artillery).

Bau: construction.

bayerisch: Bavarian.

Bayern: Bavaria.

Bedienung: i) operation, ii) gun crew.

Befestigung: i) attachment, fastening, ii) fortification.

Behälter: case.

Behörde: authorities.

Belgien: Belgium.

belgisch: Belgian.

Beobachtung: observation.

Beschiessung: bombardment.

Beschläge: fittings.

Beschreibung: specification.

Beschuss: proof.

Bestimmung: ordinance.

Bewaffnung: armament.

Bewegung: action.

Blättchen: flakes.

Blankwaffe: edged weapon.

Blech: sheet.

Blechbehälter: metal container.

Blei: lead.

Bleigeschoss: lead bullet.

Blitzkrieg: 'lightning war'.

Boden: base, bottom.

Böhmen: Bohemia.

Bohrer: drill.

Bolzen: bolt, stud.

Bombe: bomb.

Brand: fire, incendiary.

Braunschweig: Brunswick.

breit: wide.

Bremse: brake.

Breslau: Wroclaw, Poland.

brüniert: blued.

Brünn: Brno, Czechoslovakia.

Büchse: gun, rifle.

Bund: state, federation, federal.

Chrom: chrome, chromium.

Dachkorn: barleycorn (inverted 'V' or pyramidal) sight.

Dämpfer: buffer.

Dauer: continuity.

Dauerfeuer: automatic fire.

Deckel: cover, lid.

Dichtung: seal.

Dienst: service.

Donau: Danube.

Doppellauf: double barrel.

doppelt: double.

doppelte Bewegung: double-action.

Draht: wire.

Drall: twist.

Dreh: turn.

Drehstütze, pedestal mount.

Drehverschluss: rotary action.

Dreibein, Dreifuss: tripod.

dreieckig: triangular.

Druck: pressure.

Durchmesser: diameter.

Eierhandgranate: oviform grenade.
ein: one.
Einbau: assembly.
einfach: simple.
Einführung: adoption.
Einheits: standard, universal.
Einheitsmaschinengewehr: 'universal
    machine-gun'.
Einsatz: i) insert, ii) action, combat.
einschüssig: single-shot.
Einstecklauf: sub-calibre barrel
    insert.
Einzelfeuer: single-shot.
Einzellader: single-loader.
Einzellauf: single-barrel.
einzeln: singly.
Eisen: iron.
Eisenbahn: railway.
Eisenkern: iron core.
Elsass: Alsace.
Energie: power.
Entfernung: distance.
Entladung: discharge.
Entwurf: design, project.
Erhöhung: elevation.
erproben: to test.
Ersatz: substitute, replacement.
explodieren: to burst.
Fabrik: manufactory.
Fahrrad: bicycle.
Fallschirmjäger: paratrooper.
Faustfeuerwaffe: handgun.
Feder: spring.
Feld: field, land (rifling).
Feldartillerie: field artillery.
fest: compact, rigid.
Feuer: fire.
Filz: felt.

Firmenzeichen: factory sign, logo.
Flak, FLAK
    (Flugzeugabwehrkanone): anti-
    aircraft gun.
Flammen: flames.
Flammenwerfer: flamethrower.
Flieger: airman.
Fliegerpistole: signal pistol for
    airborne use.
Frankreich: France.
französisch: French.
Fremdgerät: foreign equipment.
Führung: guide.
Führungsband: drive-band.
Fussartillerie: foot artillery.
Gabelstütze: bipod mount.
Gas: gas.
gasdicht: gas-tight, gas-sealed.
Gasdrucklader: gas-operated firearm.
geändert: altered.
Gebirge: mountains.
Gebirgsjäger: mountaineer,
    mountain troops.
gebogen: curved.
Gebogener Lauf: curved barrel.
gehärtet: hardened.
Gehäuse: housing, receiver,
    breech.
geheim: secret.
Geheime Staatspolizei (Gestapo):
    secret police.
geladen: loaded.
Gelenk: joint.
Genossenschaft: association, co-
    operative.
Gemeinschaft: union, commune.
Geradzugverschluss: straight-pull
    action.

Geräte: equipment.
geriffelt: ribbed, cannelured.
Geschoss: bullet.
Geschütz: gun, cannon.
Geschwindigkeit: velocity.
Gesellschaft: company.
gesichert: secured.
Gewehr: rifle, shotgun.
Gewehrgranate: rifle grenade.
Gewinde: thread.
gezogen: rifled.
glatt: smooth.
gleiten: to slip, glide.
GmbH (Gesellschaft mit
    beschränkter Haftung): limited
    liability company.
Granate: grenade, shell.
Griff: grip, handle.
gross, groß: large.
Gurt, Gürtel: belt.
Gurttrommel: belt-drum.
Hahn: hammer.
hahnlos: hammerless.
Hannover: Hanover.
Halter: catch.
Hand: hand, shoulder.
Handfeuerwaffe: small arm.
Handschutz: handguard.
hart: hard, solid.
Hebel: lever.
Heer: army.
Heereswaffenamt (HWaA): army
    weapons office.
Hersteller: manufacturer, producer.
Hilfskorn: auxiliary front sight.
Hinterlader: breechloader.
Holland: the Netherlands.
holländisch: Dutch.

Holz: wood.
Hülse: i) case, ii) chamber (of a rifle).
infrarot: infra-red.
Inspektion: inspection, inspectorate,
    perusal, section.
Inspektion für Waffen und Gerät
    (IWG): the predecessor of the
    HWaA.
Instandsetzung: repair.
Jäger: hunter, rifleman.
kaiserlich: imperial.
Kaiserliche Marine: imperial
    navy.
Kaliber: calibre.
Kammer: bolt.
Kampf: combat, struggle, fight.
Kampfgruppe: battle group.
Kampfpistole: 'battle pistol'.
Kampfstoff: poison.
Karabiner: carbine.
Kartusche: cartridge(-case).
Kasten: box.
Kavallerie: cavalry.
Kennzeichen: marking(s).
Kimme: sight notch.
Kipplauf: dropping barrel.
Klammer: clasp, latch.
Klappschaft: folding stock.
klein: small.
Klemme: clamp.
Kompagnie (pre-1918), Kompanie
    (post-1918): company (of a
    regiment).
Köln: Cologne.
königlich: royal.
Königliche Gewehrfabrik: royal rifle
    factory.
Körper: body.

Kolben: butt.
Kolbenring: butt swivel.
Kopf: head.
Kopfzünder: nose-fuze.
Korn: front sight.
Kraft: energy, power.
Krieg: war.
Kriegsmarine: navy.
Kriminal: criminal.
Kriminalpolizei: detectives.
Krummlauf: curved barrel.
Kühlmantel: cooling jacket.
Kugel: ball.
Kunststoff: plastic.
Kupfer: copper.
Kupfermantelgeschoss: copper-
     jacketed bullet.
kurz: short.
lackiert: lacquered.
Ladestreifen: charger.
Ladung: charge, loading.
Lafette: carriage, mount.
Land: land, district.
Landespolizei: state police.
Landsturm: 'over-age' reserve.
Landwehr: the eligible reserve.
lang: long.
Lauf: barrel.
Lauflos: barrelless.
Legierung: alloy.
leicht: light, lightweight.
Leichtmetall: aluminium.
Leistung: efficiency.
Leiter: leader.
Leitfaden: instruction, order.
leuchten: to illuminate, shine.
Leuchtgeschoss, Leuchtgeschoß: star
     shell.

Leuchtpistole: flare pistol.
Leuchtspur: tracer.
Lieferung: delivery.
links: left(-hand).
Linse: lens.
Loch: hole, cavity.
Los: lot (delivery).
Luft: air.
Luftwaffe: airforce.
Luftwaffewaffenamt (LWaA): airforce
     weapons office.
Lüttich: Liége, Belgium.
Magazin: magazine.
Mahren: Moravia.
Mantel: (bullet-)jacket.
Marine: navy, naval.
Marinewaffenamt (MWaA): navy
     weapons office.
Maschinen: machines.
Maschinengewehr (MG): machine-
     gun.
Maschinenkarabiner (MKb):
     machine carbine.
Maschinenpistole (MP): machine-
     pistol or submachine-gun.
Masseverschluss: blowback action.
Maßtab: scale.
Mehrlader: repeater.
Messing: brass.
Militär: military.
Minen: mines.
Minenwerfer: mortar.
Modell: model, pattern, type.
Montage: assembly.
Mörser: mortar.
München: Munich.
Mündung: muzzle.
Munition: ammunition, munitions.

Muster: pattern, model.

Mutter: nut.

nah(e): close.

Nahkampf: close combat.

Nahpatrone: short-range (reduced power) cartridge.

Nahkampfwaffe: close-range or personal protection weapon.

Nebel: smoke.

neuer Art (n.A.): new pattern.

Nieder: lower, as in the district of Lower Saxony (Niedersachsen).

Nürnberg: Nuremburg.

Ober: upper, higher (e.g. Oberschlesien, 'Upper Silesia').

Oberkommando: high command (e.g., Oberkommando der Wehrmacht, armed forces high command).

Öffung: opening, hole.

Öl: oil.

öldicht: oil-seal(ed), oil-tight.

osterreich: Austria.

Österreichisch: Austrian.

Panzer: i) armour, ii) tank.

Panzerabwehrkanone (Pak, PAK): anti-tank gun.

Panzerbüchse (Pz. B.): anti-tank rifle.

Patrone: cartridge.

Patronengurt: cartridge belt.

Patronenhülse: cartridge case.

Patronenkasten: cartridge box.

Pistolen: pistols.

Pistolenpatrone (Pist. Patr.): pistol cartridge.

Pistolentasche (PT.): holster.

Platzpatrone: blank cartridge.

Polen: Poland.

polnisch: Polish.

politisch: political.

Polizei: police.

Prag: Praha (Prague), Czechoslovakia.

Prägeteile: stampings.

Präzision: accuracy.

Preussen, Preußen: Prussia.

preussisch, preußisch: Prussian.

Probe: experiment, trial, sample.

prüfen: to examine.

Puffer: buffer.

Pulver: propellant, powder.

Querbolzen: crossbolt.

Rahmen: frame, receiver.

Rand: rim, edge.

Rast: groove, click.

Rauch: smoke.

rauchlos: smokeless.

recht: right(-hand).

Regulierung: adjustment.

Reich: empire, state.

Reichstag: parliament (pre-1945).

Reichssicherheitshauptamt (RSHA): 'Central State Security Office'.

Reichswehr: armed forces.

Reihen: series.

Reihenfeuer: series or automatic fire.

Reihenfertigung: series or mass production.

Reinigung: cleaning.

Repetierlader: repeater.

Richtaufsatz: gunsight.

Riegel: bolt, latch.

Riffelung, Rille: cannelure, groove.

Rinne: groove, channel.

Riss, Riß: crack, split, rupture.

Röhren: barrels, tubes.

Röhrenmagazin: tube magazine.
Rost: rust.
rostfrei: stainless or non-corrosive.
Rückstoss, Rückstoß: recoil.
Rückstossverstärker: muzzle booster.
Russland, Rußland: Russia.
russisch, rußisch: Russian.
Rüstung: armament.
Sachsen: Saxony.
sächsisch: Saxon.
Schaft: (gun-)stock.
Schalldämpfer: silencer.
Schieber: slider.
Schiessen, Schießen: shooting.
Schiessplatz, shooting range.
Schlagbolzen: striker, firing-pin.
Schlaufe: swivel, loop.
Schlesien: Silesia.
Schliessen, Schließen: to shut.
Schliessfeder: recoil spring.
Schlitten: slider, sledge.
Schloss, Schloß: lock.
Schnell: fast, quick, rapid.
Schnellfeuer: rapid-firing.
Schnellwechsellauf: quick-change barrel.
Schraube: screw.
Schuss, Schuß: shot.
schussbereit, schußbereit: ready for action.
Schütze: rifleman.
Schutzstaffel (SS): defence guard.
Schwarzpulver: blackpowder (gunpowder).
schwenkbar: swivelling.
schwer: heavy.
Seitengewehr (SG): sidearm, knife or sword bayonet.

Selbstlade: self-loading.
sicher: safe, secure.
Sicherheitsdienst (SD): security service.
Sicherung: safety (catch).
Sintereisen: sintered iron.
Sockel: base.
Sonder: special.
Spange: clasp, buckle.
Spannabzug: double-action trigger.
spannen: to cock.
spitz: pointed.
Spitzgeschoss, Spitzgeschoß: pointed ('spitzer') bullet.
Sprenggeschoss, Sprenggeschoß: explosive bullet.
Spur: trace.
Stäbchen: strands, cords.
Stahl: steel.
Stahlblech: sheet-steel.
Standvisier: fixed sight.
Stange: rod, pole.
Stark: strong.
Stift: pin.
Stoss, Stoß: shock, thrust.
Stosstrupp: raiding party.
Streifen: strip, clip.
Stumpf: blunt.
Sturm: assault.
Sturmgewehr: assault rifle.
Sturmpistole: assault pistol.
Sturmtruppen: assault troops.
Tasche: pocket, holster.
Teil: part, piece, component.
Träger: carrier, support.
treffen: to hit.
Treibladung: propellant charge.
Trommel: cylinder, drum.

Trommelmagazin (TM): drum magazine.
Tropen: tropics.
tschechisch: Czechoslovakian.
Tschechoslowakei: Czechoslovakia.
überzählig: spare.
Übung: practice, training.
umgeändert: modified.
Umschalter: selector, changeover switch.
Ungarn: Hungary.
ungarisch: Hungarian.
unter: below, beneath.
Unterbrecher: disconnector.
Unternehmen: enterprise.
Untersuchung: inspection, examination.
Ursprung: origin.
veraltet: obsolete.
verbessert: improved.
Verbindung: connector.
verborgen: concealed.
Vergrösserung: enlargement, magnification.
Verriegelung: lock.
Verschluss: action, bolt, breech-lock.
verstärken: to strengthen.
Versuch: trial, experiment.
verzögern: to delay.
Visier: back sight.
Volk: people.
Volksgewehr: 'people's gun'.
Volkssturm: 'assault people', last-ditch units.
Volkswaffe: 'people's weapon'.
Vorderschaft: fore-end.
Vorrichtung: device, mechanism.
Vorsatz: muzzle adaptor.

Vorschrift: instruction.
Waffe: weapon.
Walze: cylinder.
Warschau: Warszawa (Warsaw), Poland.
Warze: lug, stud.
Wasser: water.
wasserdicht: waterproof, watertight.
Wechsel: conversion, exchange.
Wehr: defence, protection.
Wehramt: operations section of the Reichswehr ministry (post-1918).
Wehrmacht: armed forces.
Werk: factory.
Weste: waistcoat, vest.
Westentaschenpistole: vest-pocket pistol.
wiederladen: to reload, handload (cartridges).
Wien: Vienna, Austria.
Wolfram: tungsten.
Wurfkörper: projector grenade.
Zange: pliers.
Zeichen: sign.
zeichnen: to draw.
Zeichnung: drawing.
Zeiger: pointer.
Zeit: time.
Zeitzünder: time fuze.
Zerfall: disintegration.
Zerfallgurt: disintegrating-link belt.
Zeugamt: ordnance office.
Ziel: aim, objective.
Zieleinrichtung or Zielgerät, aiming equipment.
Zielfernrohr: telescope sight.
Zink: zinc.

Zinn: tin.
Zubehör: accessories.
Zubringer: follower, carrier.
Züge: rifling grooves.
Zünder: fuze.
Zündhütchen: primer.

zusammengesetzt: assembled.
Zusatz: supplementary.
Zweibein: bipod.
Zwilling: twin or double.
Zwinge: clamp, holder.
Zylinder: cylinder.

Appendix 4

Bibliography

German military periodicals

Allgemeines Heeresmitteilungen ('Herausgegeben vom Oberkommando des Heeres'). Oberkommando des Heeres, Abt. für Allgemeine Truppenangelegenheiten Schriftleitung, Berlin; various issues, 1934–43.

Armee-Verordnungsblatt ('Herausgegeben vom Kriegsministerium). E.S. Mittler & Sohn, Berlin; various issues prior to 1918.

Heerestechnisches-Verordnungsblatt ('Herausgegeben vom Oberkommando des Heeres AHA/Stab [Sonderstab A]'). Oberkommando des Heeres, Berlin; various issues, 1943–5.

Heeres-Verordnungsblatt ('Herausgegeben vom Oberkommando des Heeres'). Oberkommando des Heeres, Abt. Heerwesen/Schriftleitung, Berlin; various issues, 1922–43.

Books and pamphlets

ANON. *German Order of Battle 1944* ('The regiments, formations and units of the German ground forces'). Reprinted by Greenhill Books, London, with an introduction by Ian Hogg, 1994.

—*Liste der Fertigungskennzeichen für Waffen, Munition und Gerät* . . . Oberkommando des Heeres, Berlin, Germany; 1940–4. Reprinted by Karl Pawlas, Nürnberg, West Germany, 1977.

238

—*Organisationsbuch der N.S.D.A.P.* ('Herausgeber: der Reichsorganisationsleiter der N.S.D.A.P.'). Zentralverlag der N.S.D.A.P., Berlin; 1943.

—[Aberdeen Proving Ground Staff]: *German Submachine Guns and Assault Rifles*. Produced for restricted circulation during the Second World War, and reprinted as 'German Submachine Guns and Assault Rifles of World War II' by WE, Inc., Old Greenwich, Connecticut, U.S.A., 1966.

BAER, Ludwig: *Die leichten Waffen der deutschen Armeen 1841–1945*. Journal-Verlag Schwend GmbH, Schwäbisch Hall, West Germany, 1976.

BALL, Robert: *Mauser Military Rifles of the World*. Krause Publications, Iola, Wisconsin, U.S.A.; second (revised) edition, 2000.

CHURCHILL, [Sir] Winston L.S.: *The Second World War*. Cassell & Company, London; 1985. In six volumes: 'The Gathering Storm' (1919–40), 'Their Finest Hour' (1940–41), 'The Grand Alliance' (1941–2), 'The Hinge of Fate' (1942–3), 'Closing the Ring' (1943–4) and 'Triumph & Tragedy' (1944–5).

COOPER, Matthew: *The German Army 1933–1945* ('Its Political and Military Failure'). Macdonalds and Jane's, London, 1978.

DAVIS, Brian L.: *German Army Uniforms & Insignia, 1933–1945*. Arms & Armour Press, London, 1971.

DUNNIGAN, James F. (Ed.): *The Russian Front. Germany's War in the East, 1941–5*. Arms & Armour Press, London, 1977.

ECKARDT, Werner, and MORAWIETZ, Otto: *Die Handwaffen des branden-burgisch-preussisch-deutschen Heeres 1640–1945*. Helmut Gerhard Schulz Verlag, Hamburg, West Germany, 1973.

FISCHER, Karl: *Waffen- und Schiesstechnischer Leitfaden für die Ordnungspolizei*. Verlag R. Eisenschmidt, Berlin, Germany; fifth edition, 1944. Reprinted by Akademische Druck- und Verlagsanstalt, Graz, Austria, 1975.

GANDER, Terry: *Germany's Guns, 1939–45*. The Crowood Press, Marlborough, 1998.

GIBSON, Randall: *The Krieghoff Parabellum*. Privately published, Midland, Texas, U.S.A., 1980 and 1988.

GÖRTZ, Joachim: *Die Pistole 08*. Verlag Stocker-Schmid, Dietikon-Zürich, Switzerland, and Motor-Buch Verlag, Stuttgart, Germany, 1985.

GÖTZ, Hans Dieter: *Die deutschen Militärgewehre und Maschinenpistolen 1871–1945*. Motor-Buch Verlag, Stuttgart, West Germany, 1974. English-language edition: Schiffer Publishing, Westchester, Pennsylvania, U.S.A., 1985.

HAHN, Fritz: *Waffen und Geheime Waffen des deutschen Heeres, 1933–1945*. Bernhard & Graefe Verlag, Koblen, 1987.

HANDRICH, Hans-Dieter: *Vom Gewehr 98 zum Sturmgewehr*. Motor-Buch Verlag, Stuttgart, 1992.

HOGG, Ian V.: *German Artillery of World War Two*. Arms & Armour Press, London, 1975. Reissued Greenhill Books, London, 1996.

—*German Handguns, 1871–1945*. Greenhill Books, London, 2001.

—*German Secret Weapons of the Second World War*. Greenhill Books, London, and Stackpole Books, Mechanicsburg, Pennsylvania, U.S.A., 1999.

—*The Cartridge Guide* ('The Small Arms Ammunition Identification Manual'). Arms & Armour Press, London, 1982.

—*The Greenhill Military Small Arms Data Book*. Greenhill Books, London, and Stackpole Books, Mechanicsburg, Pennsylvania, 1999.

—and WEEKS, John: *Military Small Arms of the 20th Century*. Krause Publications, Iola, Wisconsin, U.S.A., seventh edition, 2000.

—and WEEKS, John S.: *Pistols of the World* ('A comprehensive illustrated encyclopedia of the world's pistols and revolvers from 1870 to the present day'). Arms & Armour Press, London, third edition, 1992.

HUG, Thomas: 'Das deutsche Maschinengewehr 1934. MG34. Entwicklung eines Einheitsmaschinengewehrs', in *Waffen Digest*. Verlag Stocker-Schmid, Zürich-Dietikon, Switzerland, 1984.

JARMAN, T.L.: *The Rise and Fall of Nazi Germany*. New American Library, New York, U.S.A., 1961.

KENT, Daniel W.: *German 7.9mm Military Ammunition, 1888–1945*. Privately published, Ann Arbor, Michigan, U.S.A., 1973. A revised edition was published in 1991.

LAW, Richard D.: *Backbone of the Wehrmacht. The German K98k rifle, 1934–1945*. Collector Grade Publications, Inc., Cobourg, Ontario, Canada; revised edition, 1993.

—*Sniper Variations of the German K98k Rifle* ('Backbone of the Wehrmacht volume II'). Collector Grade Publications, Inc., Cobourg, Ontario, Canada, 1996.

LEFEVRE, Eric: 'Les Maschinenpistolen MP 38 et MP 40', in *Gazette des Armes*, No. 142 (June 1985), pp. 14–18, and No. 143 (July 1985), pp. 25–30.

LIDDELL HART, B.H. [Captain Sir Basil]: *History of the Second World War*. Cassell, London, 1970.

LUCAS, James: *Last Days of the Reich* ('The Collapse of Nazi Germany, May 1945'). Arms & Armour Press, London, 1985.

—*Storming Eagles* ('German Airborne Forces in World War Two'). Arms & Armour Press, London, 1988.

—*World War Two through German Eyes.* Arms & Armour Press, London, 1987.

LUSAR, Rudolf: *Die deutschen Waffen und Geheimwaffen des 2. Weltkrieges und ihr Weiterentwicklung.* J.F. Lehmanns Verlag, München, West Germany; sixth edition, 1971.

MARKHAM, George [John Walter]: *Guns of the Reich. Firearms of the German Forces, 1939–1945.* Arms & Armour Press, London, 1989.

MASTIER, Dominique, and Stéphane Ferrard: 'Le chemin de crioix du PM MAS 38', in *Gazette des Armes,* No. 65 (December 1978), pp. 36–45.

MULLIN, Timothy J.: *Testing the War Weapons* ('Rifles and Light Machine Guns from Around the World'). Paladin Press, Boulder, Colorado, U.S.A., 1997.

MUSGRAVE, Daniel D., and OLIVER, Smith Hempstone: *German Machineguns.* MOR Associates, Friendship Station, Washington D.C., U.S.A., 1971. A revised edition was published in 1992 by Ironside International Publishers, Alexandria, Virginia, U.S.A.

NELSON, Thomas B., and LOCKHOVEN, Hans B.: *The World's Submachine Guns (Machine Pistols).* International Small Arms Publishers, Köln, West Germany, volume 1, 1964.

PALMER, A.W.: *A Dictionary of Modern History 1789–1945.* Barrie & Jenkins, London, 1973.

PARRISH, Thomas (ed.): *The Encyclopaedia of World War II.* Secker & Warburg, London, 1978.

PAYNE, Robert: *The Life and Death of Adolf Hitler.* Jonathan Cape, London, 1973.

PREUSS, Prof. Dr Johannes: *Zahlencode System des Heeres von 1925 bis 1940* ('Kennziffern für die Hersteller neu gefertigter Waffen, Munition und Gerät'). Journal-Verlag Schwend GmbH, Schwäbisch Hall, 2002.

QUARRIE, Bruce: *Weapons of the Waffen-SS. From small arms to tanks.* Patrick Stephens, Cambridge, England, 1988.

RANKIN, James L.: *Walther Models PP and PPK 1929–1945.* Privately published, Coral Gables, Florida, U.S.A., 1974.

—*Walther Volume II – Engraved, Presentation and Standard Models.* Privately published, Coral Gables, Florida, U.S.A., *c.*1977.

—*Walther Volume III, 1908–1980.* Privately published, Coral Gables, Florida, U.S.A., 1981.

REID, Alan: *A concise encyclopedia of the Second World War.* Osprey Publishing, London, 1975.

SÁDÁ, Plk.Dr. Miroslav: *Československé Rucni Palné Zbrane a Kulomety*. Nase Vojsko, Prague, Czechoslovakia, 1971.

SCHÄFER, Karl: 'Deutsche Signalpistolen', in *Waffen-Digest*. Verlag Stocker-Schmid, Zürich-Dietikon, Switzerland: two parts, 1983–4.

SCHROEDER, Joseph J., Jr, and BREATHED, John W., Jr: *System Mauser* ('A pictorial history of the Model 1896 self-loading pistol'). Handgun Press, Chicago, Illinois, U.S.A., 1967.

SENICH, Peter R.: *The German Assault Rifle, 1935–1945*. Paladin Press, Boulder, Colorado, U.S.A., 1987.

—*The German Sniper, 1914–1945*. Paladin Press, Boulder, Colorado, U.S.A., 1982.

SHIRER, William L.: *Rise and Fall of the Third Reich. A History of Nazi Germany*. Secker & Warburg, London, 1970.

SMITH, W.H.B., and SMITH, Joseph E.: *The Book of Rifles*. Stackpole Books, Harrisburg, Pennsylvania, U.S.A., fourth edition, 1972.

—(EZELL, Edward C. [ed.]): *Small Arms of the World*. Stackpole Books, Harrisburg, Pennsylvania, U.S.A., twelfth edition, 1983.

SPEER, Albert: *Inside the Third Reich*. Macmillan, New York, U.S.A., 1970.

STILL, Jan C.: *Axis Pistols* ('The Pistols of Germany and Her Allies in Two World Wars'). Privately published, Douglas, Alaska, U.S.A., 1986.

—*Imperial Lugers and Their Accessories* ('The Pistols of Germany and Her Allies in Two World Wars. Volume IV'). Published privately, Douglas, Alaska, U.S.A., 1991.

—*Third Reich Lugers and Their Accessories* ('The Pistols of Germany and Her Allies in Two World Wars. Volume III'). Published privately, Douglas, Alaska, U.S.A., 1988.

—*Weimar and Early Nazi Lugers and Their Accessories* ('The Pistols of Germany and Her Allies in Two World Wars. Volume V'). Published privately, Douglas, Alaska, U.S.A., 1993.

TAYLOR, A.J.P.: *The Course of German History* ('A Survey of the Development of German History since 1815'). Hamish Hamilton, London, 1945.

TOLAND, John: *Adolf Hitler*. Doubleday, New York, U.S.A., 1976.

TREVOR-ROPER, Hugh R.: *The Last Days of Hitler*. Macmillan, London, fourth edition, 1971.

—(ed.): *The Goebbels Diaries*. Secker & Warburg, London, 1978.

WALTER, John D.: *Central Powers' Small Arms of World War One*. The Crowood Press, Marlborough, 1999.

—*German Military Letter Codes* ('The manufacturers' marks of the Third

Reich, 1939–1945'). SARP, Hove, England, and International Military Antiques, Inc., Millington, New Jersey, U.S.A., 1996.

—*German Military Letter Codes, 1939–45.* Tharston Press, Godstone, England, and International Military Antiques, Inc., Millington, New Jersey, U.S.A., 2004.

—*Machine-guns of Two World Wars* ('Greenhill Military Manuals'). Greenhill Books, London, and Stackpole Books, Mechanicsburg, Pennsylvania, U.S.A., 2004.

—*Military Pistols of Two World Wars* ('Greenhill Military Manuals'). Greenhill Books, London, and Stackpole Books, Mechanicsburg, Pennsylvania, U.S.A., 2003.

—*Military Rifles of Two World Wars* ('Greenhill Military Manuals'). Greenhill Books, London, and Stackpole Books, Mechanicsburg, Pennsylvania, U.S.A., 2003.

—*Rifles of the World.* Krause Publications, Iola, Wisconsin, U.S.A., second (revised) edition, 1998.

—*The German Rifle* ('A comprehensive illustrated history of the standard bolt-action designs, 1871–1945'). Arms & Armour Press, London, 1979.

—*The Greenhill Dictionary of Guns and Gunmakers* ('From Colt's first patent to the present day, 1836–2001 . . .'). Greenhill Books, London, and Stackpole Books, Mechanicsburg, Pennsylvania, U.S.A., 2001.

—*The Luger Book* ('The encyclopedia of Borchardt and Borchardt-Luger hand-guns, 1885–1985'). Arms & Armour Press, London, 1986.

—*The Luger Story* ('The Standard History of the World's Most Famous Handgun'). Greenhill Books, London, and Stackpole Books, Mechanicsburg, Pennsylvania, U.S.A., revised printing, 2001.

WHITTINGTON, Major Robert D., III: *German Pistols and Holsters 1934/1945. Military – Police – NSDAP.* Brownless Books, Benton, Louisiana, U.S.A., 1969.

WIRNSBERGER, Gerhard (ed.): *Deutsche Codezeichen* ('Codezeichen auf Waffen, Geräten und Munition'). Verlag Wirnsberger, Schwäbisch Hall, West Germany, 1975.

Notes

1. Prologue

1. As many as one gun in three in German service at the beginning of 1945 may have been an impressment.

2. The First Steps, 1919–33

1. Rw. M., HL., 17 November 1922. See *Heeres-Verordnungsblatt*, 21 November 1922, p. 515, §726, 'Bräunen der Hülsen des Gewehres 98'. The finish was extended to the magazine follower, butt plate and butt-plate screw heads in October 1924, but retained only on the receiver and the magazine follower by the end of 1925.
2. Rw. M., HL., 11 October 1924; see *Heeres-Verodnungsblatt*, 21 October 1924, §387, '100m-Visier'. Rw. M., Insp. d. Inf., 25 June 1925; see *Heeres-Verodnungsblatt*, 26 June 1925, p. 60, §199, 'Unterring zum Gewehr 98'.
3. The distinction between the marks applied to the left side of the receiver, immediately ahead of the cut-out to facilitate charger-loading, was subsequently abandoned in favour of 'Mod. 98'. See Rw. M., 17 July 1930; *Heeres-Verordnungsblatt*, 2 August 1930, p. 116, §359, 'Hülsen für Schusswaffen 98'.
4. Rw. M., HL., 5 January 1927; Ch. d. HL., 4 September 1929; Ch. d. HL., 13 July 1931. See *Heeres-Verodnungsblätter*, 14 January 1927, p. 1, §2, 'Schlosshalter- und Auswerferfedern'; 17 September 1929, p. 105, §365, 'Kammerfang für Gewehr 98 und Karabiner 98b'; and 22 July 1931, p. 179, §409, 'Instandbesetzung an der Hülse und dem Auszieher der Schusswaffen 98'.

5 Rw. M., Insp. d. Inf., 29 August 1927 and 5 December 1927. See *Heeres-Verordnungsblatt*, 16 September 1927, p. 110, §373, 'Zielfernrohrgewehre', and 10 December 1927, p. 134, §496, 'Zielfernrohrgewehre'. Ch. d. HL., 4 September 1929. See *Heeres-Verordnungsblatt*, 17 September 1929, pp. 105, §366, 'Neufertigung der Riegel zum Zielfernrohrkarabiner 98b' and §367, 'Behinderung des Schlossganges am Zielfernrohrkarabiner 98b'.

6. Ch. d. HL., 5 December 1931. See *Heeres-Verordnungsblatt*, 17 December 1931, p. 234, §619, 'Zielfernrohrkarabiner 98b'.

7. Rw. M., HL., 29 June 1927. See *Heeres-Verordnungsblatt*, 22 July 1927, p. 88, §295, 'Einstecklauf 24 (E.L. 24) mit Zielmunition'.

8. Ch. d. HL., 18 January 1932. See *Heeres-Verordnungsblatt*, 19 February 1932, p. 23, §63, 'Einstecklauf 24 mit Mehrladeeinrichtung'.

9. Ch. d. HL., 8 August 1933. See *Heeres-Verordnungsblatt*, 28 August 1933, p. 121, §366, 'Anhängemagazin zum Einstecklauf 24'.

3. The Third Reich, 1933–38

1. Oberbefehlshaber des Heeres, 14 June 1935. See *Allgemeine Heeresmitteilungen*, 21 June 1935, p.80, §275, 'Karabiner 98k'.

2. O.K.H., 23 May 1936, 30 May 1936 and 3 September 1937 respectively. See *Allgemeine Heeresmitteilungen*, 10 June 1936, p. 106, §363, 'Verkürzen des Drückers zum Visier des Karabiners 98k'; 10 June 1936, p. 106, §364, 'Änderung des Lagers in Schlosshalter des Schusswaffen 98 bisherigte Fertigung bei Einstellung einer verstärkten Schlosshhalterfeder'; and 13 September 1937, p. 409, §1086. 'Änderung der Visierklappe zum K 98k bei Einstellung eines verstärkten Visierschiebers. (B).'

3. O.K.H., 4 December 1936. See *Heeres-Verordnungsblatt*, 15 December 1936, p. 442, §1193, 'Einführung enire verbesserten Mehrladeeinrichtung zum Einstecklauf 24.'

4. O.K.H., 20 May 1936. See *Allgemeine Heeresmitteilungen*, 27 May 1936, p. 1, §344, 'Schiessgerät 35 fur 3,7 cm Tak.' At this time, the guns were known as 'Tankabwehrkanone'.

5. O.K.H., 16 January 1937. See *Allgemeine Heeresmitteilungen*, 21 January 1937, p. 12, §26, 'Einstecklauf zur Pak. (für Schiessen mit Zielmunition Kal. 5,6 mm).' The designation of the gun had now become 'Panzerabwehrkanone'.

6. See, for example, *Allgemeine Heeresmitteilungen* for 6 December 1934 (p. 31, §118, 'Zielfernrohrgewehre [Karabiner]'); 13 July 1935 (p. 92, §323, 'Zielfernrohr für Gewehre'); and 21 February 1938 (p. 26, §92, 'Verkauf von Zielfernrohren').

7. O.K.H., 7 March 1938. See *Allgemeine Heeresmitteilungen*, 21 March 1938, p. 52, §150, 'Verkauf von Zielfernrohren'.
8. O.K.H., 29 June 1938. See *Allgemeine Heeresmitteilungen*, 9 July 1938, p. 265, §411, 'Maschinenpistole 38 (MP. 38)'.

4. The Road to War

1. O.K.H. (Ch. H. Rüst u. BdE.), 25 February 1943. See *Allgemeine Heeresmitteilungen*, 22 March 1943, p. 185, §273, 'Anschiessen von Gew. M. 95 (ö)'.
2. Guns found with a 12mm-high 'H' above the chamber, though otherwise comparable with the Austrian guns, were converted in Hungary. Their cartridge was known as '31.M'.
3. The renaming of stores ranging from pistols to armoured vehicles was approved by O.K.H. (Ch. H. Rüst u. BdE.) on 22 November 1939. See *Allgemeines Heeresmitteilungen*, 7 December 1939, p. 389, §874, 'Benennung übernommener tschechischer Handwaffen und M.G.'.
4. O.K.H. (Ch. H. Rüst. u. B.d.E.), 1 March 1940. See *Heeres-Verordnungsblatt*, 15 March 1940, p. 120, §345, 'Schiessen gegen Flugziele mit M.G. 26 (t).'
5. O.K.H. (Ch. H. Rüst. u. B.d.E.), 16 October 1939. See *Allgemeine Heeresmitteilungen*, 7 November 1939, p. 367, §765, 'Anschiessen tschechischer Handfeuerwaffen und M.G.'.
6. O.K.H. (Ch. H. Rüst. u. B.d.E.), 10 December 1939. See *Allgemeine Heeresmitteilungen*, 16 December 1940, p. 528, §1161, 'Verwendung für Platzptronen 33 für M.G. (t.).'
7. O.K.H. (Ch. H. Rüst. u. B.d.E.),30 July 1940, 30 January 1942 and 6 August 1942 respectively. See *Allgemeine Heeresmitteilungen*, 5 August 1940, p. 292, §813, 'Platzpatr. (t)'; 7 February 1942, p. 73, §110, 'Änderung der Seitengewehre (t) und (p)'; and 21 August 1942, p. 365, § 697, 'Seitengewehre 24 (t)'.

5. Lightning Strikes

1. O.K.H., 29 April 1940. See *Allgemeine Heeresmitteilungen*, 7 May 1940, p. 233, §534, 'Abgabe polnischer und tschechischer Jagdwaffen'.
2. O.K.H. (Ch. H. Rüst. u. B. d. E.), 19 April 1941. See *Allgemeine Heeresmitteilungen*, 7 May 1941, p. 231, §462, 'Jagdwaffen aus den besetzten Gebieten'.
3. O.K.H. (Ch. H. Rüst. u. B. d. E.), AHA/Inf. 2, 6 May 1944. See

Heeres Verordnungsblatt, 'Beiblatte Infanteriegerät Nr. 19', 15 September 1944.

4. O.K.H. (Ch. H. Rüst. u. B. d. E.), 26 April 1940. See *Allgemeine Heeresmitteilungen*, 7 May 1940, p. 238, §559, 'Anschiessen mit Gewehre und Karabiner (p.)'.

5. O.K.H. (Ch. H. Rüst. u. B. d. E.), 18 June 1941. See *Heeres-Verordnungsblatt*, 25 June 1941, p. 374, §554, 'Gewehre (p)'.

6. O.K.H. (Ch. H. Rüst. u. B. d. E.), 30 April 1942. See *Heeres-Verordnungsblatt*, 11 May 1942, p. 268, §405, Seitengewehr (p)'.

7. O.K.H. (Ch. H. Rüst. u. B. d. E.), 6 November 1941 and 3 September 1942. See *Heeres-Verordnungsblatt*, 15 November 1941, p. 660, §983, 'Vorkommnis an einer Beutewaffe'; and 15 September 1942, p. 501, §564, 'Karabinerriemen (h)'.

8. The 'P. 640 (b.), Belg. G.P.' was added to the ammunition-interchangeability lists of April 1940 on 21 October 1941. See *Allgemeine Heeresmitteilungen*, p. 546, §1014, 'Verschiessen von Pist. Patr. 9 mm (b) aus deutschen Waffen'.

9. The list of foreign-equipment numbers given in Karl Fischer, *Waffen- und schiesstechnischer Leitfaden für die Ordungspolizei* (1944 edition, p. 59) seems to suggest that some guns in the '553' group had receivers marked 'MLE 07-15'. These would be adaptations of the full-length Mle. 07 *Tirailleurs Sénégalais* colonial rifles, and could hardly have been considered as carbines unless cut-down to Mle. 90 or Mle. 92 proportions.

10. O.K.H. (Ch. H. Rüst. u. B. d. E.), 2 July 1942. See *Heeres-Verordnungsblatt*, 11 July 1942, p. 336, §544, 'Ausweisung für das Laden, Sichern und Entladen des Gewehrs (f) M 16'.

11. O.K.H. (Ch. H. Rüst. u. B. d. E.), 7 September 1942. See *Allgemeine Heeresmitteilungen*, 21 September 1942, p. 416, §798, 'Änderung von Beute-Seitengewehren'.

12. Many details extracted from Dominique Mastier & Stéphane Ferrard, 'Le chemin de croix du PM MAS 38', *Gazette des Armes*, no. 65 (December 1978), pp. 36–45.

13. O.K.H. (Ch. H. Rüst. u. B. d. E.), 29 December 1939. See *Allgemeine Heeresmitteilungen*, 22 January 1940, p. 30, §81, 'Kolbenkappe und Schutzplatte zur Kolbenkappe'. This introduced the 'Kolbenkappe mit hochgezogenen Seitenwänden' for the Kar. 98k, and a protective plate ('Schutzplatte') to accompany the butt plate of the 'Gew. 33 (t) k' (which subsequently became the Gewehr 33/40).

14. O.K.H. (Ch. H. Rüst. u. B. d. E.). See *Allgemeine Heeresmitteilungen*, 21 November 1940, p. 499, §1161, 'Gewehr 33/40'.

15. Manual D 167/1 was published by the H.WaA.–Wa.Z.4 on 25 September 1942, but was presumably preceded by an older version.
16. This was included in manual D 167/2, published by H.WaA.–Wa.Z.4 on 11 December 1942, but its exact purpose (and advantage over two conventional three-magazine pouches) remains unclear.

6. The Great Adventure

1. Richard D. Law, *Sniper Variations of the German K98k Rifle*, p. 65, quoting *The Halder War Diary 1939–1942* by Charles Burdick and Hans-Adolf Jacobsen.
2. O.K.H. (Ch. H. Rüst. u. B. d. E.), 31 January 1942. See *Heeres-Verordnungsblatt*, 5 February 1942, p. 57, §66, 'Russische Beutegewehre mit angebohrten Läufen'.
3. O.K.H. (Ch. H. Rüst. u. B. d. E.), 31 July 1942. See *Allgemeine Heeresmitteilungen*, 7 August 1942, p. 328, §646. And if it should be thought that these tricks were unique to the Russians, a German directive dating from January 1944 blamed the British for dropping similarly altered ". . . brass-cased cartridges with lacquered red primer annuli and the headstamp 'P 490 S* 16 39' . . .": *Heerestechnische Verordnungsblatt*, 1 February 1944, p. 35, §61, 'Englische Gewehr- und MG. Patr. mit Sprengstofffüllung'.
4. O.K.H. (Ch. H. Rüst. u. B. d. E.), 30 January 1942. See *Allgemeine Heeresmitteilungen*, 7 February 1942, p. 74, §113, 'Änderung der Seitengewehre (t) and (p)'
5. O.K.H. (Ch. H. Rüst. u. B. d. E.), 18 May 1942. See *Heeres-Verordnungsblatt*, 27 May 1942, p. 281, §442, 'Beutegewehre (j)'.
6. O.K.H. (Ch. H. Rüst. u. B. d. E.), May 1942 and 27 March 1943 respectively. See *Heeres-Verordnungsblatt*, 26 May 1942, p. 287, §346, 'Seitengewehre (j)'; and *Allgemeine Heeresmitteilungen*, 7 April 1943, p. 220, §321, 'Änderung an Beuteseitengewehren'.
7. O.K.H. (Ch. H. Rüst. u. B. d. E.), 17 April 1942. See *Allgemeine Heeresmitteilungen*, 7 May 1942, p. 222, §405, 'Auschiessen der russischen Selbstladegewehr "Tokarew" (Mod. 1940)'. See also *Heeres-Verordnungsblatt*, 5 November 1942, p. 632, §694, 'Waffentechnische D-Vorschriften'.
8. O.K.H. (Ch. H. Rüst. u. B. d. E.), 4 December 1942. See *Allgemeine Heeresmitteilungen*, 21 December 1942, p. 633, §1113, 'Anschiessen von Beutegewehren (r)'. The guns were tested with Soviet 'Munition 262 (r)'.
9. O.K.H. (Ch. H. Rüst. u. B.d.E.), 31 September 1943 and 8 September 1944 respectively. See *Heerestechnische Verordnungsblatt*, 15 September

1943, p. 181, §301, 'Inf.-Patr. Tschechischer Herkunft'; and 1 October 1944, p. 415, §688, 'Verschiessen von Beute-Gewehrpatronen'.

10. The origins of the Walther G.A. 115 project have been increasingly questioned in recent years. Instead of a prototype for the Gew. 41 (W) or MKb. 42 (W), it may be a 'simple rifle' project dating from 1943–4. No examples could be obtained for examination.

11. Manual D 191/1, *Beschreibung, Handhabungs- und Behandlungsanleitung für G41 (M)* was published on 26 May 1941. No Walther equivalent has yet been authenticated from the same period, and it is likely that the Mauser project progressed much faster in its initial stages than the rival design.

12. O.K.H. (Ch. H. Rüst. u. B. d. E.), 2 December 1942. See *Allgemeine Heeresmitteilungen*, 12 December 1942, p. 633, §1112, 'Gewehr 41'.

13. O.K.H. (Ch. H. Rüst. u. B. d. E.), 30 April 1943. See *Heerestechnisches Verordnungsblatt*, 15 May 1943, p. 16, §30, 'Gewehr 43'.

14. O.K.H. (Ch. H. Rüst. u. B. d. E.), 4 January 1945. See *Heerestechnisches Verordnungsblatt*, 15 January 1945, p. 18, §38, 'Storüngen am K 43 mit Schutzschiebern alter Ausführung'.

15. The post-war US Army trial undertaken in 1946 produced 'bench rest' group diameters of about 3.6 inches at 100 yards, and 11.4 inches at 300 yards. These were regarded as 'satisfactory'. However, trials undertaken in Germany in March 1945, with two different K. 43, had given 12-shot groups of 187×114cm and 174×119cm (both height$\times$width) at 1200 metres. This was deemed to be extremely unsatisfactory. See Richard D. Law, *Sniper Variations of the German K 98k Rifle*, pp. 160–5.

16. The date of introduction is confirmed by O.K.H. (Ch. H. Rüst. u. B. d. E.) in a directive of 9 December 1944. See *Heerestechnisches Verordnungsblatt*, 2 January 1945, p. 4, §6, 'Sturmgewehr 44'. Manual D 1854/1, *Sturmgewehr 44, Beschreibung, Handhabung und Behandlung*, was published on 1 December 1944.

17. O.K.H. (Ch. H. Rüst. u. B. d. E.), July 1941. See *Allgemeine Heeresmitteilungen*, 21 July 1941, p. 379, §726, 'Karabiner 98k – Z.F. 41 (Zielfernrohrkarabiner)'.

18. O.K.H. (Ch. H. Rüst. u. B. d. E.), 16 April 1943. See *Heerestechnisches Verordnungsblatt*, 1 May 1943, p. 3, §7, 'Aufsteckfilter für Zielfernrohr 41'.

19. O.K.H. (Ch. H. Rüst. u. B. d. E.), 13 October 1941. See *Allgemeine Heeresmitteilungen*, 21 October 1941, p. 545, §1012, 'Gewehr 98/40'.

20. O.K.H. (Ch. H. Rüst. u. B. d. E.), 4 September 1942. See *Heeres-Verordnungsblatt*, 11 September 1942, p. 414, §708, 'Änderung des Schlosshalters zum Gew. 98/40'.

21. O.K.H. (Ch. H. Rüst. u. B. d. E.), 18 April 1942. See *Allgemeine Heeresmiteilungen*, 7 May 1942, p. 223, §407, 'Gewehrgranatgerät'.

22. A pamphlet, *Merkblatt über Mitführung, Verwendung und Handhabung der Gewehr-Spreng-Granate (G.Sprgr.), der Gewehr-Panzergranate (G.Pzgr.) und der Gewehr-Sprenggranate Üb (G.Sprgr.Üb.)* was published on 1 March 1942.

23. O.K.H. (Ch. H. Rüst. u. B. d. E.), 6 January 1943. See *Allgemeine Heeresmiteilungen*, 21 January 1943, p. 37, §77, 'Unfälle durch Gewehrgranatblindgängen'.

24. O.K.H. (Ch. H. Rüst. u. B. d. E.), 9 June 1942. See *Allgemeine Heeresmiteilungen*, 22 June 1942, p. 283, §521, 'Gewehrgranatgerät'.

25. O.K.H. (Ch. H. Rüst. u. B. d. E.), 18 September 1942. See *Allgemeine Heeresmiteilungen*, 7 October 1942, p. 441, §845, 'Austattung mit Gewehrgranatgerät'.

26. O.K.H. (Ch. H. Rüst. u. B. d. E.), 8 September 1942. See *Heeres-Verordnungsblatt*, 28 September 1942, p. 433, §739, 'Beutegewehre – Änderung des Zubringers'.

27. For details, see Ian Hogg's book *German Artillery of World War Two*, Greenhill Books, 1999).

7. Seeds of Doubt

1. O.K.H. (Ch. H. Rüst. u. B. d. E.), December 1944. See *Heerestechnisches Verordnungsblatt*, 15 December 1944, p. 507, §866, 'Zielfernrohr K 43'.

2. O.K.H. (Ch. H. Rüst. u. B. d. E.), 11 August 1944. See *Heerestechnisches Verordnungsblatt*, 1 September 1944, p. 321, §541, 'Schiessen mit Gewehrgranaten'.

8. A Bitter End

1. Richard D. Law, *Sniper Variations of the German K98k Rifle*, pp. 205–6.

2. The 'VG-6' is known to have been a bolt-action Mauser carbine.

3. However, manual D 1864, *8,8cm R Pz B 54 mit 8,8cm R Pz B Gr 4322. Gebrauchsanleitung*, apparently dated from October 1943. An update, D 1864/1, had appeared by November.

4. Gen.St.d.H./Gen.Qu./Qu.3, 22 August 1944, and AHA/In. 2, 31 August 1944. See *Heerestechnisches Verordnungsblatt*, 15 September 1944, p. 361, §595, 'Kennzeichen von umgebauten Beutewaffen'.

5. Fritz Hahn, *Waffen- und Geheimewaffen des deutschen Heeres* (1987), p. 32.

6. O.K.H. (Ch.H.Rüst. u. B.d.E.), 10 October 1944. See *Heerestechnisches Verordnungsblatt*, 1 November 1944, p. 443, §749, 'Winterabzuge für K 98k und MP 40'.

7. D 1867, *Gebrauchsanleitung für den Winterabzug Modell 98*. O.K.H. (Ch.H.Rüst. u. B.d.E.)/WaZ-4, September 1943. See also preceding note.

8. O.K.H. (Ch. H. Rüst. u. B. d. E.). See *Allgemeine Heeresmitteilungen*, 225 July 1942, p. 300, §695.

Appendix 1. Small-arms ammunition

1. O.K.H. (Ch. H. Rüst. u. BdE.), 30 August 1943, See *Heerestechnisches Verordnungsblatt*, 15 September 1943, p. 181, §300.
2. O.K.H. (Ch. H. Rust. u. B. d. E.), 11 August 1944. See *Heerestechnisches Verordnungsblatt*, 15 August 1944, pp. 311–13, §532, 'Gewehrgranaten'.
3. O.K.H. (Ch. H. Rust. u. B. d. E.), 8 September 1944. See *Heerestechnisches Verordnungsblatt*, 1 October 1944, p. 415, §687, 'Neue Treibpatrone für Gewehrsprenggranate'.
4. O.K.H. (Ch. H. Rust. u. B. d. E.), 28 November 1939. See *Allgemeine Heeresmitteilungent*, 7 December 1939, p. 390, §875, 'Munition für Handfeuerwaffen und M. G.'
5. O.K.H. (Ch. H. Rust. u. B. d. E.), 19 May 1944. See *Heerestechnisches Verordnungsblatt*, 15 June 1944, p. 226, §387, 'Verschiessen von Platzpatronen (j) und (t)'.
6. O.K.H. (Ch. H. Rust. u. B. d. E.), 12 August 1943. See *Heerestechnisches Verordnungsblatt*, 15 September 1943, p. 180, §298, 'Gew. und M. G. Mun. griech. Herkunft für Übungszwecke'.
7. O.K.H. (Ch. H. Rust. u. B. d. E.), 17 October 1942. See *Allgemeine Heeresmitteilungen*, 7 November 1942, p. 511, §953, 'Grosse Gewehr-Panzergranate'.
8. O.K.H. (Ch. H. Rust. u. B. d. E.), 16 March 1943. See *Allgemeine Heeresmitteilungen*, 7 April 1943, p. 219, §319, '1. Munitionsaustattung'.
9. O.K.H. (Ch. H. Rust. u. B. d. E.), 6 September 1944. See *Heerestechnisches Verordnungsblatt*, 1 October 1944, p. 385, §642, 'Beschreibung der Gewehrblendgranate 42. (Gw B Gr 42)'.

Index